A Failure of Vision

Michael Harrington and the Limits of Democratic Socialism

A Failure of Vision

Michael Harrington and the Limits of Democratic Socialism

Doug Greene

zer0 books

Winchester, UK
Washington, USA

JOHN HUNT PUBLISHING

First published by Zero Books, 2021
Zero Books is an imprint of John Hunt Publishing Ltd., No. 3 East St., Alresford, Hampshire SO24 9EE, UK
office@jhpbooks.com
www.johnhuntpublishing.com
www.zero-books.net

For distributor details and how to order please visit the 'Ordering' section on our website.

ISBN: 978 1 78904 723 3
978 1 78904 724 0 (ebook)
Library of Congress Control Number: 2020942272

A CIP catalogue record for this book is available from the British Library.

Design: Stuart Davies

UK: Printed and bound by CPI Group (UK) Ltd, Croydon, CR0 4YY
Printed in North America by CPI GPS partners

Contents

Also by the author

Communist Insurgent: Blanqui's Politics of Revolution,
ISBN: 9781608464722

Dedicated to the memory of my father. I hope it would have changed his mind.

Acknowledgments

Writing a book is a collective endeavor. Considering this is my second book, I think that is even more so. In the process of exploring the life and ideas of Michael Harrington, I am indebted to many friends, family and comrades. I want to thank Harrison Fluss for giving me the idea to write on Harrington in the first place. Both Harrison and his fiancée, Sam Miller, have been constant sources of ideas and encouragement. You are also two of the finest people I have ever met. Thank you to Stefanie Reis for helping me with interviews. I would also like to thank Peter Bloom for reading an early draft of my book and offering feedback. A special thank you to Michael Yates and C. Derick Varn for your efforts to get my book published. It meant a lot to me.

The following comrades and friends have also been constant sources of support. Forgive me if I miss anyone since there are so many of you: Abdullah Al-Haddad, Amy Banelis, Jeffrey Baker, Nathaniel Flakin, Brian Kelly, Marc Luzietti, Chris Persampieri, Donald Parkinson, James Rotten, Matthew Strauss, Sam Wells Pagano and Fanshen Wong. To Ian Horst, you are one of my closest friends and comrades. I am also glad that you listened to me as I shared my findings on Michael Harrington with you. Andrew and Christine Shelton, you are two of the best friends I have ever had.

I owe a special debt to the following members of my family: my mother and grandmother for their tireless support and always asking me how the writing was going. To Danny and Teri, thank you for listening to me. Lauren, your pets were a source of encouragement when I wrote, especially Socks.

Lastly, there is Shalon van Tine. Without your help, this book would not have been written or published. You not only checked up on my writing progress, but you believed in me. I want you to know that you mean the world to me.

Introduction[1]

> *To build a new American majority for social change, there must be a precise program, bold enough to respond to the challenges confronting our society, politically astute enough to appeal to millions of men and women. A program located on the left wing of realism!*
>
> Michael Harrington[2]

On the weekend of August 2, 2019 one thousand delegates of the Democratic Socialists of America (DSA) held their biannual convention in Atlanta, Georgia to discuss their internal structure and future organizational strategy. It was a momentous occasion. Normally, most socialist conventions are ignored in the mainstream press, but DSA's convention was covered in *The Guardian*, CNN and the *New York Times*. Since 2016, members swarmed into DSA as "democratic socialism" gained in popularity with the 2016 and 2020 presidential campaigns of Bernie Sanders. In just 3 years, DSA has gone from an older-aged paper membership of 6500 to a vibrant and younger one approaching an impressive 60,000, and it is now the largest socialist organization in the United States in over 60 years.

DSA's momentum and size puts it in a unique place to play a major role in placing "democratic socialism" at the center of American politics. In some respects, the convention marked a major left turn for the organization. A number of important resolutions were passed in favor of open borders, the creation of an anti-fascist working group, opposition to American imperialism and support for a rank-and-file strategy in the labor movement. However, DSA's overwhelming priority remains electoral politics. At the convention, DSA pledged that if Bernie Sanders loses the Democratic Party nomination, then they will not support any other Democrat in the 2020 election.

DSA's convention was distinguished by a great deal of consensus on the question of the Democratic Party. The Democratic Party is not only one of the major parties of American capitalism, but it presents itself as the "party of the people," which historically neutralizes any left-wing challenges inside their ranks and co-opts independent social movements. In other words, the Democrats function as a force of controlled opposition and lend "popular" legitimacy for imperialist policies.

Even though there are differences within DSA regarding the Democrats, no organized center exists inside the organization that calls for an immediate and clean break from the Democratic Party. DSA's convention passed a resolution in support of a "dirty break" from the Democrats and the creation of an independent working-class party, but this decision remains something for the distant future. For now, DSA is still tied to the Democrats, who set the boundaries for their political action. Currently, nearly one hundred self-described democratic socialists and DSA members hold elected office ranging from school boards to the halls of Congress, including representatives Alexandria Ocasio-Cortez and Rashida Tlaib, nearly all of whom are Democrats. Despite rhetorical commitments to the contrary, it seems that DSA has no intention of breaking with the Democrats and bourgeois politics, but merely hopes to pressure its liberal wing. In other words, DSA does not seek to organize and mobilize American workers as a class, but rather, it fosters the illusion that change comes from electing a better class of Democrats.

All of this is perfectly in line with the strategy of Realignment, developed by DSA's founder, Michael Harrington, to shift the Democrats to the left. Michael Harrington (1928-1989) was the most important advocate for democratic socialism in the United States in the latter half of the twentieth century. He is widely, and deservedly, recognized for writing *The Other America*, a seminal exposé of poverty in the United States that inspired

President Kennedy and President Johnson's Great Society and the War on Poverty programs. Over the course of Harrington's life, he wrote 14 books on many topics ranging from socialism to Marxism to religion to poverty to American politics and the Third World.

However, Harrington was more than simply an outspoken public intellectual. From his early days in the International Socialist League to leading the Socialist Party and founding DSA, he was also a committed political activist. Even though democratic socialism was a marginal force in the United States, Michael Harrington had a plan to change that. To break out of its isolation, Harrington argued that socialists needed to undertake patient and pragmatic work to create a new political majority.

The main arena for this work would take place inside the Democratic Party. Harrington believed that the main constituents of the Democratic Party – labor unions, blacks, women and farmers – contained the future base for a new majority and, ultimately, the socialist movement. So long as the Democrats remained under the control of racists and business interests, this new majority remained politically impotent. Therefore, Harrington argued for realigning the Democratic Party by driving out its racist, conservative and wealthy elements so that the party would truly represent the interests of ordinary people. After the Democrats were transformed, they would support meaningful and genuine reforms to strengthen the welfare state, overcome poverty and lay the foundations for democratic socialism. Michael Harrington's name may not be widely known today, and his works may be collecting dust, but his Realignment strategy remains very alive inside DSA and the wider American left.

If Michael Harrington returned from the dead and saw DSA today, he would largely feel vindicated. Harrington would believe that DSA's growth in membership was largely the result of pursuing Realignment. True, he would object to DSA only supporting Bernie Sanders in the 2020 Democratic Party primary, since he would want to leave room open to supporting the eventual nominee as a "lesser evil" to defeat the Republicans. Despite this, Harrington would be pleased that the majority of DSA stayed true to his Realignment strategy.

The opening moments of the 2020 Democratic primary seemed to further justify Michael Harrington's Realignment strategy for DSA. Bernie Sanders generated tremendous enthusiasm and won several early primaries. After Sanders' primary win in Nevada, DSA members such as Dustin Guastella and Connor Kilpatrick proclaimed that the Democratic Party was "Bernie's party now."[3] Sanders appeared on the road to winning the nomination and the White House. Just as quickly the optimism faded. Sanders lost heavily on Super Tuesday in March and withdrew from the race the following month. Shortly thereafter, Sanders ended up endorsing Joe Biden as the presumptive Democratic nominee. Now the former "anti-establishment" Sanders, along with Ocasio-Cortez, are circling the wagons around Biden and foregoing any criticism in the name of "party unity." Similar to democratic socialist experiments of SYRIZA in Greece and Jeremy Corbyn in Great Britain, the Bernie Sanders campaign was soundly defeated. So what is next for Realignment and DSA?

The 2020 Democratic Party primary was not the first failure of the Realignment strategy. Ever since Michael Harrington adopted Realignment in the 1960s, it has been an unmitigated disaster for democratic socialism and the wider left. Realignment was based on a flawed characterization of the Democratic Party as a coalition of equal interest blocs. In reality, the Democrats are a capitalist-controlled party where business interests not only determine the political agenda, but block any serious initiatives to transform the party. By focusing socialist efforts around electoral politics and the Democratic Party, Michael

Harrington wound up with a reformism that could not even reform. In the end, the obstacles that Harrington confronted paralyzed his Realignment efforts, and he found himself doing little more than rationalizing the subordination of the labor bureaucracy to the Democratic Party.

Ultimately, the entire Realignment strategy reveals Michael Harrington's failure of vision. Despite his avowed socialism, Harrington espoused an uninspiring and conservative socialism. His orientation to liberals and the Democratic Party meant he prized tactics of moderation and compromise for fear of alienating potential allies. Whenever radicals acted outside of and against the limits accepted by the Democratic Party and the labor bureaucracy, Harrington attempted to rein them in. This political strategy required kowtowing to liberal prejudices and prizing loyalty to American institutions. Whatever his socialist desires may have been, Michael Harrington reconciled himself to acting as the "loyal opposition" to the powers that be. The 2020 elections are simply the latest example of Realignment's bankruptcy. In the end, Michael Harrington and his legacy have proved to be a disaster for the development of socialist politics.

Chapter 1

Jesuit

The Harringtons

Despite being known as the "Man Who Discovered Poverty," Michael Harrington's beginnings were anything but impoverished. He was born into a well-off Irish-American and Catholic family in St. Louis, Missouri. His father, Edward Michael Harrington, fought in the First World War as part of the American Expeditionary Force. After coming home, Edward became a lawyer, specializing in patent law. In the early 1920s, Edward met a local teacher named Catherine Fitzgibbon and after a brief courtship, the two married. Even though Catherine was forced to give up teaching following her marriage, she refused to become a dutiful housewife. Instead, Catherine continued her education and took an active role as a volunteer in the Catholic Church. As a result of her fiercely independent nature, it was only after 5 years of marriage that Catherine gave birth to the couple's only child – Edward Michael Harrington Junior – on February 28, 1928. Both parents expected great things of their son.

Harrington's well-off background shielded him from the catastrophe of the Great Depression. The fierce class struggles and miserable poverty of the 1930s were foreign to him. As he wrote later: "though I vaguely recall breadlines and the shiny union buttons on the caps of truck drivers, it is from afar."[1] This is not to say that he had no interest in politics. When Harrington came of age, the terms Catholic, Irish and Democrat were practically synonymous. His immediate and extended family were just as devoted Democrats as they were faithful Catholics. Michael's grandfather, Patrick Fitzgibbon, was a passionate and loyal supporter of the St. Louis Democratic Party. Patrick was such a dedicated Democrat that he refused to take communion from a priest whom he suspected of being a Republican. On election day 1944, Patrick, who lay on his death bed, insisted on voting for a fourth time for Franklin Roosevelt (he died on April 17, 1945 just 5 days after the death of his beloved president).[2] Despite a brief lapse into revolutionary radicalism in the mid-1950s, Michael himself would maintain his allegiance to the Democratic Party for the remainder of his life.

Unlike many Irish-Americans, the St. Louis community was not nurtured on militant Irish nationalism like their brethren in Boston or New York but was far more assimilated. As Michael Harrington recalled, his parents "did not partake of that suffering, angry identity eight centuries of British savagery had imposed upon the Irish people. We were Americans."[3] All that remained of their Irish identity was "a vague, somewhat stagy Irish sentimentality and a cultural nostalgia perpetuated by wakes and tenors."[4] By contrast, it would be difficult to underestimate the role of the Catholic Church in forming the character and worldview of Michael Harrington. The Catholic Church was still looked upon with suspicion in America and sought to shield the faithful from the pernicious and godless influence of the modern world, resulting in its own intellectual ghettoization. If the Catholic Church felt under siege, then the Jesuit Order were the advance guard in militantly and boldly defending the faith against any secular onslaught. The Jesuits were prominent in St. Louis having founded a university, medical school and other educational and charitable institutions.

Since the Harringtons were God-fearing, they wanted Michael to receive a rigorous Jesuit education. However, there were other, more "materialistic", reasons for getting a Jesuit education. As Michael's biographer Maurice Isserman noted, Catherine Harrington understood that "alumni of Jesuit schools were well represented among the city's professional, business, and political classes. Catherine knew she was providing him with the personal network he would need to make his mark in St. Louis society, as well as the opportunity to gain a first-rate education."[5] A Jesuit education would not only steel Michael in his faith, but secure his financial future.

Harrington recalled later that when he attended Jesuit schools their "heroic period was long since dead. But something of the spirit of being shock troops of Christ on the perimeters of the faith still persisted."[6] Still, Michael absorbed the lessons of Jesuits that "ideas have consequences, that philosophy is the record of an on-going debate over the most important issues before mankind."[7] Even after he left the Church, a residual Jesuit spirit remained in Harrington's later political and philosophical writings. Harrington excelled at St. Louis High School, earning academic honors during his last 2 years. Michael joined a number of clubs and wrote for the school paper during all 4 years of high school, rising to editor in his senior year. In a foretaste of things to come, Harrington was noted as a skilled debater by the school. By the time he graduated high school, Harrington possessed not only a rigorous Jesuit education, but was recognized by his graduating class as "one of the most famous and popular '44 graduates."[8] Like the young men of his generation, Harrington followed the Second World War with rapt attention. Most of the class of 1944 expected to fight in the war after graduating (14 ended up killed or missing in action).[9] Michael was eager to fight too, but he was still too young to be drafted in 1944. Instead of going off for glory, the disappointed young Harrington proceeded to Holy Cross College in Massachusetts to continue his Jesuit education.

Holy Cross

At Holy Cross, Michael Harrington again stood out among his peers. He wrote for and edited the school paper, *The Tomahawk*. Harrington also edited the school yearbook and the literary journal, the *Purple*. He was also a member of the school debating society and assisted the college priests in the celebration of mass. A profile of Michael published by the *Purple* described his "most distinguishing characteristic" as "balance."[10]

There was not much in the way of student activism when Michael Harrington attended Holy Cross. The political atmosphere was charged with anticommunism in celebration of Spanish dictator Francisco Franco and support for the House on Un-American Activities in rooting out subversion. Michael Harrington shared the prevailing anticommunism, but otherwise his ideas remained confused and in flux. At first in a fit of teenage rebellion, he outraged his family by becoming something worse than an atheist – a Republican. He identified with Ohio Senator Robert A. Taft because he was a "civil libertarian...an opponent of the big businessmen of the Northeast, an Adam Smith anarchist."[11] At the same time, Harrington's social and economic ideas were largely in line with support for Pope Leo XIII's condemnation of unbridled capitalism made in the 1891 encyclical *Rerum Novarum*. This social Catholicism was perfectly consistent with his support for New Deal reforms. As Harrington said later, "I came of age at the very last moment when the philosophical preoccupations of the Great Depression were still primary."[12]

Michael graduated second in his class in 1948. His father hoped that his son would follow in his footsteps and become a lawyer. The law had little appeal for Michael, who now had dreams of becoming a poet. However, he didn't want to disappoint his parents and after being accepted to Yale Law School, he agreed to attend it for at least a year.

Road to Damascus

At Yale, Michael found his political and philosophical assumptions under assault. By the 1940s, Yale Law School was a bastion of unabashed liberalism. As Harrington recalled: "The professors were mainly liberals and my classmates, most of them returned veterans, were left liberals, Henry Wallacites, socialists and communists."[13] Harrington attempted to defend his conservatism in many debates with his classmates. He held his ground for a while, but slowly he was won over until no trace of his allegiance to the Republican Party remained.

Beyond debating with classmates, Harrington largely stayed out of politics aside from one cause: the Zionist struggle against the British Empire in Palestine. According to his own recollection: "I was Irish enough to accept without question the truth of Zionist attacks on British imperialism, and the holocaust of the European Jews seemed to me the most monstrous evil since time began."[14] Indeed, Harrington could recite the words of "Hatikva," the Israeli national anthem, by heart.

Harrington's Zionist sympathies were in agreement with the mainstream of New Deal liberalism. For instance, the Progressive Party candidate Henry Wallace (Franklin Roosevelt's vice president from 1941-45) criticized Harry Truman for hesitating to arm Israel after it declared independence and for "playing politics with the lives of the people of Israel." Harrington was very much part of the liberal consensus supporting Israel, something that he remained committed to for the remainder of his life. Despite his parents' hopes, Harrington's time at Yale left him even less interested in becoming a lawyer than before he began. He spent his free time in the school library reading poetry or taking weekend trips to explore the cosmopolitan atmosphere of New York City. He was determined to become a writer. He applied to and was accepted into the University of Chicago's graduate program for English literature. Even though his parents were disappointed, they accepted Michael's decision. In the fall of 1948, Michael moved to Chicago to chart his own path.

Unlike Holy Cross or Yale, Chicago was politically charged where many of the battles that characterized the thirties between communists, socialists, Trotskyists and liberals were still on-going.

Harrington stayed away from organized politics. Instead he was drawn to the Bohemian culture of Chicago where "everyone... had a poem or play or novel in the works."[15] Among these free spirits, Harrington read voraciously to grasp ideas and their implications. Michael was so caught up in his books that the night before an important exam, he read Joseph Conrad's *Victory*, which he described as "a poignant account of how man cannot hide himself from life and love" and read the whole thing that night.[16] We do not know whether or not Harrington failed that particular exam, but in any event his grades did not suffer.

While Harrington soaked in the Bohemian atmosphere, his radicalism did not identify with the oppressed and exploited, but was "distinctively aesthetic and elitist...Capitalism was not so much cruel and exploitative as crass and vulgar: the bourgeoisie was hated as a boor rather than a thief."[17] Later, Michael Harrington nostalgically mourned for the aristocratic rebels of Bohemia who truly cared about ideas and passions, saying: "we were, to be sure, pampered rebels. Some of us received allowances from home that provided us with the material security to disdain the middle class. But what made us something more than just privileged and posturing youths having a fling on the edge of society was that we were really serious, even passionate, about ideas for their own sake."[18] By contrast, Harrington believed the sixties counterculture was "not a continuation of the Bohemian tradition, but a radical departure from it," since it was truly a mass phenomenon.[19]

At Yale, Michael Harrington had endured the mocking and criticism of his Catholicism from his classmates, but it was only in Chicago that he had his first crisis of faith. The catalyst was that he could no longer accept that people could be condemned to hell, no matter the offense. This called his entire Jesuit worldview into question, since it was based upon an integral system "in which every thesis was intricately wired to every other thesis and each part, no matter how small, was therefore indispensable."[20] When Harrington graduated in 1949 with his MA, he not only lacked his religious belief, but was unsure about his future plans. He had vague ideas about settling in New York City as a poet, but until then he returned home to St. Louis. It was an awkward time since he kept his parents in the dark about his break with the Church. While there, Michael took a job as a social worker where he had a sudden moment of realization like Paul on the Road to Damascus:

> In my case, my convictions began to become deadly serious one day in the fall of 1949. I needed money so I could stake myself to go to New York and write poetry. Without any idealistic thought on my part, and through the influence of a cousin and ward leader, I was given a job in the Pupil Welfare Department of the Saint Louis Public Schools. I was assigned to the Madison School, located in an Arkansas sharecropper district down near the river, not far from a "Hooverville," one of those colonies of driftwood and tincan shacks that had survived from the Depression. One rainy day I went into an old, decaying building. The cooking smells and the stench from the broken, stopped-up toilets and the murmurous cranky sound of the people were a revelation. It was my moment on the road to Damascus. Suddenly the abstract and statistical and aesthetic outrages I had reacted to at Yale and Chicago became real and personal and insistent. A few hours later, riding the Grand Avenue streetcar, I realized that somehow I must spend the rest of my life trying to obliterate that kind of house and to work with the people who lived there.[21]

It remains an open question if those events transpired exactly as Harrington recalled. Still, it would be months before Michael would translate his affirmation to fight poverty into something beyond an abstract vow. For the moment, he decided to finally reject his parents' plans that he pursue a doctorate. In December 1949, Harrington decided to move to Greenwich Village to become a writer. Bohemia still beckoned him.

Greenwich Village

More so than Chicago's Bohemia, New York's Greenwich Village was the center of the intellectual, political and artistic avant-garde in the United States. For Harrington and so many others, Greenwich Village represented a chance to escape the "routine of the nine-to-five, to find a space in which to think, perhaps just to dribble away a life."[22] Since the beginning of the twentieth century, those who frequented Greenwich Village represented a veritable honor roll of American communism and anarchism including Emma Goldman, John Reed, Max Eastman and Big Bill Haywood. Artists and cultural innovators found their way to the Village too such as the dancer Isadora Duncan, writers William Faulkner and Norman Mailer, the playwright Eugene O'Neill and the poet Dylan Thomas. By the time Harrington arrived in late 1949, Greenwich Village possessed not only hubs of political radicals, free-thinkers, artists and intellectuals, but a lively club scene too.

Michael's first priority was to find some means of support. He worked a number of jobs such as writing for the *Columbia Encyclopedia*, apprenticing at *Life* magazine (making the large sum of $90 a week), and employment as a soda jerk and as a machine operator.[23] The machine shop was owned by socialist friends and Harrington recalled "bosses and the workers discussed the Russian Revolution at lunch break."[24] Michael's refusal to work a normal nine-to-five job meant that he had a lot of down time. During the day, he spent his free time writing poetry while his nights were spent absorbing politics, culture and drinking lots of alcohol at taverns such as the White Horse.

Ever the Jesuit, Harrington saw himself as part of the Bohemian elite. Whereas the great majority of people were kept in "cultural darkness," Harrington described the atmosphere of Greenwich Village as "an outcast minority of aesthetic aristocrats even when some of them were starving. One of the virtues of that cruel necessity was that the Bohemian scale was intimate."[25] Later in life, Harrington lamented the uninhibited and confused mass radicalism of the sixties that destroyed the individualism and upper-class rebels of Greenwich Village. He was revolted at the mass elements of the later counterculture, saying in disgust that "it is something else again when hundreds of people gather at a Woodstock Festival to listen to highly commercialized and collectivized rites of liberation."[26] While Harrington freely admitted that Bohemia – like the counterculture – had its phoniness, he hastened to add that "our phoniness had high standards. We postured about the first rate, about Proust and Joyce and Kafka, the later Beethoven quartets and Balanchine choreography, Marx and Lenin. So there was always the possibility that the sophisticated inanities could become serious and substantial, that one would hear or say a truth or even be incited to create. The proof is in the production."[27] For Harrington, mass society destroyed all that was good and noble in Bohemia by replacing it with nihilistic mediocrity.

While Harrington reveled at being among Greenwich Village's cultural elect, he still agonized over his career and future. His job at *Life* magazine provided a decent income, but he found the corporate environment alienating and deadening: "All of those trite statements about 'selling your soul' and the enervating effect of work for *Life* are true."[28] He desperately looked for other work. He applied without success to a position at the American Friends Service Committee, a Quaker social organization. As a result, he neglected his poetry and sunk into a spiritual crisis.

Harrington's moment of crisis came just as the Cold War turned hot with the outbreak of the Korean War. On June 25, the war began as soldiers of the Korean People's Army crossed the 38th parallel dividing North and South to begin their march to Seoul. Within days, General Douglass MacArthur, Supreme Commander of United States Far Eastern Command, organized an expeditionary force to meet the North Koreans in battle. On July 7, the United Nations Security Council approved American-led action on the Korean peninsula. It appeared that the outbreak of World War III was at hand.

Shortly after the war began, Harrington received a draft notice. This further compounded his spiritual crisis. He volunteered for the Army Medical Reserve. He was a convinced pacifist and unwilling to bear arms. Michael could not register as a conscientious objector because that was only available for religious believers. He faced the prospect of prison for refusing the draft. His family in St. Louis were opposed to his stand, but Harrington held his ground. He waited anxiously for orders to be sent to Korea, which he intended to refuse.

His orders never came. As Harrington recalled: "Some bureaucrat in the Pentagon thereupon changed my life. He decided that the federal reserves would not be called upon, so in January 1951, I transferred to the New York unit."[29] Even though he was not sent to Korea, he had to attend military drills as a member of the reserve. During active duty training in the summer of 1951, he was sent to the infantry. Earlier, Harrington had explained his pacifism to his superiors and was assured that he would not have to bear arms. An army captain chewed him out and Michael expected to be sent to the stockade. Instead, he was returned to the medics. Eventually, Harrington resigned his position, but the army refused to let him go. Finally in 1953, when his original term of enlistment expired, Michael Harrington was released from the army with an honorable discharge.[30]

The Wager

While dealing with the prospect of fighting in a war he didn't believe in, Michael Harrington's spiritual crisis finally came to a head. In February 1951, he made a conscious choice to return to the Catholic Church:

> But then, after two years of indecisive apostasy, I read myself back into the Church. Both of my mentors in that reconversion were the authors of forbidden books, Blaise Pascal and Søren Kierkegaard. One night while reading the *Pensées* after a long immersion in Kierkegaard, I decided in a most unjesuitical fashion to return to Catholicism. I no longer felt that I could prove my faith, but now I was willing to make a wager, a doubting and even desperate wager, on it: *Credo quia absurdam*. I believe because it is absurd.[31]

The following day, after giving confession in a local church, Michael walked into the offices of the Catholic Worker to put his new-found faith into practice.

The Catholic Worker Movement was one of the most vibrant expressions of left-wing Catholicism in the United States. As Harrington said, "it was as far Left as you could go within the Church."[32] The Catholic Worker Movement was founded by the charismatic Dorothy Day in 1933, whom Harrington described as "a saint, which means, among many other things, that she was utterly human, complex, inconsistent."[33] Day was born into a Brooklyn middle-class family in 1897 and was attracted to both Christianity and revolutionary politics. At first, Day's commitment to the red flag outweighed her devotion to the cross. In the mid-1910s, Day joined the Socialist Party and worked on leftist journals such as the *Call*, *Masses*, and the *Liberator*, where she made the acquaintance of revolutionary luminaries such as Max Eastman and Mike Gold.

Day converted to Catholicism in 1927 after a failed marriage and an abortion that she called "the great tragedy of her life."[34] Despite taking communion, she remained very much a radical and wanted the Church to take an active role in helping the poor. In December 1932, Day witnessed communist-led hunger marches in Washington DC and was saddened that the Catholic Church was nowhere to be found: "I could write, I could protest, to arouse the conscience, but where was the Catholic leadership in the gathering of bands of men and women together, for the actual works of mercy that the comrades had always made part of their technique in reaching the workers?"[35]

The following year, Day met the eccentric French immigrant Peter Maurin, who shared her vision of social Catholicism. Maurin's ideal of social justice was deeply inspired by Pope Leo XIII's encyclicals and the example of St. Francis of Assisi. Together, the two kindred spirits began the Catholic Worker Movement to improve the lives of the poor and "live in accordance with the justice and charity of Jesus Christ."[36] According to Harrington, "The core of The Catholic Worker, then and now, was a commitment to the 'corporal works of mercy,' like feeding and clothing and sheltering the poor in 'houses of hospitality' around the country."[37]

By the time Harrington joined the Catholic Worker, the movement had fallen on hard times. During the Korean War, Day's absolute pacifism appeared to many Catholics such as Cardinal Spellman as dangerously subversive and a step removed from communism. Still, the Catholic Worker never pushed the boundaries of what the Church accepted as permissible too far. As Harrington noted: "For Dorothy, and the rest of us, were Catholics, however politically radical we might be."[38]

The Catholic Worker Movement was something that a young idealist like Michael Harrington could eagerly throw himself into.[39] He worked at the soup kitchens and wrote for the *Catholic Worker* on subjects such as book reviews, labor struggles, repression in Spain and poverty in America. He also had an opportunity to put his antiwar beliefs into action for the first time. The Catholic Worker braved the pervasive atmosphere of McCarthyism and the stigma of being labeled "subversive" to protest the Korean War. At a demonstration to mark the first anniversary of the Korean War on June 25, 1951, a "motley little band" in Central Park composed of the Catholic Worker, War Resisters League and the Fellowship of Reconciliation came out against the war, where they were met with violence. It was at this demonstration that Michael Harrington met Dave Dillinger and Bayard Rustin (the latter would later be a close collaborator in the civil rights movement and the Socialist Party).[40]

Michael was something of a misfit among the faithful of the Catholic Worker. One volunteer, Betty Bartelme, remembered him as "not the favorite of the people who came in off the street. They were not taken with Mike. I think that's because he didn't really understand them. He was sympathetic towards them, but he really didn't communicate with them."[41] Harrington's upper-class attitudes remained, and he despised the asceticism of the Catholic Worker:

> Even when I was a Catholic worker, I hated the lousy food, the bedbugs, the smells – poverty actually stinks, did you know that? Closed off buildings, reeking with odors of food, urine...anyway, you'd have to be an absolute nut to want to live like that. I'm willing to put up with it if necessary, but I happen to like nice food, good wine...and I've never made any secret of it.[42]

Indeed, Michael did not quite live up to the Catholic Worker's Credo of voluntary poverty. He had several hundred dollars saved up from his time at *Life* and could rely on his parents for funds if he needed. After a few months of abstaining from alcohol, Harrington retreated to his old habits.

Harrington also found it difficult to square being a member of the US armed forces with the pacifism of the Catholic Worker.

Despite his opposition to the Korean War, Michael was viewed by many in the Catholic Worker as a hypocrite by continuing to attend drill training. Harrington describes the experience as follows: "On drill nights I felt myself an outcast. I waited until everyone was at dinner and sneaked out of the house in my uniform, the livery of my compromise. There was constant discussion of how I could be so unprincipled."[43]

Whatever his misgivings or charges of hypocrisy, Michael Harrington at last felt he was living his faith. As he wrote in a letter to a friend: "this catholicism is sensational. have become insufferably religious...and have found it wonderful."[44]

The Catholic Worker Movement allowed Harrington to reach a mass audience for the first time. In November 1952, he represented the Catholic Worker in a debate against a young and up-coming conservative intellectual, William F. Buckley, at the University of Vermont in Burlington. The question under discussion was, "Is Our Educational System leading us down the road to Socialism?" Harrington defended his position well and impressed Buckley, who later recalled:

> [Harrington] was so much in command of his own arguments and pitch that was effective. He was a very, very good polemical slugger. In the first place, he was very quick. Secondly, he was very fluent, extremely keen in seizing the weaknesses of his opponent, whether those were analytical philosophical weaknesses, or whether or not they were exploitable in terms of the sentiments of the audience.[45]

It was the start of a friendly adversarial relationship between Buckley and Harrington that would continue for many decades.

Harrington's writing also reached wider audiences. He began writing for *Commonweal,* a liberal Catholic journal, and contributed nearly four dozen articles by the end of the 1950s. He also had a fateful encounter with the writer Dwight Macdonald, then writing a profile on Dorothy Day for the *New Yorker*. Macdonald was a founder of the journal *Partisan Review* and an anticommunist leftist. The two hit it off almost right away and began a productive friendship (Macdonald's review for the *New Yorker* of *The Other America* helped propel Harrington to celebrity status). Through Macdonald, Harrington entered the world of the denizens of the New York Intellectuals "who, in keeping with Bohemian tradition, rose up against the new philistines of the [Communist Party] in the name of high standards."[46] Harrington found himself quite at home among this elite crowd. It was thanks to Macdonald that Michael finally had his poetry published, only to realize that he "had no talent, or at least no genius."[47]

As Harrington reached beyond the confines of the Catholic Worker, he found himself questioning the Catholic Workers' political efficacy. For one, it:

> does not have a mass base – either among the workers or the middle class...Let us plead guilty for having sometimes been arrogant toward the immediate needs of the worker. Let us plead guilty for having lost an orientation toward the working class. Let us plead guilty for having been uncompromising in a hostile fashion that alienated many. And I am quite serious. We are guilty of these.[48]

He was in search of a different path that would lead out of the self-imposed isolation of the Catholic Worker. His time in Chicago and New York had already exposed Harrington to the different groups on the political left, but his ideas remained unformed. In searching for new ideas, Michael began to explore Marxism. By January 1952, he was reading Marx, Lenin, Trotsky and Bertolt Brecht.[49] Even though his understanding of Marxism remained superficial, he devoured the literature. Michael's vocal interest in Marxism brought him into conflict with Dorothy Day. The two engaged in long arguments over the merits of socialism, where Day hoped to win the wayward Harrington away from godlessness. He stubbornly defended his ground.

Whether he knew it or not, Michael Harrington was looking for a leftist group to recruit him. That opportunity was not long in coming. In March 1952, in a protest at the Spanish embassy in support of imprisoned labor activists, Michael met Bogdan Denitch, a member of the Young People's Socialist League (YPSL). Denitch had an instinct for locating talent and Harrington caught his eye very quickly: "I immediately noticed this smart guy who didn't look as flaky as the rest of the Catholic Workers, or as nutty as the anarchists."[50] Denitch gave the eager Harrington newspapers and books to read (including the anti-Stalinist novelist Victor Serge).[51] Within a few weeks, Michael Harrington applied for membership of the YPSL.[52] When he showed his red card to Dorothy Day, she was shocked and refused to speak to Michael for days.

Michael Harrington's decision to join the YPSL effectively meant the end of Pascalian wager with the Catholic Church. By December 1952, he admitted that, "I no longer believed in the faith, not even by way of an existential leap."[53] Even though he would always consider himself culturally Catholic, or a "pious apostate", and look with sympathy on moderate forces inside the Church, this time Michael Harrington's break with both religion and God was permanent.

Chapter 2

Shachtmanite

Young People's Socialist League

After joining the YPSL, Michael Harrington's first problem was not how to make a revolution, but how he was going to pay the bills. A solution was not long in coming. In early 1953, he was hired as executive secretary by the Workers Defense League (WDL), which was formed in 1936 to defend union organizers. His legal training made him an ideal fit for the WDL. By the time Harrington was hired, the WDL was focused more on the civil liberties of those targeted by Joseph McCarthy's anticommunist crusade. Over the next 18 months, Michael handled the organization's correspondence, recorded minutes at meetings and put out the newsletter.

While the WDL was opposed to McCarthyism, it was equally opposed to the Communist Party (CPUSA). Their anticommunism stemmed from several sources. First were anticommunist union leaders and WDL board members James Carey and Charles Zimmerman. The unions they led – the Union of Electrical Workers (UE) and the International Ladies Garment Workers Union (ILGWU) – had a long history of fighting perceived communist control in the labor movement.[1] Zimmerman was also a member of the Socialist Party of America (SPA) and his opinions aligned closely with the anticommunist views of their leader, Norman Thomas, who was also a founder of the WDL.

By the early 1950s, the SPA was a dying organization. At the height of its power in 1912, when the Socialist Party had captured 6 percent of the presidential vote on the ticket of Eugene Debs, it had counted over one hundred thousand members and its influence could be found in the labor movement and among the intelligentsia. In 1952, the SPA was reduced to a rump of only 2000 members.[2] The party now served more as a retirement home for aged radicals who reminisced about their glory days. The YPSL, the party's youth wing, had only 134 members nationwide in 1952. They recruited just 62 that year, counting Michael Harrington among their number.[3]

Under the impact of the Cold War, the Socialist Party accepted the reigning anticommunist imperative to militarily resist totalitarianism. Norman Thomas, long known as a pacifist, abandoned that position in 1948 when he wrote a letter to President Harry Truman expressing support for his hard line against the Soviets.[4] That same year, Thomas went even further and supported the creation of NATO to counter the Soviet threat to Western Europe. In 1950, the Socialist Party's National Action Committee voted unanimously to support the US in the Korean War, viewing it as an "international police action" under the auspices of the United Nations to hold back communist aggression.[5] Thomas was also a supporter of the American Congress of Cultural Freedom (ACCF), an advocacy group formed in 1950 composed of left-wing anticommunist intellectuals to uphold intellectual freedom against communism. Unbeknownst to most members of the Congress of Cultural Freedom, including Dwight Macdonald, the organization was generously funded by the CIA. Thomas himself knew the source of funds and when money was short, he personally phoned CIA director Allen Dulles to plead for more cash.[6]

Almost immediately after joining the YPSL, Michael Harrington found himself in opposition to the Socialist Party's open support for the Korean War. Harrington's antiwar sentiment was shared by many in the YPSL, notably Bogdan Denitch. It was in leading the charge against the Socialist Party's pro-war position that Michael first learned to play dirty in the world of politics. In the rough and tumble world of internal party battles, Harrington worked closely with Denitch. Denitch played the role of "bad cop" by delivering provocative and uncompromising speeches, while Michael played the part of "good cop" by offering a more compromising tone to win over potential allies. As Denitch later recalled: "Mike was very much of a party-building type, which is something that people who write about Saint Michael will not tell you."[7]

Bogdan Denitch was more than Michael Harrington's comrade-in-arms in inner-party feuds, he was also a fervent supporter of Max Shachtman's Independent Socialist League (ISL). To Norman Thomas, the ISL was a "totalitarian" organization, whose worldview was fundamentally at odds with democratic socialism. As a result, collaboration between the Socialist Party and the ISL was strictly forbidden. Since Denitch and the ISL were opposed to the Korean War, Michael ignored the Socialist Party's warnings. He continued to work closely with Denitch and began working with the ISL to sponsor events. Relations between the YPSL and SPA reached their nadir in April 1953, when the former called for a Young Socialist Unity Conference, sending out invitations to Max Shachtman and other prominent figures in the ISL. In a further rebuke to Thomas, both Denitch and Harrington were elected to leadership positions in the YPSL. Thomas flew into a rage, demanding that the Socialist Party formally condemn Harrington and Denitch for their association with Shachtman: "He is a modified Trotskyist and our trouble with Trotskyists, Shachtman among them, is a matter of history. I think it is a very serious matter when our youth section shows such decided Trotskyist sympathy."[8]

The Socialist Party presented an ultimatum to the YPSL by cutting off all financial support and called upon them to cease all collaboration with the ISL. They refused. Instead, Harrington and Denitch polled all YPSL members in good standing – all 63 of them – about whether they should stay affiliated to the Socialist Party. In August, 39 YPSL members voted to formally cut ties with the Socialist Party.

In February 1954, YPSL fused with the Shachtmanites and formed the Young Socialist League (YSL) with a total membership of 83.[9] Harrington and Denitch were awarded the prominent positions of co-editors of the YSL's "Young Socialist Challenge," that was a weekly insert in the ISL's paper *Labor Action*. Harrington later wrote of these early years of the YSL: "Our Marxist sophistication stood in reverse ratio to any possibility of changing the world... Indeed, our isolation may have been an advantage. Little sects, Marx had once remarked, are only justified in times when there is no mass working-class movement of the Left, but under such circumstances they play a necessary role."[10] Despite the YSL's small members, Michael Harrington was optimistic that they would lead the forthcoming socialist revolution.

Max Shachtman

For Michael Harrington, Max Shachtman was his most important political mentor, who shaped his understanding of Marxism and socialism. This influence was something that Harrington acknowledged even after he drifted apart from Shachtman in later years. In the dedication to the 1970 work, *Socialism*, Harrington said: "Even though I have some serious disagreements with him on issues of socialist strategy, I am permanently and deeply indebted to Max Shachtman, who first introduced me to the vision of democratic Marxism and whose theory of bureaucratic collectivism is so important to my analysis."[11] Harrington took from Shachtman a deep-rooted anticommunism that the Soviet Union was a bureaucratic collectivist evil empire.[12] As we shall see later, Harrington also took up Shachtman's politics in other respects: an adaptation to social democracy, alliances with the labor bureaucracy and support for "Realignment" in the Democratic Party. This is not to say that Michael Harrington's views were identical to those of Max Shachtman. He would expand on Shachtman's ideas at times and was willing to break with him in certain cases when it became necessary.

So who then was Max Shachtman?

Max Shachtman (1904-1972) was one of the most brilliant, charismatic and controversial figures of American radicalism. Shachtman was born into an immigrant Jewish family who immigrated from the Russian Empire. While still a teenager, Shachtman was inspired by the Russian Revolution and joined the fledgling American Communist Party in 1921. The talented young man rose quickly through communist ranks, writing for the *International Labor Defense* and the *Young Worker*. In 1928, Shachtman was expelled from the party after being won over to the politics of Leon Trotsky. Shachtman joined forces with other expelled Trotskyists, James P. Cannon and Martin Abern, to form the Communist League of America (CLA) to carry on the fight for Trotskyism in the United States. While Cannon was the movement's acknowledged leader, it was Shachtman who was a far better orator and a favorite of young Trotskyist militants.

Even later in life, Harrington observed that Shachtman could still captivate audiences:

> when Max gave a speech, which sometimes lasted for about three hours, his presentation of socialist theory was usually suffused with personal emotion and experience. In 1956 during the upheaval in Poland I heard him speak to an audience primarily composed of students. None of us, not even those who had been working with Shachtman for some years, knew the names of the Polish Communists reviled, and sometimes murdered, by Stalin when he purged the party in Poland in the thirties. Yet as Max recited their names, sometimes with just an identifying tag – "a trade unionist, a working-class militant" – it was like hearing the roll call of revolutionary martyrs who were bone of our bone, flesh of our flesh.[13]

Shachtman faithfully followed Trotsky's orders when he called for entryism into the Socialist Party, known as the "French Turn" (so named because it was first carried out by French Trotskyists), to win over sections of its membership to a revolutionary program before splitting off.[14] In June 1936, Norman Thomas welcomed the Trotskyists into the SPA in the hope of making the socialists into an all-inclusive party to the left of the communists. The Trotskyists managed to win over the YPSL and were making inroads on the membership before they were expelled the following year.[15] The whole experience left Thomas and older socialists bitter and distrustful of radicals.

In 1938, the Trotskyists formed the Socialist Workers Party (SWP) with 1500 members.[16] The SWP had proven themselves as stalwart militants in trade unions. Their leadership was in the hands of capable men such as Cannon and Shachtman. In fact, Shachtman was the most well-known face of the Trotskyist movement after Trotsky himself and the latter's trusted lieutenant.

A little more than a year after its founding, the SWP was torn apart with Shachtman and Trotsky on opposite sides. The impetus for the split came in 1939-1940 following the Molotov–Ribbentrop Pact and the Soviet Union's invasion of Poland and Finland. Cannon and a majority of the SWP, supported by Trotsky, upheld the traditional position of unconditional support of the USSR. Shachtman led a minority who condemned the invasion as imperialist and refused to support the Soviet Union.

At the heart of this debate was the famous "Russian question" or the class character of the Soviet Union. Trotsky and Cannon argued that the USSR was a degenerated workers' state that rested on collective and planned property, which was originally supposed to produce genuine workers' democracy. Instead, the rule of the workers was usurped by a new bureaucratic caste. To restore the rule of the working class, Trotsky and Cannon believed that a political revolution was needed to overthrow the bureaucracy. Despite the Russian Revolution's degeneration, Trotsky argued that the USSR was still a workers' state and that the main enemy remained imperialism. Therefore, in any direct conflict with imperialism, it was imperative upon communists to defend the USSR.[17] Shachtman refused to accept the SWP's position and argued that all the belligerents in the war were imperialists. In April 1940, Shachtman, along with 40 percent of the membership and most of the youth wing, left the party. Shortly thereafter, they formed the Workers Party (WP).

In contrast to Trotsky and Cannon, Shachtman argued that the Soviet Union was no longer a workers state, but a bureaucratic collectivist regime engaged in imperialist expansion.[18] At first, Shachtman argued that the USSR was superior to capitalism, stating: "I consider nationalized property in the Soviet Union a historically superior form of property to any form of private property in history."[19] In December 1940, Shachtman argued that in the event of a war between the USSR and imperialist powers that the former should still be defended: "should the character of the present war change from that of a struggle between the capitalist imperialist camps into a struggle of the imperialists to crush the Soviet Union, the interests of the world revolution would demand the defense of the Soviet Union by the international proletariat."[20] However, 6 months later when the Germans invaded the USSR, he made an abrupt about face and refused to defend it.

In breaking with Trotskyist orthodoxy on the Russian Question, Shachtman and the WP developed the idea of a "third camp." Shachtman's perspective was that World War II was a struggle between different warring empires and Marxists should support none of them. Instead, Shachtman offered a positive program of supporting the third camp:

The masses of the people can find a way out of the horrors

> of the Second World War only under the banner of the Third Camp!
>
> The Third Camp has nothing in common with the two imperialist war camps – it is their deadly enemy.
>
> The Third Camp is the camp of the workers in factory and field, in mine and on railroad. It is the camp of the slaves of all colors who yearn and fight for their independence from imperialism. It is the camp of labor, fighting against the profit-lusting employers. It is the camp of labor fighting against the governments of the employers. It is the camp of the peasants and sharecroppers and farmers fighting against the grasping trusts, the railroad magnates, the bank sharpers. It is the camp of the Irish people, the Indian people, the Indo-Chinese and Moroccan peoples, the Filipinos and the Puerto Ricans, the Chinese people, the Polish and Czech and Slovakian and Scandinavian people, the people of the Soviet Union – the people who are at war today or will be at war tomorrow against the imperialist tyranny of the United States, England, France, Germany, Italy, Japan and the bureaucratic dictatorship of the Kremlin.
>
> The Third Camp is the camp of the hundreds of millions who yearn for peace, for security, for freedom, for independence.
>
> The Third Camp is the banner carried by the Workers Party, Section of the Fourth International![21]

In line with the third camp position, Shachtman backed independent working-class action. Thus, he refused to support the "no-strike pledge" adopted by the two major labor federations – the American Federation of Labor (AFL) and the Congress of Industrial Organizations (CIO) – and the CPUSA after the United States entered the war. Shachtman believed that there would be a renewed militancy in the labor movement during the war in the face of speed-ups and the increased demand for production. The WP sent its members into industry to win recruits and foster rank-and-file activity. At its wartime height, the WP had about 80 percent of their membership in industry and grew to 500 members.[22]

The Shachtmanites found a receptive audience among workers, winning elections as shop stewards, presidents of union locals and grievance committees through their dedicated organizing and defiance of the "no-strike pledge."[23] One union where the Shachtmanites gained noticeable influence was in the United Auto Workers (UAW). The UAW, led by Walter Reuther, was one of the major unions that built the CIO during the great class struggles of the 1930s. During World War II, the UAW and Reuther enthusiastically supported the "no-strike pledge" and the war effort. However, UAW membership was opposed to the disproportionate sacrifices they made while businesses made enormous profits. As a result, opposition developed inside the UAW supported by the Shachtmanites in support of rescinding the "no-strike pledge" and favoring of new union leadership.

Despite their small numbers, the Shachtmanites had enough support to force a referendum on the issue at a UAW convention held in September 1944.[24] The UAW upheld its support for the "no-strike pledge" by a two-thirds majority, but as Peter Drucker observed: "Many more union members than voted for the pledge in the referendum violated it in practice by going out on strike in 1944 and 1945. Around the country there were more strikes in 1944 than in any other year this century."[25]

The Shachtmanites found themselves fighting not only Walter Reuther, but the Communist Party. As Peter Drucker noted: "Wartime battles with the Communist Party pushed Shachtman and his party toward a stance of more rigid hostility. Communists would do anything to keep war production going, including trying to ban *Labor Action* from plants, informing to the bosses on troublemakers, and getting them fired from their jobs."[26] By 1945, the WP's theoretical journal, *The New International*, saw the CP as enemies: "The time is fast approaching when whoever seriously aspires to leadership in the American working class and refuses to align himself in merciless struggle against the Communist Party will thereby prove himself either a traitor or a blind fool."[27]

Shachtman's growing hostility to the CP dovetailed with a new assessment of the Soviet Union. By July 1943, he believed that Stalin's counter-revolution had been completed and it made no difference if the USSR won or lost the war. In fact, he warned that a Soviet victory "means the extension of a new slavery...a totalitarian slavery that Stalinist rule represents, a slavemaster oppression which crushes everything that is noble, progressive, democratic, socialist and internationalist in the working class that comes under its heel."[28]

If Stalinism in the USSR represented a new form of "barbarism," then the logical extension was to view domestic communists in the labor movement as Stalinist agents who were more dangerous than the bourgeoisie. In order to defeat the Stalinists, Shachtman believed that socialists should abandon their hostility to reformists and the labor bureaucracy, but offer them critical support:

> It should go without saying among genuine militants that in any struggle for leadership and control of the labor movement, or any section of it, they will always seek to counterpose a policy of class independence and class struggle against both the Stalinist and reformist bureaucracies. But where, as is the general rule nowadays, the militants are not yet strong enough to fight for leadership directly; where the fight for control of the labor movement is, in effect, between the reformists and the Stalinists, it would be absurd for the militants to proclaim their "neutrality" and fatal for them to support the Stalinists. Without any hesitation, they should follow the general line, inside the labor movement, of supporting

> the reformist officialdom against the Stalinist officialdom. In other words, where it is not yet possible to win the unions for the leadership of revolutionary militants, we forthrightly prefer the leadership of reformists who aim in their own way to maintain a labor movement to the leadership of the Stalinist totalitarians who aim to exterminate it.[29]

In line with Shachtman's new position, the WP supported Walter Reuther in 1946-1947 against the Communist Party.[30] Shachtman's original Marxist anti-Stalinism was quickly morphing into Cold War anticommunism. After World War II, many WP militants lost hope in a breakthrough of the third camp. The postwar boom and the Cold War ended labor militancy. Many WP cadre began looking instead to advance their professional careers. Those cadre who remained in the labor movement were increasingly in staff positions and no longer rank-and-file leaders.

As a sign of its lowered expectations, the WP transformed itself into the ISL in 1949. In contrast to the WP, the ISL no longer saw itself as a vanguard party. As *Labor Action* explained: "While it has been the custom for small socialist propaganda groups to assign themselves the name of a party, the WP has decided to break with this custom and to call itself what in actuality it is and has been – a socialist propaganda group."[31] Shachtman ritualistically upheld continuity with Trotskyism for several years afterward, but his impetus now was in a non-revolutionary direction.

Shachtman's conception of socialism changed from that of a mass revolutionary movement from below led by the workers to identifying with progressive union bureaucrats like Walter Reuther who represented the "democratic labor movement." To that end, Shachtman believed it was urgent to increase the political power of unions since they were the key to socialist transformation. To increase labor's political power, Shachtman began looking positively at ways to support labor candidates in the Democratic Party. The first ISL maneuvers in the Democratic Party took place in August 1949 when the ISL pledged support for union candidates who ran in Democratic primaries and to support them if they won since they "would deepen and sharpen the conflict of interests between the bureaucracy of the official of the capitalist parties and the labor leadership."[32] Shachtman still called for an independent labor party, but in practice he supported the union leadership and their subordination to the Democrats. It was the foundation of the strategy of Realignment.

By 1952, Shachtman was saying:

> The Democratic Party is a big bourgeois political machine. Ever so shrewd labor leaders may join it...There is no sure way of telling at present which of two forms this pressure will take in the next period: forcing the labor leaders out of the Democratic Party and toward an authentic, representative, independent party of the working class, or forcing the labor leaders to take such actions inside the Democratic Party as will precipitate the muted conflict between the old machine and the new "interlopers" and lead by another road – an indirect, tortuous, discreditable and foul one – to the same inevitable conclusion: the declaration of, political independence of the American working class.[33]

Concurrently with Shachtman's Realignment strategy, the perspective of a revolutionary third camp receded. As we mentioned above, Shachtman believed the Soviet Union was a new form of barbarism and Western capitalism was a lesser evil in comparison. The surest sign that Shachtman's third campism was giving way to qualified support for the camp of imperialism came during the Korean War.[34] Initially, Shachtman equally condemned both sides and demanded that America withdraw its troops. His verbal opposition to the war did not translate into deeds since Shachtman refused to support any actions that would weaken the US war effort (a position that was not shared by the wider ISL membership). Instead Shachtman argued that the working class supported national defense and that their patriotism was identical "with its own class interests: with the preservation of its organizations, its relatively high standard of living, its hard-won democratic rights, as well as the right to rule as a free and independent nation... [and] that all the things that the working class identifies with national defense are actually threatened by Stalinism."[35] In a perverse reading of Lenin, Shachtman argued that socialists needed to transform the Korean War from an imperialist war into a democratic one in order to defeat the Stalinists. Shachtman's position on the Korean War could be seen as a dry run for Michael Harrington's position on the Vietnam War: a verbal antiwar position that stays within the boundaries of respectable opinion and refuses to engage in any concrete action to actually end the war.

Even though ISL had dropped almost all programmatic commitments to Leninism by the mid-1950s, its radical dynamism was not completely spent as evidenced by its youth wing, the YSL. After the failure of their expectations for resurgence of postwar labor radicalism, the YSL looked to the campuses as a source of new recruits. While student activism was at a low point during the McCarthy era, the YSL was one of the only independent left-wing student groups not controlled by the Communist Party. To Michael Harrington, YSL with its youthful élan and anticommunist radicalism was far more promising than the moribund Socialist Party.

However, the movement that Harrington joined was moving away from revolutionary Marxism. In the postwar world, the ability of anti-Stalinists such as Shachtman to sustain a revolutionary political outlook no longer appeared viable. During the 1930s, capitalism appeared impotent in the face of the Great Depression and class struggles such as the rise of the CIO appeared to portend the beginnings of socialism. International events such as the Spanish Civil War and the Resistance and anticolonial movements during World War II provided another source of inspiration that a revolutionary alternative to both the Soviet Union and Western capitalism might emerge. By the end of the 1940s, everything had changed with the Cold War and the postwar boom, and the space for an independent revolutionary perspective vanished. As a result, Max Shachtman's third campist opposition to both Moscow and Washington gave way to viewing the latter as not only a lesser evil, but as the best defense against the threat from Stalinist totalitarianism. The Shachtmanite definition of "socialism" was purged of its revolutionary content and sought to reconcile itself with social democracy and the aims of the labor bureaucracy. Michael Harrington himself was swept along with this current.

Young Socialist League

Later in life, Harrington claimed: "I never thought of myself as a Trotskyist." In the mid-1950s he certainly expressed no doubts about his commitment to the world revolution.[36] Many YSL cadre were similar to Harrington in being intellectuals with a passion for ideas. This was no longer Bohemia where ideas were debated for their own sake. Like the Jesuits, the Shachtmanites also believed that ideas had consequences. Harrington describes the thrill of political debates inside the YSL:

> One of the most distinctive aspects of learning Marxist theory and history in the radical movement rather than in the classroom was that the process was existential. When we debated [the decisions of the Bolsheviks]...it was not an issue of the dead past. Each one of us was asking himself what he would have done under the circumstances. As a result, the disagreements over events that took place thirty years earlier

often took on the intensity of a debate over future policy.[37]

As much as any cadre, Harrington was determined to put Marxist ideas into action.

While Harrington awaited the return of class struggle, the Shachtmanites remained isolated during the quiet 1950s. They appeared to thrive in isolation. As Harrington observed:

> Indeed, our isolation may have been an advantage...We could, therefore commit our stupidities in private and painfully work out our ideas without being required to defend them before a television camera. Since we were so short on practice we had nothing else to do but become long on theory.[38]

In the tiny ranks of the YSL, there was plenty to do, if someone was dedicated or talented enough. Michael possessed large quantities of both traits. A former ISL member, Tim Wohlforth, describes Harrington's work ethic and the respect he earned from his comrades:

> Mike Harrington was a handsome Irish fellow whose brown hair even then was salted with gray. He had a ready smile, a winning personality, and could effortlessly do almost anything requiring the assembling of words. He spoke well and wrote well. Sometimes he would get an idea, find an unused typewriter at [ISL headquarters] sit down and knock out a fifteen-page theoretical article for the discussion bulletin in the evening.[39]

From 1954 to 1958, he wrote for *Anvil, Labor Action* and *The New International* on a wide range of topics: McCarthyism, literature, civil liberties, academic freedom, elections, the burgeoning civil rights movement, an obituary for Bertolt Brecht ("Poet of the GPU"), imperialism, India, China, de-Stalinization in the USSR and class struggles in Eastern Europe. Like the rest of the far left, Harrington followed the Hungarian Revolution of 1956 with rapt attention. Michael also had an opportunity to put his knowledge of foreign languages to use by translating the opening chapter of Georg Lukács' *History and Class Consciousness*, "What is Orthodox Marxism?" for *The New International* in 1957.[40]

In his capacity as a YSL organizer, Michael traveled widely across the United States to different college campuses to speak and establish contacts. Harrington's increased political prominence and the fact that the ISL was on the Attorney General's List of Subversive Organizations (it would only be removed in 1958 after a lengthy court battle) brought Michael to the attention of the FBI. In 1955, he was placed on an FBI "Security List" as one of 12,000 radicals who were to be imprisoned in the event of a national emergency.[41] Harrington said later that the FBI's surveillance on the 250 YSL members was far out of proportion to the threat they represented: "We could not, I used to say, overthrow the Fourteenth Street subway stop on the Seventh Avenue line. Yet the federal police lavished the kind of attention on us that would have been appropriate to a mass armed revolutionary movement."[42]

Michael reached out beyond the ranks of the YSL and maintained his contact with left-leaning New York intellectuals. He also wrote for *Commonweal* and *Partisan Review*, slowly building his reputation as a serious thinker. It was during these years that Michael met a life-long friend and comrade named Irving Howe. Despite their age difference (Howe was 8 years older), the two had much in common. They were intellectuals who loved literature, and they both frequented radical and Bohemian circles. They also shared similar political backgrounds and trajectories. During the 1940s, Howe was a fervent Shachtmanite and hoped for victory of the third camp, but with the onset of the Cold War, his optimism faded. In 1952, Howe rejected any identification with the third camp and threw his support behind the "democratic west," arguing: "We believe in the need to cooperate with whatever forces resist this tendency while also resisting the advances of Stalinism. But as democratic socialists our place is in the...democratic world, no matter how sharp our criticisms of its bourgeois leadership."[43] Howe's Cold War anticommunism was something that Michael could easily embrace.

In 1955, Howe founded the journal *Dissent*, which rejected both third campism and vulgar McCarthyite anticommunism. To advance the fight against communism, Howe argued that the United States should support a third force to "undercut the hold of Stalinism by a genuine appeal for radical democracy." The third force should be indigenous and anticommunist revolutionaries who would offer people an alternative to both communists and authoritarian dictators whether in Guatemala or Vietnam.[44] On the domestic front, *Dissent* originally balked at support for the Democrats and liberalism. By 1958 Howe changed his mind and argued that "the decisive political struggles during the next few years will occur in the Democratic party." While the left should continue to offer a "long-range socialist perspective," it was now necessary to support and cooperate with liberals in taking progressive action.[45] Howe's position was very much in line with the growing evolution of the ISL and Michael Harrington. Considering the ugly split between the ISL and Howe, Shachtman forbade anyone from writing for *Dissent*. However, Michael was not deterred and the YSL passed a resolution welcoming *Dissent* as a "new forum for socialist views."[46] Shortly thereafter, Harrington began writing for *Dissent* and would be a regular contributor for the rest of his life.

Harrington's first article in *Dissent* was an exposé on the American Committee for Cultural Freedom. According to him, the ACCF's anti-Stalinism was, "crude, promiscuous, and often without positive content...[it] has enthusiastically laid itself open to the pressures and shaping influences of the State

Department policies and rationales."[47] By contrast, Michael argued that the European affiliates of the Congress of Cultural Freedom were better than their American counterpart since they remained concerned with intellectual freedom and maintained independence from their governments. Instead, the ACCF was too closely identified with the American government and therefore too "crude" in its battle with communism. Harrington argued that if the ACCF wanted to effectively battle communism, then they must fight against intellectual conformity and the violations of civil liberties, including those of communists, in the United States.

This was not Harrington's only attempt to challenge the anticommunist consensus. In October 1954, he was contacted by a liberal friend named John Codley to do a study on the Hollywood blacklist for the Ford Foundation's Fund for the Republic. He quickly accepted and soon found himself in Los Angeles. For the next year, Michael interviewed people on all sides – communists, suspected communists and McCarthyites – for his study. According to him:

> talking to so many people who hated one another was an emotional exhausting experience. The executives who enforced the blacklist were, for the most part, frightened liberals. Most, but not all, of the Communists pretended to be mere liberals and anyone who mentioned their masquerade was charged with "red-baiting." There were lies and hypocrisy all around, and though Codley and I unambiguously defended the victims, including the Stalinists among them, they did not always charm us.[48]

When the study was published in June 1956, it comprehensively demonstrated that there was indeed an elaborate blacklist in Hollywood to keep out heretical ideas. The report brought both Codley and Harrington to the attention of the House on Un-American Activities Committee (HUAC). Codley was called to testify before HUAC where he was questioned about Harrington's political affiliations. Michael recalled that the behavior of men like Codley showed that:

> the anti-Communist Left was not at all as cowardly as some of the recent interpretations of the fifties suggest. A good number of us fought against both Stalinism and American repression and for the same democratic reasons. The thesis that any and all anti-Communism is an ally of reaction is not simply wrong in theory; my friends and I proved it wrong in practice.[49]

His time at the Fund for the Republic and Codley's integrity convinced Michael that liberals were not irredeemable, but they could work with socialists in pursuit of progressive causes.

Michael believed that collaboration between liberals and socialists would be ineffectual if the latter had no organization of their own in order to undertake joint work. Unfortunately, the American left in the 1950s possessed tiny and besieged groups who were shunned by the mainstream of society. It appeared hopeless that socialists could create a viable mass organization of their own in the near future. Suddenly hope came from the most unexpected corner – the Communist Party.

Despite the repression of the McCarthy years, the CP still had tens of thousands of members and was the largest left-wing organization in America. It is entirely possible that the CPUSA would have survived the decade intact if not for events in the Soviet Union. On February 25, 1956 Soviet leader Nikita Khrushchev delivered a "secret speech" to the Twentieth Congress of the Soviet Communist Party, condemning the crimes and terror of Joseph Stalin. The Khrushchev speech prompted wide-ranging debate inside CPUSA on their links to the USSR and their conception of socialism. For a few months, it seemed possible that the Communist Party might be renewed with new ideas.

Debate inside the CPUSA was shut down after mere months due to the Hungarian Revolution. Khrushchev's speech had signaled a liberal Soviet approach to Eastern Europe, but the Hungarians took it a step further and rose up in a popular revolution.[50] The pro-Soviet communists were replaced by a new reform-minded government led by Imre Nagy, who announced plans to leave the Warsaw Pact. This was too much for Khrushchev, who sent tanks into Hungary the following month to crush the revolution. The CPUSA leadership reaffirmed their allegiance to the USSR and orthodoxy by supporting the suppression of the Hungarian Revolution. This not only ended the Communist Party's openness, but drove thousands of dissidents out of the party, leaving just 5000 members in 1958.[51]

Harrington and the ISL followed events in the USSR and CPUSA with great interest. The Khrushchev revelations appeared to be a vindication for the ISL's anti-Stalinism. Harrington wrote sympathetically on the CP dissents led by John Gates, who were challenging party orthodoxy:

> The thing that makes the Gates faction different, qualitatively different, from the [orthodox CP] is that it seems to contain people who are reacting honestly, if after so many years in the intellectual prison of Stalinist ideology, to the events that have been shaking the Communist world...[this was] evidence of something which I once wrongly thought was impossible: that even those who have participated in the Stalinist movement for years...can begin to make independent criticisms.[52]

Harrington concluded: "We can no longer rule out dialogue with these people, at least as long as they maintain their newly-won independence of thought."[53]

The CPUSA was full of people revolted by Stalinism who wanted a new political home, but where would they go? The tiny ISL offered little in the way of an attractive or viable alternative to the CP. None of the splits from the Communist Party produced a significant pole of attraction. Once the dissidents were out of the CP, they wandered into the political woodwork. As Maurice Isserman observed: "In the heat of their battle with [the party], they had not had time to create a meaningful alternative political program or vision...No longer bound together in common opposition to the old guard, they soon found themselves drifting apart politically and personally."[54]

Michael Harrington and the ISL were not the only ones watching the implosion of the Communist Party and asking what came next. The Socialist Party was following events too. Since the YPSL left, the SPA had shrunk even further. They no longer ran presidential candidates. In 1956, the Socialist Party had only 691 dues-paying members, who were mostly concentrated in four states (New York, Pennsylvania, Wisconsin and California). In an attempt to stave off decline, the socialists had merged with the even smaller Social Democratic Federation (SDF) to form the Socialist Party of America-Social Democratic Federation (SP-SDF) in 1956. This allowed the SP-SDF to reaffiliate to the Socialist International, but little more. The Socialist Party appeared destined for a quiet dissolution.

David McReynolds, one of the few remaining youthful voices, was determined to change that. He believed that with the decline of the communists the possibility existed to create a new revitalized and activist Socialist Party that would regroup the entire left. To that end, McReynolds hoped to reach out to independent radicals such as the ISL and bring them into the Socialist Party. Norman Thomas was opposed to this since he still had bitter memories of Shachtman from the French Turn in the 1930s and the defection of the YPSL to the ISL. When McReynolds' proposal for regroupment was put to a vote, the

Socialist Party overwhelmingly voted it down.

This was not the last word on regroupment. By 1956, Shachtman saw the ISL as dead political weight instead of the nucleus of a future Leninist party. He was determined to find a new path. While he did not have much hope in recruiting ex-communists, he was hopeful about the civil rights movement and the prospects of the labor movement after the merger of the AFL and CIO in 1955. When Shachtman heard about McReynolds' proposal, he welcomed it with gusto as a way out of the political ghetto. In a signal that the ISL was serious about shedding old dogmas, Shachtman announced his formal disavowal of the Leninist and communist tradition in a lengthy review article of Theodore Draper's "Roots of American Communism" in *The New International*. He argued that the whole split between the socialist and communist parties back in 1919 was a tragic mistake:

> everything positive that the Communists did contribute to the cause of socialism in this country, could have been contributed just as well, with tenfold better results, with tenfold more effectiveness and durability, and with a hundredfold more assurance of correctives for shortcoming and error, if they had worked, as they could have done without serious difficulty, as an integral part of a broad, united socialist party.[55]

Now Shachtman argued that the American left needed a Debsian style broad-tent social-democratic party that would be untainted by communism. Socialism could only be effective by basing "itself upon American soil, upon American social conditions as they really are, upon the American working class as it really is, upon the language as it is really spoken."[56] The winds changed quickly in the ISL. In February 1957, Shachtman's proposal for a merger with the socialists was voted down, but in July he was supported by a majority.

Norman Thomas was encouraged by Shachtman's moves away from Leninism and the prospect of capturing the youthful and energetic YSL. Thomas reached out to Shachtman and received promises from the latter that his followers would not act as an organized faction in the party. Now that Thomas was reassured, the SP-SDF voted in favor of merger in the summer of 1958. At the same time, the ISL voted in favor of its own dissolution:

> The Democratic Socialist Movement must be democratic first and foremost in its internal life, so that its membership may be able to arrive freely and fairly at decisions on policy and activity, where the views of the majority prevail at all times with scrupulous assurances that the rights and conscience of minorities are in no way violated. This requires in turn a movement that is broad in its composition, its outlook, its concepts; that avoids iron and sterilizing dogmas which it seeks to impose upon all others, including dissenters in its own ranks; that avoids the demand for conformity on all questions and problems that are of interest to it; that rejects all concepts of a "monolithic" party and barrack-room discipline. All "monolithic" parties have had their day to the full; all of them have yielded disastrous results, the Communist Parties more than any other.[57]

While the Shachtmanites did not want to appear to be usurping control from the Socialist old guard, they ended up taking over the party quickly. Michael himself ended up as the de facto leader of the reconstituted YPSL without much effort. As Harrington recalled:

> When we went into the SP Max was very concerned that we not take it over. And the problem was that the SP was a total

> shell that if you could breathe you would take it over. It was almost impossible not to take it over. The fruit kept falling off the tree, and Max kept putting it back up on the tree.[58]

The ISL and Socialist Party merger went unnoticed by the rest of the world, but it left Michael Harrington hopeful about the prospects for the future. The American left finally had an organization of its own and was on the way to breaking out of its isolation. Harrington could see that McCarthyism was in retreat and the civil rights movement was picking up steam. As he said: "This was to be a particularly fateful fact for us socialists for it meant that we had the opportunity to become part of a vibrant development and found, *mirable dictu*, that the theories we had been debating in that Fourteenth Street loft actually referred to reality."[59]

Chapter 3

Realignment

Compromise

As one of the most youthful and well-known members of the newly enlarged and reinvigorated Socialist Party, Michael Harrington was a natural choice as the party's public face. From September to December 1958, Michael traveled to college campuses across America to generate interest and recruit students to the Socialist Party. Michael described the tour as "a personal and political epiphany."[1] As he explained:

> The experience was the final, existential proof of a basic Marxist proposition I had been struggling to formulate for some time: If you consider your country capable of socialism, you must love it and trust it deeply. You must sense the dignity and humanity of the people that survive and even grow despite the injustices of the system. You must be – if the word be purged of every bit of jingoism – a patriot, for you hold to the astounding conviction that your land and its people can be socialist.[2]

His faith in America was further reaffirmed in signs that political life was coming alive after years of passivity and McCarthyite paranoia.

In a report that he delivered to the Socialist Party the following February, Michael noted "a mood of change" in America. Of special interest to Michael were events taking place inside the California Democratic Party. The labor unions, who provided reliable votes to the Democrats, were opposed to the proposed "right to work" law in opposition to the party leadership. Harrington believed this showed "the bosses have politicalized the labor movement better than eighteen million pieces of socialist literature could."[3] That same year, Michael took his first step into the Democratic Party by joining the Village Independent Democrats (VID) in New York City. VID had grown out of the 1952 and 1956 Democratic presidential campaigns of Adlai Stevenson, a hero to many liberal reformers. The VID wanted to continue that work by shaping a progressive agenda and electing officials committed to change. Michael believed the VID was waging a "very serious fight" against the local machine.[4] While he still believed that the Democrats were a bourgeois party, he accepted that they were "the only game in town."[5] He reasoned that if socialists refused to work with Democrats, then they were displaying sectarian purism: "How could one be pure in an institution that was unprincipled on principle? So it was my radicalism that made me into something of a realist. If, I thought, you were going to play piano in a whorehouse, you might as well do so with gusto and flair."[6] Michael's support for the VID was a break with his earlier view "that there was no 'real' difference between the major parties."[7] Following in the wake of Shachtman, he rejected that perspective because it was based on Trotsky's "dying vision" of a "revolutionary apocalypse." However, Michael saw his turn to the Democrats not as an abandonment of socialism, but a result of him losing his romantic illusions and making "real contact" with workers.[8] Concurrently with his positive appraisal of work inside the Democrats, he changed his view of the labor bureaucracy, particularly of progressives like Walter Reuther. Instead of seeing labor bureaucrats as obstacles to the development of class consciousness, Michael said the "Reutherites were the genuine, and utterly sincere and militant, Left-wing of American society."[9] He was no longer concerned with the revolutionary seizure of power, but with pragmatic and "realistic" questions about using the existing institutions to effect genuine change. For now, Michael saw himself as only helping local reformers and as of yet he didn't have a fully worked out political strategy.

Travels Abroad

The merger of the ISL and the Socialist Party came just as the former was removed from the Attorney General's list of subversive organizations. This meant that Michael could apply for a passport and travel abroad, something he had long wished to do. He planned to go to Vienna to attend the World Festival of Youth and Students being sponsored by communist youth organizations. His anticommunism meant he wouldn't be there as a delegate, but merely as an observer.

Since this was the first communist youth festival being held outside of the Eastern Bloc, the CIA was particularly interested in those attending it. As a result, the CIA nearly financed Harrington's trip after he stumbled upon a CIA front in Los Angeles. After discussing the matter with YPSL, he presented the CIA with an ultimatum:

> It was decided that I would tell the front group that I would accept an airline ticket from them only if I could go on my own, completely independent of their organization, and with the explicit understanding that I would attack American capitalism and foreign policy as vigorously as Communism. That did it. The offer to help was withdrawn forthwith and I paid my own way, having nothing to do with what turned out to be the CIA's dirty games.[10]

As it was, Michael traveled to Europe without their help.

After a stopover in London, he went to Paris and found himself at home in its Bohemian circles. He followed closely debates over the war raging in Algeria, which was supported by the French Socialist Party. Michael himself was personally opposed to the war and supported a French withdrawal. Later, he made his way to Berlin to attend a meeting of the International Union of Socialist Youth, the youth wing of the Socialist International. The mayor of West Berlin was the future German chancellor and leader of the Socialist International, Willy Brandt, who would become a close personal friend. Since the Berlin Wall hadn't been constructed yet, he traveled to East Berlin where, "I was repelled by the drab city with 1984 banners everywhere proclaiming 'Work for Us Is a Joy, for We Work to Build Socialism.'"[11] After Berlin, Harrington finally arrived in Vienna. Even though he couldn't attend the festival, he observed it from afar with horror:

> In the stadium at one of the mass rallies the Russian delegation released "peace parachutes" when it entered; everyone had to rise, and had to chant rhythmically, hypnotically, *Mir y Drujba, Paix et Amirté,* Peace and Friendship. It was my first totalitarian rally and it reminded me of the newsreels I had seen of Hitler at Nuremberg.[12]

Afterwards, Harrington stayed in Europe for another month before finally returning to the United States where the civil rights movement was capturing the radical imagination.

Bayard Rustin

Michael Harrington had been involved in civil rights since joining the ISL and recalled that his comrades were overwhelmingly white and "none of us had any real contact with the black community. We were initially moved, not because we had any living relationship with the human suffering and dignity in the black ghetto of our city, but because we sensed the emergence of a new Social Force in American life. Our analysis was simplistic and inaccurate but it pointed us toward some important truths."[13] They were not completely isolated from key players in the movement, though. The ISL managed to win the support of the brilliant civil rights organizer named Bayard Rustin.

Rustin began his radical career at a young age as a member of the Young Communist League (YCL). In 1941, Rustin left the YCL after he refused to prioritize the war effort over civil rights. Instead, Rustin worked as an organizer for A. Philip Randolph and his March on Washington. Since Rustin was a pacifist, he refused to serve in the US army and was imprisoned. After the war, he continued his pacifist activism, leading the War Resisters League and protesting the Korean War, where he first met Michael Harrington. By 1956, Rustin was working with two of Shachtman's lieutenants, Tom Kahn and Rochelle Horowitz, in support of the Montgomery Bus Boycott. The three continued to work closely together in the coming years, often going to Shachtman's home along with Harrington to discuss strategy. Rustin not only shared Shachtman's perspective on allying the civil rights movement with organized labor, but on the necessity of anticommunism. When the Student Non-Violent Coordinating Committee (SNCC) was formed in 1960, Rustin tried to get them to adopt an anticommunist clause. SNCC activist James Forman describes Rustin's efforts as follows:

> When SNCC set out to draw up its constitution that fall, a chorus of liberals and conservatives tried to get the new organization to insert a totalitarian disclaimer. This kind of clause barred from membership anyone advocating a totalitarian form of government. Ostensibly, it applied to everything from fascists to communists but actually it had meaning only for the Left. The League of Industrial Democracy, in which Bayard Rustin was active, had gotten SDS to put such a clause in its early constitution. Rustin tried to get SNCC to do it, too; but SNCC refused all such pressure...[14]

Anticommunism was not simply something that Rustin, Shachtman and Harrington supported in principle, but they believed opposing radicalism was necessary if the civil rights movement was going to be taken seriously by their potential allies in the labor bureaucracy and the Democratic Party.

The Crusader

After sit-ins in Greensboro North Carolina in February 1960 over segregation led to protests across the country, Michael Harrington took on a more prominent role in the civil rights movement. Michael helped organize the movement in New York by bringing white students and black activists together. He also worked with Rustin to organize "The Committee to Defend Martin Luther King" who was then facing trumped up charges of tax evasion. During all of this, he proved himself to be a dedicated organizer. To Harrington, the civil rights movement was a great crusade for justice where black and white were joined together in a common cause for justice. The atmosphere of camaraderie was great enough for him to momentarily forget old ideological differences with communists and fellow-travelers. One such moment occurred when traveling on a bus to Washington DC for a protest:

> As the buses rolled toward Washington, the ride was usually dominated by the small group of socialists and a larger, but still tiny, delegation of "red diaper babies"...Whatever our attitudes toward the Soviet Union or China, we all knew the same songs, so the buses would reverberate to "This Land Is Your Land," the national anthem of the Left, and the ballads of the Spanish Civil War.[15]

Michael's stature in the movement had grown so much that he was chosen to serve as a spokesperson for Dr Martin Luther King Jr during a meeting at the National Students Association in support of the sit-ins. As Harrington recalled: "It was not then considered preposterous for a white radical to be a spokesman for a black leader."[16] A few months later, Harrington would work with King again when the movement planned demonstrations at the Republican and Democratic conventions in support of the sit-ins and for enforcing the Fourteenth Amendment.

After a great deal of difficult organizing, Martin Luther King Jr led a 5000-person demonstration during the week of the Democratic Convention. While the march received little media coverage, Harrington believed it to be a great symbolic victory since the Democrats passed a liberal platform on civil rights. While in Los Angeles, Harrington spent time with Martin Luther King Jr discussing political strategy. Harrington found many points of agreement with King, whom he believed had a quiet socialist orientation. There was one major point of disagreement; King supported the Democratic presidential nominee John F. Kennedy while Harrington did not. As he recalled: "I was against it. In part, my reasons were stupid and sectarian, having to do with a lingering inability to advise anyone to back a 'bourgeois' candidate."[17] In November, Harrington did not cast a vote for JFK. It was a decision that he came to regret.

Realignment

Throughout 1960, Michael's responsibilities within the Socialist Party increased. He was made the editor of a new biweekly paper named *New America*. While *New America* had a small staff and limited resources, it managed to cover many of the social and political struggles of the day. While *New America* did criticize the Democrats, particularly on their lukewarm support for the civil rights movement, it was mostly friendly criticism. As Harrington wrote in the first issue:

> American socialism must concentrate its efforts on the battle for political realignment, for the creation of a real second

> party that will unite labor, liberals, Negros, and provide them with an instrument for principled debate and effective action. Such a party as the Democratic Party will be when the Southern racists and certain corruptive elements have been forced out of it. Political realignment is a precondition for the resurgence of a meaningful Socialist politics in America; it is also a precondition for meaningful and progressive social welfare, labor, and civil rights legislation.[18]

The center of democratic and socialist struggle for the foreseeable future was no longer in the streets, but in the corridors of the Democratic Party.

While Michael Harrington did not originate the idea of political realignment, he not only supported it, but was its foremost champion within socialist circles for the remainder of his life. Far more than Max Shachtman and Socialist Party resolutions, Michael Harrington worked to develop Realignment into a full-blown strategy for not only transforming American politics, but as a necessary part of a socialist transition. According to Harrington, Realignment was "the only place where a beginning can be made" and without it, all socialist efforts would ultimately fail.[19]

He claimed that Realignment was a strategy based on a Marxist analysis of the changing class nature of American society. Michael Harrington still upheld the central role of the organized working class in any socialist transformation, but he argued that after World War II its social weight had declined. If there was going to be a majority for socialism in America, then the working class couldn't rely solely upon themselves, but they needed allies. As he argued: "There is no single, 'natural' majority in the United States which can be mobilized behind a series of defined policies and programs. Rather, there are several potential majorities at any given time and which one will actually emerge depends on a whole range of factors."[20]

Harrington believed that the most important allies of the working class were located in the "new class" of scientists, technicians, teachers and professionals in the public sector.[21] The rise of the new class was a sign of change in the capitalist economy which was "inexorably moving toward collective forms of social life."[22] On the one hand, in the USSR, China and Eastern Europe the collectivist trend took the shape of the new tyranny of "bureaucratic collectivism." On the other hand, in the United States and Western Europe, collectivism took the form of the welfare state where "markets give way to political decisions...[and] bureaucrats, both private and public, become much more important than entrepreneurs or stockholders."[23] He concluded from his analysis that society faced the choice of two possible futures: "These extensions of Shachtman's theories have led me to a basic proposition: that the future is not going to be a choice between capitalism, Communism, and socialism, but between bureaucratic collectivism, advantageous to both executives and commissars, and democratic collectivism, i.e. socialism."[24] This was an updated version of Rosa Luxemburg's warning of "socialism or barbarism."

The pressing question was not how to reverse these collective trends, but whether the future would be democratic or totalitarian. The key to that answer depended on whether or not the new class allied with workers. In the new class, there was the potential of anti-democratic forces prevailing: "With so much economic, political and social power concentrating in computerized industry, the question arises, who will do the programming? Who will control the machines that establish human destiny in this century? And there is clearly the possibility that a technological elite, perhaps even a benevolent elite, could take on this function."[25] Michael believed that the new class "by education and work experience...is predisposed toward planning. It could be an ally of the poor and the organized workers – or their sophisticated enemy. In other words, an unprecedented social and political variable seems to be taking shape in America."[26] The expansion of education was needed in order to instruct the "new class" of planners and bureaucrats, which also allowed students new opportunities for social advancement and prestige within the established order. However, Harrington argued that students were not destined to "act bureaucratically and use sophisticated means to keep the black and poor in their proper place."[27] As the 1960s student movements demonstrated, "a school is a dangerous place, for it exposes people to ideas...Increasing education, all the data indicates, means greater political involvement."[28] This all meant the future political allegiance of the new class was left undecided. Therefore, the possibility existed of the working class allying with the new class, along with blacks and the poor (Harrington would later include groups such as feminists, peace activists, and environmentalists in this coalition) to build a new majority or the "conscience constituency."[29] And it was only this new majority that could bring real democratic socialist change to America.

By the 1960s, Harrington believed that the new majority would seek political expression. For Harrington, it didn't so much matter if there was a new party for the new majority, rather he thought "it is therefore quite possible that a new party will bear an old label: the Democratic Party."[30] He argued that the Democrats were a site of struggle for socialists, since they contained not only segregationists and capitalists, but also held the traditional allegiance of labor unions and blacks along with the new class. In other words, there was a contradiction within the Democratic Party between its base and its racist and capitalist leadership. As the Socialist Party Platform of 1968 put it: "That the most progressive elements in American life thus belong in the same Party as the most reactionary is one of the most outrageous contradictions in the society. But it is not enough simply to denounce the scandal. We must abolish it."[31] Harrington was emphatic that work within the Democratic Party "does not constitute a commitment either to its program or leadership... So the democratic Left does not work in the Democratic Party in order to maintain that institution but to transform it."[32] In 1973, Harrington succinctly described the Realignment strategy as "the left wing of realism" because it was only there that the "mass forces for social change are assembled; it is there that the possibility exists for creating a new first party in America."[33] Harrington believed that the AFL-CIO was the leading force for Realignment. While American labor unions had eschewed independent political action in the shape of a labor or socialist party like their European counterparts, Michael argued that despite their avowed allegiance to capitalism, they had created one in all but name. In fact, Harrington asserted that the American labor movement's socialism was unknown to most: "There is a social democracy in the United States, but most scholars have not noticed it. It is our invisible mass movement."[34]

According to Harrington, it was thanks to the labor movement that the New Deal had a "social democratic tinge."[35] However, the New Deal and other social-democratic reforms of the 1930s were left incomplete because FDR refused "to apply Keynesian principles in any systematic fashion."[36] It was only in the 1960s with the Kennedy and Johnson administrations that the federal government applied Keynesianism in a systematic way thanks to the pressure of the AFL-CIO. That meant the politics of AFL-CIO president George Meany were "quite analogous to that of the mainstream of European socialists."[37] Harrington concluded that this was proof that unions were not just another interest group in the Democratic Party, but they "had clearly made an on-going, class-based political commitment and constituted a tendency – a labor party of sorts – within the Democratic Party."[38]

However, he argued for caution in pursuing Realignment. Michael believed that the next step of Realignment "will not be revolution or even a sudden dramatic lurch to the socialist left. It will be the emergence of a revived liberalism – taking that term to mean the reform of the system within the system – which will of necessity be much more socialistic even though it will not, in all probability, be socialist."[39] With a new robust liberalism as the short-term goal for Realignment, this meant socialists should look to liberals as natural allies.

The Realignment strategy required patience and playing a long game, but the promised result was the creation of a left-liberal, if not a social-democratic, party that would take over the Democratic Party. This new "first party" of the people would proceed to enact needed reforms that would lead to the creation of democratic socialism.

For all its theoretical sophistication, Realignment rested on several faulty assumptions. Firstly, Harrington's contention that the Democratic Party could be "captured" by socialist forces. This assumed that the Democrats were a loose coalition of diverse interest groups who were more or less equally balanced. Rather, the Democrats were (and are still) a capitalist-controlled party representing the interests of more liberal elements among the ruling class. Harrington is correct that the Democrats do traditionally command the support of a progressive and working-class constituency, but that does not make the Democrats the "party of the people."[40] Thanks to the overwhelming capitalist control, labor unions and other progressive groups hold no power in the Democratic Party. In turn, capitalist hegemony in the Democrats enables them to thwart any internal challenge or to co-opt them as the need arises. This is a reality that Michael Harrington never understood.

Secondly, the liberal-labor alliance was an illusion of Harrington's own imagination. As Kim Moody observed: "Post-World War II liberalism, although embraced by much of the union leadership, was mostly a middle class phenomenon...As a political current it never challenged the corporate or private form of property in the means of production, while it rapidly abandoned such New Deal-expanding programs as a national health care system by the early 1950s."[41] In other words, liberals were not reliable allies for social change. To win the support of liberals, Harrington argued that socialists needed to practice moderation and respectability by playing nice in the Democratic Party. Since the Realignment strategy saw the Democrats as the only political arena for socialists, they ended up accepting the logic of lesser-evilism that led them to supporting any Democrat, no matter how right-wing, ultimately thwarting their whole project.

Lastly, the Realignment strategy was doomed because it refused to develop an independent socialist organization. The Socialist Party did view themselves as playing a unique role in Realignment as "an independent organization, free of any compromising ties with the old party machines. It can and it will play the role of the most courageous and intransigent force for realignment."[42] However, this was never something seriously carried out in practice because it went against the entire logic of Realignment. As Christopher Lasch argued:

> [Harrington] is correct in saying that there are no new social forces automatically evolving toward socialism (which is what "democratic planning" comes down to). Presumably this means that radical change can only take place if a new political organization, explicitly committed to radical change, wills it to take place. But Harrington backs off from this conclusion. Instead he seems to predicate his strategy on the wistful hope that socialism will somehow take over the Democratic party without anyone realizing what is happening. He admits that "there is obvious danger when those committed to a new morality thus maneuver on the basis of the old hypocrisies." But there is no choice, because radicals cannot create a new movement "by fiat." It is

> tempting, Harrington says, to think that the best strategy for the Left might be to "start a party of its own." But this course would not work unless there were already an "actual disaffection of great masses of people from the Democratic Party."[43]

Harrington forgot the cardinal lesson of Lenin that, "In its struggle for power the proletariat has no other weapon but organization."[44] Without political independence, there was no room for socialists to develop strategies and actions to advance the interests of the working class. Instead, Realignment forced socialists to maintain good relations with liberals in the hopes of reform at the expense of revolutionary militancy from below. Considering the capitalist control of the Democratic Party, there was no reason for them to advance the interests of the working class. According to the Trotskyist George Novack, the final result of Realignment was that it reduced the Socialist Party to "an off-stage noise in the Democratic Party."[45]

Chapter 4

The Other America

The Man Who Discovered Poverty

Even though Michael Harrington wrote dozens of articles and published 14 books on a diverse array of subjects, his name is generally synonymous with just one: *The Other America*. This short book was a groundbreaking and moving exposé of poverty in the United States of America. *The Other America* established Michael's reputation as a respected public intellectual and advocate for the poor. Michael's work stirred the conscience of people from all walks of life, who were shocked at the grinding poverty that existed in the richest country in the world. As Martin Luther King Jr once jokingly said to Michael Harrington: "You know, we didn't know we were poor until we read your book."[1] The impact of *The Other America* extended beyond the circles of idealistic students and liberals and into the corridors of power by catching the attention of presidents Kennedy and Johnson to develop the programs of "The Great Society" and launch a "War on Poverty." Needless to say, *The Other America* was Michael Harrington's crowning achievement.

The inspiration for *The Other America* came modestly enough over a casual lunch. In December 1958, Michael met Anatole Shub, an editor of *Commentary*, who asked him to write an article on poverty in America for the journal. The subject of poverty was not one much in vogue in the late 1950s; most middle-class saw America as an "affluent society," which had ended the great social problems of the modern era. Michael's experiences as both a Catholic worker and a socialist convinced him that poverty remained very present in America, so he agreed and produced "Our Fifty Million Poor," which was published the following summer. His article was well-received and soon publishers were contacting him to expand it into a book. He was reluctant to do so, remarking: "I filed them in the wastebasket because I had more important socialist work to do."[2] However, he changed his mind after speaking to a fellow socialist, Herman Rosen, who insisted he had a moral duty to tackle the subject. Since the letters were still coming in, he signed a book contract with Macmillan for five hundred dollars, which Michael considered a lot of money. Stealing time away from his activism in the Socialist Party and the civil rights movement, Michael completed the manuscript in 1961 and it was released in March 1962.

Michael relied on three major sources to make his argument on the persistence of American poverty. First were federal government statistics and figures, which allowed him to empirically prove his claims. However, numbers and charts by themselves would have only produced a dry text more suited to a graduate sociology textbook. For his second source, *The Other America* utilized interviews with the poor themselves: black and white, men and women, farmers and those in the ghettos, and the outcasts who were forgotten by affluent America. According to Michael, this would increase the impact of the work "because the American people are much more receptive to dramatic moments and vignettes than to accounts of socio-economic structures."[3] His last source were his own first-hand experiences working with the poor. As a social worker in Missouri and administering to the poor with the Catholic Worker in New York, this enabled him to be "an American Dickens to record the smell and texture and quality of their lives"[4]

The central argument of *The Other America* was that poverty had not disappeared in America, but in a population of 180 million people, there were between 40 to 50 million people living in poverty.[5] Michael claimed that despite the great advancements and abundance of the United States, the poor were a victim of this progress: "In a nation with a technology that could provide every citizen with a decent life, it is an outrage and a scandal that there should be such social misery."[6] According to *The Other America,* the poor were caught in a cycle of poverty that they couldn't escape: "All the most decisive factors making for opportunity and advance are against them. They are born going downward, and most of them stay down. They are victims whose lives are endlessly blown round and round the other America."[7] This created a "culture of poverty" which was not a simple economic condition, but touched upon all aspects of life:

> Taken as a whole, poverty is a culture. Taken on the family level, it has the same quality. These are people who lack education and skill, who have bad health, poor housing, low levels of aspiration and high levels of mental distress. They are, in the language of sociology, "multiproblem" families. Each disability is the more intense because it exists within a web of disabilities. And if one problem is solved, and the others are left constant, there is little gain.[8]

Contrary to conservative claims that the poor could escape their condition through hard work, the "culture of poverty" made it impossible for the poor to lift themselves up by their own bootstraps.[9]

If the poor couldn't escape by themselves, then how could poverty be eliminated? Ultimately, it was the task of the United States government to eradicate poverty: "It is clear that only one agency in America is capable of eradicating both the slum and slum psychology from this land: the Federal Government."[10] Despite the advancements of the New Deal, he argued that the welfare state was not designed to help the poor: "Indeed, the paradox that the welfare state benefits those least who need help most is but a single instance of a persistent irony in the other America. Even when the money finally trickles down, even when a school is built in a poor neighborhood, for instance, the poor are still deprived."[11] Michael advocated a welfare state that truly lived up to its name: that not only expanded existing programs, but included civil rights legislation and planning to uproot the sources of social inequality. While Michael looked to the enlightened liberal elites and the government as saviors of the poor, he deplored them for failing in their mission: "Yet those who could make the difference too often refuse to act because of their ignorant, smug moralisms."[12] What liberals needed was a political will and a crusading spirit in order to eradicate poverty.

Notwithstanding Michael Harrington's political background, *The Other America*'s call to action did not advocate for socialism. Indeed, this was not a book written for socialists or workers, but for "the good America, the decent America, that survives even in the age of mass culture."[13] He penned a call to enlightened liberals for action to rescue the poor: "As usual, the fate of the poor hangs upon the decision of the better-off."[14] Since his audience were liberals, Michael argued that bringing up socialism would serve as a distraction from seriously discussing poverty: "I decided that if I even mentioned the word socialism, I would divert attention from the plight of the poor, evoke all the misconceptions Americans had about the term and would then have to deal with the myths the word had conjured up."[15]

In the first few months after *The Other America*'s release, there were no signs of its future impact. The book sold modestly and received positive reviews. Michael was just glad to receive a royalties check before leaving for an extended trip to Europe to marry Stephanie Gervis, a staff writer for the *Village Voice*. By the time he returned to the United States at the end of 1963, he found himself propelled to stardom. Michael Harrington's rise to fame owed a great deal to his old friend Dwight Macdonald. Just before Michael left for Europe,

Macdonald was commissioned by *The New Yorker* to write an extended review of *The Other America*. When Macdonald's review appeared several weeks later, it hailed *The Other America* as "an excellent book – and a most important one" and echoed the call for a War on Poverty:

> The solution is also obvious: to provide, out of taxes, the kind of subsidies that have always been given to the public schools (not to mention the police and fire departments and the post office) – subsidies that would raise incomes above the poverty level, so that every citizen could feel he is indeed such. "*Civis Romanus sum*!" cried St. Paul when he was threatened with flogging – and he was not flogged. Until our poor can be proud to say "*Civis Romanus sum*!," until the act of justice that would make this possible has been performed by the three-quarters of Americans who are not poor – until then the shame of the Other America will continue.[16]

The fame of *The Other America* owes as much to Dwight Macdonald's review as to the book itself, something that Michael readily acknowledged: "Macdonald's review of my book had the effect of a second publication date and made poverty a topic of conversation in the intellectual-political world of the Northeast corridor."[17] By 1965, *The Other America* had sold over 70,000 copies and gone through at least five editions.

Michael was shocked at his new-found fame: "I was thirty-five when it came out and until then I'd never made any money in my life. Earning a living as a writer in this country sucks...But all of a sudden there were all these lecture invitations, and they paid quite well, and it freed me to write my subsequent books."[18] *The Other America* had transformed an obscure socialist activist into a public intellectual and a household name.

The Advisor

The popularity of *The Other America* also came at an opportune political moment. At the end of 1962, the Kennedy administration was planning to launch an anti-poverty campaign. To prepare for such an undertaking, Walter Heller, Kennedy's Economic Advisor, needed to gather information on poverty in America. Heller came across Macdonald's review of *The Other America* and showed the book to the president, who was very impressed.

During the spring and summer of 1963, the Kennedy administration assembled an anti-poverty task-force. According to James Sundquist, a member of the task-force, *The Other America* helped to focus them on their mission:

> The measures enacted...and those proposed, were dealing separately with such problems as slum housing, juvenile delinquency, unemployment, dependency, and illiteracy, but they were separately inadequate because they were striking only at some of the surface aspects of a bedrock problem, and that bedrock problem had to be identified and defined so that it could be attacked in a concerted, unified, and innovative way. Perhaps it was Harrington's book that identified the target for Kennedy and supplied the coordinating concept: the bedrock problem, in a word, was "poverty." Words and concepts define programs; once the target was reduced to a single word, the timing became right for a unified program.[19]

On November 19, Kennedy told Heller that he planned to formally launch the anti-poverty campaign in 1964. Just 3 days later, John F. Kennedy was assassinated in Dallas and Lyndon B. Johnson ascended to the presidency. Johnson intended to fulfill Kennedy's legacy and launch a "War on Poverty," which he formally launched in his 1964 State of the Union Address.[20] On February 1, Johnson assigned the Director of the Peace Corps, Sargent Shriver, to create another anti-poverty task-force. Naturally, Shriver reached out to Michael Harrington to be a part of the task-force.

Even though Michael was publicly critical that the Johnson administration's War on Poverty didn't go far enough, he readily accepted. He believed that this was a practical opportunity to implement change:

> Once the government had determined to do something about poverty, should I simply have said that its efforts were inevitably going to be inadequate and that in the not-so-long-run they might benefit the rich more than the poor? That, it seemed (and seems) to me, would have been to turn my back on the hungry, hopeless people who needed all the advocates they could find to push reform to its farthest limits.[21]

For the next 2 weeks, Michael worked with Shriver and other advisors in preparing a presentation on strategy for the president. He remained critical of the limited scope of the programs: "At my first meeting with Shriver, I told him that the billion dollars the White House then planned to invest in the project was 'nickels and dimes' ('Oh really, Mr Harrington,' Shriver said. 'I don't know about you, but this is the first time I've ever spent a billion dollars')."[22] Michael argued candidly for massive planned investments and social planning to tackle poverty. To his surprise, Shriver agreed and included Michael's proposals in his presentation to President Johnson. Supposedly, Johnson said: "That if it took such innovations to complete the work begun by the New Deal, then we'd just have to make them."[23] While Michael's account makes it appear that he played a central role in shaping the War on Poverty, Isserman says he did little to shape the proposed legislation.[24] Members of the Johnson administration concur that Harrington's role in drafting the legislation was actually "negligible."[25] However, the most important role that Michael Harrington played in the War on

Poverty was not in the realm of policy, but as an independent and passionate public spokesman for the White House's agenda.

All the Way With LBJ

Whatever his doubts about the War on Poverty, Michael knew that any chance to improve it would be lost if Johnson was not re-elected. Unlike in 1960 when he refused to support Kennedy, now Harrington wholeheartedly supported Johnson. Michael saw the Republican candidate, Barry Goldwater, as a dangerous right-wing extremist supported by "a united front of reaction, particularly joining together the overt forces of Klan racism and the covert forces of white backlash racism."[26] In an essay in the left-wing journal *New Politics*, Harrington said defeating Goldwater was the precondition to serious reform. He argued that a Goldwater victory would result in attacks on civil rights, labor and the welfare state. Johnson was the only "practical alternative" to Goldwater. Michael argued that the left should use the election to mobilize the people because it was necessary to overwhelmingly

> defeat Goldwater by registering millions of Negroes, trade unionists and unorganized poor whites, such an accomplishment will be a permanent gain which will have implications far beyond election day. These people will not be drawn into political activity on the basis of a completely negative proposition: Defeat Goldwater. They will be motivated to the degree to which they see the campaign as a means of struggling for civil rights, increased minimum wage, Medicare, and the like. And the existence of organized millions committed to such programs will be felt after election day as much as on it.[27]

Michael believed that after electing Johnson, the mass movement behind him would now have an advocate in the

While House and continue its forward motion: "If Johnson wins, it will not be Utopia or anything like it, but the victory will contain the possibility of important developments."[28] Harrington could not understand the rationale of socialists who were not open to the possibilities the campaign opened for Realignment. He thought they were clinging to sectarian politics and overly obsessed about being corrupted by the Democratic Party. He condemned them in no uncertain terms for being out of touch:

> Socialists in isolation might maintain their program and preserve it for the initiated, but they would lose all relevance, all communication with the people (and, from the socialist point of view, these people are the most decisive means of production of the future society). Now, however, it is clearer than ever that the old ways amount to an abstention from politics, not a political abstention.[29]

By contrast, Michael believed now was the time for radicals to get out the vote and dispense with fantasies about revolution. Even though the central issue of the 1964 election was not socialism, it was clearly the first election in his lifetime where the stakes were unbelievably high.

As it turned out, Harrington's fears that Johnson would be defeated were overblown. Johnson was not only elected in a landslide, but with Democratic majorities in both houses of Congress. The president was supported not only by liberals and labor unions, but by the majority of the capitalist class, who found Goldwater's "extremism" unappealing. Now with an impressive mandate, the Johnson administration finally not only launched the War on Poverty, but supported both the Civil Rights Act and the Voting Rights Act.

While Michael hailed the anti-poverty programs and civil rights legislation, he hoped that Johnson would do more. To that end, he collaborated with Rustin and A. Philip Randolph in drafting and lobbying for a "Freedom Budget" at the White House Civil Rights Conference of 1966. The Freedom Budget envisioned full employment for all Americans and the elimination of poverty over a period of 10 years.[30] This was the high point of Michael Harrington's political optimism. Nonetheless, the Freedom Budget never got past the planning stages and was ultimately a casualty of the Vietnam War. As Harrington recalled: "If Lyndon Johnson had not escalated that tragedy in 1965, if the huge Presidential and Congressional majorities of 1964 had held together and been used to implement Freedom Budget programs, if the demands of black people had been partly met, then many things might have been different. As it was, Vietnam caused Johnson to miss the greatest opportunity in recent American history."[31]

Later on, Michael adamantly defended the Great Society from its conservative critics, but he was personally reserved on its accomplishments.[32] He argued the War on Poverty was not fought like a real war and in the end, "what was supposed to be a social war turned out to be a skirmish and, in any case, poverty won."[33] This was partly due to the fact that there was no overarching vision for the Great Society, so precious energies were needlessly spent: "When the moment for action finally came, practical men were hamstrung because not enough visionaries had preceded them."[34] The Great Society's lack of vision was partly by design because its architects were "part of a structured system which tended – tended, not was predetermined – to place fundamental ideological limits upon liberal reform."[35] Due to the defense of capitalism, Michael argued that liberals were incapable of truly undertaking a War on Poverty, but just fell back on Keynesian measures. In order for liberals to truly carry out a War on Poverty and fulfill their radical potential, they needed the support of visionary socialists like Harrington, who recognized the limits of reform and the welfare state.

The Welfare State

Even though he hailed the welfare state for prioritizing basic human needs over profit, Michael Harrington was under no illusions that it was the realization of socialism itself: "The welfare state is a hybrid, too socialist to be completely capitalist, decidedly too capitalist to be socialist."[36] He saw the Western European welfare state as the result of an uneasy compromise between mass movements from below and capitalists willing to concede reforms. Since the capitalists still held power, they undermined the gains of the welfare state. While the welfare state fulfilled longstanding socialist demands to nationalize large swaths of industry, Harrington said its main beneficiaries were capitalists:

> More to the point...[nationalization] also reveals a central flaw in the notion of socialist capitalism. As long as the system is dominated by private corporations and wealth, that fact will tend in the long run to make all collectivist measures discriminate in favor of the status quo. So there is yet another dilemma for the social democrats: if state property within a capitalist system is run on a social rather than a profit-making calculus, it will usually subsidize the private sector; if state property operates according to the profit calculus, it then behaves like, and often in concert with, the capitalists.[37]

Even though the welfare state would not solve the contradictions of capitalism, Harrington claimed it was still a necessary stepping stone on the road to socialism (something we will discuss at length in the appendix):

> Capitalism "socializes" private priorities and is institutionally opposed to any redistribution of the relative shares of wealth. This is related to its propensity for crisis and, ultimately, its self-destruction. In this context, the welfare state is seen as

> an ambiguous and transitional phenomenon, the temporary salvation of the system, but also the portent of its end.[38]

Therefore, it remained the task of socialists to not only defend the programs of the welfare state, but to expand them. In the long run, Michael believed that the struggle to make the welfare state provide for the pressing needs of the people would reveal its inherent contradictions and lead to demands to go past it and create socialism itself. Michael Harrington believed *The Other America* and participation in the Great Society were a means to that end.

Chapter 5

The Anticommunist

The New Mood

In 1960, the Socialist Party was still a small organization, numbering roughly a thousand members and appeared uniquely placed to take advantage of the new political mood. One of the sources of socialist strength was YPSL, which benefited from an energetic and talented new membership. The new dynamism of YPSL caused its membership to jump from 300 in 1960 to over 800 by 1962.[1] According to older socialist Debbie Meier:

> [The new recruits]...they were ambitious. We saw that as a hopeful sign. They were competent. In the 1950s we had had the feeling that we could only attract 'nudniks.' Who would join an organization that isn't going anywhere? If we were attracting people with ambitions, they must see in us that we have a future.[2]

As opposed to the doldrums of the 1950s when only a brave few could be found at demonstrations, YPSL was now participating in demonstrations of thousands across the country.

Long before Berkeley became synonymous with New Left radicalism, YPSL had a solid base of supporters there who were active in the civil rights movement and five members were among the Freedom Riders arrested in 1961.[3] When Michael Harrington traveled to Berkeley in the late 1950s, he recalled that it was vibrant and open to left-wing politics: "There on the edge of the Pacific a radical-Bohemian world existed that was very much like the one I had known at the University of Chicago in the late forties. At the Steppenwolf and Blind Lemon there was an ambiance of folk music, Marxism, and sexual freedom, the Left-wing trinity of that period."[4] Even though Michael Harrington's membership of YPSL lapsed in 1959 when he aged out at 31, he remained a mentor to the young socialists. They treated him with a respect and formality that he wasn't used to by calling him "Sir" instead of "Mike."[5]

Michael's prestige and esteem was not just limited to the ranks of Young Socialists. A young Tom Hayden, who first met Michael in 1960, described him as "easily one of the most charismatic political intellectuals" he ever encountered.[6] The following year, when Tom Hayden wrote "Who are the Student Boat-Rockers?" about student radicalism, he listed just three men over 30 who were respected by the younger generation: Norman Thomas, C. Wright Mills and Michael Harrington.[7] It was a great honor for Michael Harrington.

The appearance of youthful radicalism made Michael hopeful that they could revitalize the American left. In "The American Campus," written for *Dissent* in 1962, he observed that the young were full of:

> a sort of frenzy of introspection and self-consciousness, with groups spending almost as much time in front of a mirror as on the picket line...Its mood was more radical than liberal, oriented toward single "issues" rather than finished ideologies (but conscious politicals have often played a decisive organizational role). Its tone is moral, focusing on questions like peace, capital punishment, and human equality, ignoring economic and social planning.[8]

He warned that the New Left would squander their potential if they lacked proper guidance. Otherwise, they would embrace "totalitarian" ideas such as communism. Michael argued that older socialists needed an approach of "patient education" in order to win over the young:

> Students today distrust adult leaders and organizations (and particularly the liberal establishment)...And often, the break with the hypocrisy of American society generates a suspicion of anyone who comes down hard on Communist totalitarianism. In the first radical flush, these students fail to distinguish between the official anti-Communist slogans of the status quo and the critique of a democratic left.[9]

Michael's patient approach to the New Left should not be confused with any flexibility on the question of communism. He was adamant that any pro-communist "attitudes must be faced and changed."[10] On that, there could be no compromise.

Students for a Democratic Society

The question remained about how student radicals could be nudged away from the dangers of communism and embrace the democratic left? A broad organization was needed to welcome young radicals, but one that was not connected with a political party nor doctrinally socialist. YPSL did not qualify since it was not only openly socialist, but too small and riven with factionalism. The solution appeared to lie in reviving the moribund Student League for Industrial Democracy (SLID). SLID was a descendant of the Intercollegiate Socialist Society founded in 1905 by Upton Sinclair to promote socialist ideas on campuses. By the 1940s and 1950s, SLID was controlled by trade unions such as the ILGWU who were bitterly opposed to "communist totalitarianism." Their anticommunism extended to all radicals, even anti-Stalinist ones. In 1951, Bogdan Denitch, then a young Shachtmanite, was driven out of SLID's City College of New York's chapter as a "clear and present danger."[11] When Michael was in the YSL, he derisively said that SLID played "a pro-American, Cold War, State Department kind of role."[12] As Kirkpatrick Sale observed, SLID's anticommunism did not attract many followers: "Membership crises were recurrent, and throughout the fifties the number of paid-up members probably never got beyond a hundred – with perhaps another hundred occasional hangers-on – at no more than a dozen campuses altogether."[13] In 1958, their annual convention attracted a total of only 13 students. If SLID didn't want to fade out of existence, then they needed to make major changes. Al Haber, who became president of SLID in 1960, knew it was time to make the organization relevant to a new generation. For one thing, the name of the organization was anachronistic and held little meaning to young people. According to Sale:

> the stated reasons were simple – "industrial democracy" was too narrow an idea, it made the organization sound too labor oriented, it was too hard to recruit on college campuses with an antiquated and cumbersome name – but the overriding reason was that SLID felt, perhaps mostly unconsciously, the need to dissociate itself from the old and tired leadership of the League for Industrial Democracy in response to the new college mood.[14]

A majority of SLID agreed with Haber and the name was officially changed to Students for a Democratic Society (SDS).

Now with a new name, SDS made their first effort to reach out to the broader world by holding a conference in Ann Arbor in support of the civil rights movement, known as "Human Rights in the North." SDS's timing couldn't have been better since the conference was held just after the Greensboro Sit-Ins that galvanized students across the country. This touched the souls of white students, who were inspired by the fearlessness of blacks standing up to Jim Crow terror. It also raised the possibility of a multi-racial alliance of white and black who could create a new America. As a result, "Human Rights in the North" attracted an impressive array of student and civil rights activists including not just Socialist Party stalwarts like Michael

Harrington and Bayard Rustin, but also James Farmer from the Congress of Racial Equality. No concrete actions emerged from the conference, but SDS was now on the map as a pole of attraction for radical students.

Among the new recruits to SDS was Tom Hayden, a recent graduate, a journalist and an activist in the civil rights movement. When Harrington met Hayden, he tried to win the latter to socialism. Later, he recalled with frustration that Hayden "accepted much of my analysis, yet he balked at the socialist idea itself. My analysis, he said, was too bound up with dogma and obsolete bookish controversies. What radicalism needed was a fresh start, a rethinking of perspectives that would avoid the old rhetoric, with its sectarian Europeanisms, and speak in the authentic vocabulary of America."[15] Hayden embodied the new generation of SDS, who were eager for change and action, but little interested in theory or the controversies of the past.

If SDS was going to bring major change, then they needed more than just a crusading spirit, but a positive vision to present to their members. A planned manifesto was the major point on the agenda for SDS's 1962 conference at a UAW retreat in Port Huron, Michigan. Tom Hayden was charged with writing this manifesto; he worked with not only other members of SDS such as Al Haber, but also with Michael Harrington and SDS's parent body, the League for Industrial Democracy (LID) to develop a statement. Even though Hayden was hostile to a lot of the existing left, Michael recalled that there was "harmony and even euphoria" as they worked together.[16]

On June 15, 1962 the *Port Huron Statement* was released to the world. Nearly 80 percent of the *Port Huron Statement* is taken up with criticism of American society and institutions ranging from political parties, big business, the military, labor unions and racism. The authors called for the revitalization of American democracy in place of apathy and alienation that currently pervades the country. The measures proposed were not revolutionary, but reformist with calls for greater spending on welfare, civil rights programs, and tackling poverty to create a "participatory democracy," where all citizens take part in directly running things. Its middle-class orientation was apparent by locating students, not the working class, as the main agents of social change. According to Sale, the *Port Huron Statement* not only gave coherence to a new generation of students, but "it gave to those dissatisfied with their nation an analysis by which to dissect it, to those pressing instinctively for change a vision of what to work for, to those feeling within themselves the need to act a strategy by which to become effective. No ideology can do more."[17] Throughout the *Port Huron Statement*, many of Harrington's ideas are quite visible.[18] For instance, the manifesto recognized that the student movement needed the civil rights movement and labor unions as allies if they were going to win:

> a new politics must include a revitalized labor movement: a movement that sees itself, and is regarded by others, as a major leader of the breakthrough to a politics of hope and vision. Labor's role is no less unique or important in the needs of the future than it was in the past; its numbers and potential political strength, its natural interest in the abolition of exploitation, its reach to the grass roots of American society, combine to make it the best synthesis of the civil rights, peace, and economic reform movements.[19]

The *Port Huron Statement* also accepted the strategic orientation of Realignment that liberals and socialists were natural allies. However, this "new majority" had no political expression, which was due to the "Democratic Party which tolerates the perverse unity of liberalism and racism, prevents the social change wanted by Negroes, peace protesters, labor unions, students, reform Democrats, and other liberals."[20] Therefore, if the new majority was to prevail, they needed to Realign the Democratic Party in order to implement real change such as expanding the welfare state and ending Jim Crow:

> An imperative task for these publicly disinherited groups, then, is to demand a Democratic Party responsible to their interests. They must support Southern voter registration and Negro political candidates and demand that Democratic Party liberals do the same (in the last Congress, Dixiecrats split with Northern Democrats on 119 of 300 roll-calls, mostly on civil rights, area redevelopment and foreign aid bills; and breach was much larger than in the previous several sessions). Labor should begin a major drive in the South. In the North, reform clubs (either independent or Democratic) should be formed to run against big city regimes on such issues as peace, civil rights, and urban needs. Demonstrations should be held at every Congressional or convention seating of Dixiecrats. A massive research and publicity campaign should be initiated, showing to every housewife, doctor, professor, and worker the damage done to their interests every day a racist occupies a place in the Democratic Party. Where possible, the peace movement should challenge the "peace credentials" of the otherwise-liberals by threatening or actually running candidates against them.[21]

The *Port Huron Statement* explicitly condemned communism as well:

> As democrats we are in basic opposition to the communist system. The Soviet Union, as a system, rests on the total suppression of organised opposition...The Communist Party has equated falsely the "triumph of socialism" with centralised bureaucracy. The Soviet state lacks independent labour organisations and other liberties we consider basic...

> Communist parties throughout the rest of the world are generally undemocratic in internal structure and mode of action...The communist movement has failed, in every sense, to achieve its stated intentions of leading a worldwide movement for human emancipation.[22]

When it came to questions of the new majority, Realignment and anticommunism, the fundamentals of Michael Harrington's worldview were clearly present in the *Port Huron Statement*.

However, the *Port Huron Statement* diverged from Harrington on a number of points. Labor unions were criticized for a crisis of vision and their bureaucratic structures that were "cynical toward, or afraid of, rank-and-file involvement in the work of unions."[23] Michael claimed that he:

> was painfully aware of the limitations of American unions. But I also knew many militants who were trying to build a democratic and social labor movement, and I thought that the established union leadership played a progressive role, particularly on domestic issues...I argued that American liberalism, for all of its flaws, was the mass Left of the society, and that radicals had to speak to what was positive in it and what made it possible to move liberals to the Left – not simply focus on its inadequacies.[24]

More seriously, SDS also rejected the logic of anticommunism, seeing it as an obstacle to movements for social change: "An unreasoning anti-communism has become a major social problem for those who want to construct a more democratic America...Even many liberals and socialists share static and repetitious participation in the anti-communist crusade and often discourage tentative, inquiring discussion about the 'Russian question.'"[25] SDS's rejection of anticommunism also challenged the rationale for the Cold War that the Soviet Union was bent on world domination and that the United States was a force for democracy in the world. Rather, anticommunism served as a shield for the United States to support anticommunist dictatorships who protected corporate interests:

> With rare variation, American foreign policy in the Fifties was guided by a concern for foreign investment and a negative anti-communist political stance linked to a series of military alliances, both undergirded by military threat. We participated unilaterally – usually through the Central Intelligence Agency – in revolutions against governments in Laos, Guatemala, Cuba, Egypt, Iran. We permitted economic investment to decisively affect our foreign policy: sugar in Cuba, oil in the Middle East, diamonds and gold in South Africa...[26]

The *Port Huron Statement* on communism was in line with the old Shachtmanite tradition of third campism by rejecting both Washington *and* Moscow. Ironically, SDS's challenge to Michael Harrington's anticommunism went too far: "My anti-Communism was formed in the traditions of revolutionary anti-Stalinist Marxism. It was not simply a theory, but an emotion as well."[27]

When Michael arrived at the Port Huron conference, he was more than ready for a fight. At one of the opening panels, he ferociously denounced Hayden's draft. The latter was stunned but refused to concede any ground. The argument between Hayden and Harrington continued throughout the night. The following day, Michael had to leave Port Huron for a speaking engagement, but nothing was resolved. On top of fights over the *Port Huron Statement*, another argument erupted. This centered over whether to allow the seating of Jim Hawley, who was at the conference as an observer on behalf of the Communist Party. To Harrington's allies, Horowitz,

Kahn and former YPSL chairman Richard Roman, the seating of a 17-year-old communist was like being in the same room as Joseph Stalin. The majority of SDS were confused by the whole affair. By the time the issue was settled in favor of Hawley being seated, he had already left for home.

In light of the objections from Harrington and the League of Industrial Democracy, the delegates redrafted the statement to make it more acceptable. Criticism of liberals and labor unions were toned down. The section on communism was also changed, but it still ended up rejecting the kind of virulent anticommunism favored by Harrington. SDS's rejection of anticommunism also found expression in their new constitution, which removed the clause barring adherents of "totalitarianism" from membership.[28] Michael Harrington and his allies were dissatisfied with the outcome, despite the fact that SDS had conceded to them on almost all major points, except the cardinal sin of communism. After the convention, Horowitz told Harrington that SDS had made no substantial changes to the draft. He called an emergency meeting of the LID to deal with the wayward SDS. According to LID's executive secretary, Vera Rony, the old guard was horrified at what SDS had done:

> To our amazement...the SDS convention adopted a policy statement which placed the blame for the cold war largely upon the US...The students placed the blame for the present impasse on nuclear disarmament largely upon the US and bitterly scored our foreign policy as a whole, while making the merest passing criticism of Soviet actions in this sphere. In addition, Communist youth observers were seated at the convention and given speaking rights...After these events, the LID Executive Committee met to decide the position of the adult organization. It was the general view that we could not countenance a student body which disagreed with us on basic principles and adopted a popular front position.[29]

LID took immediate action and demanded that both SDS leaders Hayden and Haber explain themselves. As Kirkpatrick Sale observed: "SDS, by the tone of the summons, was clearly condemned in advance."[30] Until the issue was resolved, LID forbade SDS from mailing or distributing any material under its own name. When the hearing began on July 6, Harrington wasted no time in getting to the point:

> Let's get to the broad problem. There is no SDS as a functioning organization with a political life. It does not exist. So how can you get a representative convention from a nonorganization? Besides, this document of cosmic scope was given to the delegates – that's obviously not representative. It would require a year's discussion to get a really representative document. This can't even try to express the view of the people who were there – even that's not possible in such a short meeting. A founding convention should take ten days to two weeks and a year of discussion.[31]

Hayden and Haber objected that SDS was a functioning organization and they did hold a convention. Furthermore, the *Port Huron Statement* was not meant to be the last word on radicalism, but was seen as the beginning of a wider dialogue.[32]

After Harrington's charges had been presented, the attack on Haber and Hayden began in earnest:

> Rony: "Do you think that the LID would allow a communist-front group to be seated at a convention? Do you think you're trying to run SDS within LID as the elders would?"
>
> Harrington: "There is a basic clash here between SDS's and Lid's concept of how to deal with other groups...PYOC is the youth group of the CP! – it's not a front group. There's a tradition, and a good one, not to give it a voice or vote in the community."

Hayden: "But we just allowed him to be seated, without any declaration implying support or condemnation."

Harrington: "We should have nothing to do with those people."

Fleishman: "Would you give seats to the Nazis too?"

Harrington: "United frontism means accepting reds to your meeting...You knew this would send LID through the roof. This issue was settled on the left ten or twenty years ago – and that you could countenance any united frontism now is inconceivable. And you voted down the authoritarianism section [of the constitution], too."

Hayden: "United frontism is a slanderous charge. We're not supporting these groups but merely stating our opinions procedurally."

Harrington: "Document shmocuments. Slaimon and I said that this was antithetical to the LID and everything it's stood for."

Hayden: "There was no notion at Port Huron that these differences were irreconcilable. The document doesn't confuse community and fraternity."[33]

The interrogation of Hayden and Haber continued for 2 hours. Michael condemned them for working with communist youth groups and people who associated with communists. To no avail, Haber protested that Harrington's objections to the statement draft were taken to heart in the final version. The trial ended without any formal resolution, but as far as Michael Harrington was concerned, they were guilty. LID not only cut off the salaries of Hayden, Haber and field secretary Steve Max, but they cut off all funding to SDS and changed the locks to the office door.

Afterward, Haber and Hayden met in Steve Max's apartment to determine their next move. Paul Booth, who was also present, recalled how Hayden felt betrayed: "They were vicious, personally vicious...It taught me that social democrats aren't radicals and can't be trusted in a radical movement. It taught me what social democrats really think about civil liberties and organizational integrity."[34] After the initial shock wore off, the SDSers decided not to throw in the towel. They went back to the office and picked open the locks.

After reclaiming their office, SDS wrote a formal appeal to the LID board condemning their treatment and defending the *Port Huron Statement*. SDS extended an olive branch, saying that differences between them and LID were actually beneficial to a growing movement: "Friction between the generations represented in the LID is both necessary and proper – and a spark of hope for change in our times."[35] It worked. A break between LID and SDS was avoided thanks to the intervention of Norman Thomas and calmer heads on the LID board. After tempers cooled, a compromise was reached and the major gains of Port Huron – statement, officers and constitution – were allowed to stand. The keys to SDS's office were returned. Michael apologized and a formal reconciliation of sorts was reached at the end of the summer when he met with SDS leaders at the University of Ohio. Still, bitter feelings remained between Michael Harrington and the young radicals: "But at that Columbus meeting I was aware that I had lost the confidence and trust of the young people. At the end of our tense reconciliation Casey Hayden said, 'Well, I know now what it must have been like to be attacked by the Stalinists.'"[36]

Later on, Michael deeply regretted how roughly he handled SDS and felt the need to apologize for the incident whenever it came up. He said that feelings of anger and betrayal got in the way of his better judgment.[37] Michael also acknowledged that his objections to the *Port Huron Statement* were based on earlier drafts and that the final version actually incorporated most of his suggested changes. He believed that some of his problems with SDS were due to a clash between generations and jealousy on his part: "There was a new generation on the scene and I was threatened, not simply by a political disagreement over Communism and liberalism, but by my own middle-aging as well. So I fought back, stupidly and bureaucratically, as much out of wounded ego as from ideological convictions."[38]

While Harrington acknowledged his own lack of diplomacy in handling SDS, he would not admit that he had been wrong on the larger political issues: "But if I am quite ready to acknowledge my personal failings in this unhappy history, I am not at all prepared to concede political error on all points in the dispute."[39] Michael admitted that even if he had been more tactful over his disagreements with SDS, it would not have changed anything: "The conflict was, I think inevitable, and had I acted on the basis of better information, more maturity, and a greater understanding of the differences at stake, that I would only have postponed the day of reckoning."[40]

In the final analysis, the problem for Harrington was not just that many radicals were "soft on communism," but they rejected moderation and liberalism. Central to Harrington's Realignment strategy was responsible work within the Democratic Party and coalition politics to build a new majority for progressive change. By contrast, radicals considered Democrats to be an integral part of the capitalist system, who carried out wars and were beholden to the interests of segregationists and Wall Street. Michael was right that these worldviews were diametrically opposed and that conflict between him and the radicals was inescapable.

Chapter 6

The Necessary Compromise

In 1964, the civil rights movement seemed to be putting Michael Harrington's Realignment strategy into action in the form of the Mississippi Freedom Democratic Party (MFDP). It was the MFDP's intention to not only register black voters, but to drive racists out of the Mississippi Democratic Party in order to make the Democrats truly represent the people. However, once the MFDP was forced to appease segregationists by liberals and the labor bureaucracy, Michael Harrington was perfectly willing to make this necessary compromise since the needs of pragmatism trumped his strategy.

Due to restrictive voting laws and Jim Crow terror, Mississippi had one of the worst records of black voting in the country with less than 7 percent registered, even though they comprised 40 percent of the state's population.[1] In 1964, after SNCC failed to get help from the federal government in registering black voters, they decided to change tactics. Now SNCC planned to expose Mississippi's racist system on the national stage by recruiting a thousand white students from the north to come down and register voters. SNCC believed that public opinion would not tolerate racists attacking young white students with impunity. Considering that the official Mississippi Democratic Party had denounced the Civil Rights Act and was open only to whites, SNCC activists created their own organization – the MFDP. Since the MFDP was open to all citizens of Mississippi, they planned to elect delegates to the Democratic National Convention in Atlantic City in 1964 and have them seated as the Mississippi delegation instead of the segregationist party.

MFDP activists had a Realignment perspective and believed that by driving out the racists, they could capture the Democratic

Party as a vehicle for social change. As activist Cleveland Sellers recalled: "We were thinking far beyond Atlantic City. If our venture there was successful, we intended to utilize similar tactics in other Southern states, particularly Georgia and South Carolina...With the Dixiecrats deposed, the way would have been clear for a wide-ranging redistribution of wealth, power and priorities throughout the nation."[2]

The MFDP had allies in liberal and labor unions such as the UAW, who believed it was in their interests to support the civil rights movement. According to Peter Levy:

> After a decade of retreat, social activist unions were beginning to reassert their interests in progressive causes, including the drive for racial equality...When the civil rights movement emerged, they welcomed it as their own cause. Many trade unionists had joined the labor movement with an understanding that racial equality was a necessary precondition for economic and political equality for working men and women...By allying with the disadvantaged and unorganized and supporting racial equality, labor improved its general reputation and discredited the claim that it was merely a special interest group.[3]

With the coming together of labor, students and blacks in the MFDP, it appeared that Michael Harrington's Realignment strategy was finally being realized.

The summer of 1964, known as Freedom Summer, was one of the most violent of the civil rights movement. The police, Ku Klux Klan and white mobs terrorized the activists with bombings, burnings, arrests and at least six murders. As expected by SNCC, Freedom Summer garnered national media attention, particularly after two white and one black civil rights activists – James Chaney, Andrew Goodman and Michael Schwerner – were murdered. Still, the murders did not produce federal protection for civil rights activists or enforcement of voting laws in Mississippi.

Since he was on a speaking tour and writing a book, Michael Harrington did not participate in Freedom Summer. However, many of the student activists, who had braved racist terror, were inspired by his ideas. According to one student volunteer, writing to his parents from a jail cell: "One of the guys had a battered copy of *The Other America* so we divided it into chapters. I got the dismal one on the problems of the aged...To be old and forgotten is certainly a worse sentence than mine (I wouldn't recommend the book for those planning to do time)."[4]

Despite the high cost, Freedom Summer was a success and registered more than 63,000 blacks, who elected 68 "Freedom Delegates" (64 black and four white) to head to Atlantic City. When the MFDP delegates arrived in Atlantic City, they demanded to be seated as the official Democratic delegation since they held the only primaries open to all citizens. The MFDP delegates also pledged their loyalty to Johnson, noting that the segregationist Democrats supported Barry Goldwater.

The MFDP delegates made their case to be seated on television in front of the whole country. During the coverage, Fannie Lou Hamer recounted the terror she endured which included being beaten and losing her job. At one point, Hamer declared:

> If the Freedom Democratic Party is not seated now, I question America. Is this America, the land of the free and the home of the brave where we have to sleep with our telephones off the hooks because our lives be threatened daily because we want to live as decent human beings in America?[5]

Johnson called a press conference to deflect attention away from Hamer, but to no avail. Hamer's speech was replayed across the country. The Democrats were suddenly deluged with demands to seat the MFDP delegation. Even the Socialist Party declared: "The fight over the seating of the Mississippi Freedom delegation will be a test of organized liberalism's commitment to put its principles into action."[6]

Johnson had no intention of seating the delegation since he wanted to prevent the southern white vote from going to Goldwater. As Texas Governor John Connally told the president: "If you seat those Black buggers, the whole South will walk out."[7] Johnson planned to just make a minimal concession to the civil rights movement in the hopes that the whole affair would quietly go away. Minnesota Senator Hubert Humphrey, a stalwart liberal, was instructed to offer the MFDP a compromise. He said that two of their delegates would be seated alongside the entire white segregationist delegation from Mississippi. The MFDP delegation erupted in outrage after hearing this. Hamer declared: "We didn't come all this way for no two seats, 'cause all of us is tired."[8]

The Johnson camp knew that this compromise was a bitter pill to swallow. Humphrey enlisted Walter Reuther and Bayard Rustin for help. Reuther threatened to fire MFDP activists employed by the UAW if they refused to get in line. Reuther even warned Martin Luther King Jr, who supported the MFDP: "Your funding is on the line…The kind of money you got from us in Birmingham is there again for Mississippi, but you've got to help us and we've got to help Johnson."[9] Fearing the implications of a Goldwater victory and the loss of financial support, King quickly supported the deal.

Rustin argued that the MFDP needed to support the deal since this was "serious politics" as opposed to simple protest. SNCC activist James Forman recalls Rustin's lecture:

> Yes...there is a difference between protest and politics. The former is based on morality and the latter is based on reality and compromise. If you are going to engage in politics then you must give up protest…

> You must be willing to compromise, to win victories and go home and come back and win some more...
>
> That is politics. And those of you, my friends, who are here from Mississippi and who have made such a valiant struggle, you are now engaged in politics. You must accept the compromise. If you don't, then you are still protesting.
>
> We must think of our friends in labor, Walter Reuther and the others, who have gone to bat for us. If we reject this compromise, we would be saying to them that we didn't want their help. In making our decision, we must remember our friends in labor for we will need their help in other matters.[10]

In response to Rustin, SNCC activist Mendy Samstein said: "You're a traitor, Bayard, a traitor! Sit down!"[11] In the end, the MFDP accepted the deal, but even two seats were too much for the official Mississippi Democrats. They walked out of the convention after the two MFDP delegates were seated. Even with the absence of the entire state delegation from Mississippi, the Democrats still refused to seat the MFDP delegation. Even now, the Democrats were afraid of antagonizing the South.

Michael Harrington was not in Atlantic City for the Democratic National Convention, but he had followed events closely. Even though the MFDP was in line with Realignment, he supported Rustin and the two seat compromise: "For [MFDP], even to have considered the possibility of something less than total and complete victory – to argue on grounds of political practicality – was treasonous."[12] The political "realism" of Realignment meant Michael was willing to make whatever deals were necessary in order not to be isolated from the Democratic Party.

Many of those watching events in Atlantic City on their televisions drew different lessons than Michael Harrington. The experience showed them that the Democratic Party were not allies in the struggle for civil rights, but they had lined up with the Ku Klux Klan. As James Forman recalled:

> Atlantic City was a powerful lesson, not only for the black people from Mississippi but for all of SNCC and many other people as well. No longer was there any hope, among those who still had it, that the federal government would change the situation in the Deep South. The fine line of contradiction between the state governments and the federal government, which we had used to build a movement, was played out. Now the kernel of opposites – the people against both the federal and state governments was apparent. Five years of struggle had radically changed the thought processes of many people, changed them from idealistic reformers to fulltime revolutionaries. And the change had come through direct experience.[13]

Soon Michael Harrington would be affected by the growing divisions in the movement. The 1964 Democratic Convention showed that his "beloved community" that would create the "new majority" was starting to fracture. As he recognized later: "In protest there is the possibility of beloved community; in politics there is not."[14]

Chapter 7

The Moderate

Vietnam

Due to his time in the Independent Socialist League, Michael Harrington was aware of the struggles of the colonial world, including in Vietnam. As early as November 1945, Max Shachtman hailed the anti-imperialist struggles of the Vietminh and Ho Chi Minh: "The Indonesian and Indo-Chinese revolts were the first struggles of the Third Camp to emerge during the war free from compromising entanglements in one or the other imperialist camp."[1] Shachtman's support for the Vietminh didn't change even after they massacred Trotskyists that same year. In fact, the Shachtmanites picketed French consulates in 1947 in solidarity with the Vietnamese. The Workers Party knew that Ho Chi Minh was a communist, but they argued that he was not a mere Soviet puppet:

> It should be kept in mind that though Ho Chi Minh is the president of Viet Nam [sic], the Stalinists are far from controlling that republic in any way comparable to their control of Poland or Yugoslavia. Ho Chi Minh, since he is not aided by the immediate presence of the terror organization of the GPU and the Russian army, can only maintain his leadership only so long as he represents, in some way at least, the strivings of the people for independence from French imperialism.[2]

After Ho Chi Minh strengthened his ties with both the Soviet Union and China in the early 1950s, Shachtman's support for him cooled. Shortly after the Vietnamese victory over the French at Dien Bien Phu, the ISL had become hostile: "The Vietminh is decisively dominated by its Stalinist leadership and functions in practice as the power instrument of Stalinist imperialism in Indochina."[3]

When Michael Harrington joined the YSL, they supported the general line of the ISL, but also celebrated the Vietminh victory at Dien Bien Phu. Years later, Michael recalled the discussions in the YSL on Vietnam:

> What, precisely, should we say to the workers in Saigon and Hanoi? Should we advise them to create a new movement which would fight both the French colonialists and the Stalinists within the Viet Minh? Or should they enter into the Viet Minh and contest with Ho Chi Minh for leadership? There were appropriate quotations from Marx and Lenin on the national question and Trotsky on the Chinese Revolution. We decided by a majority that the Indochinese proletariat should organize independently.[4]

After 1954, Vietnam dropped from Michael's immediate concerns. He was more focused on the civil rights movement, the Socialist Party and Realignment.

By 1964, American intervention in Vietnam was increasing and it cast a shadow over his support for Johnson. In his *New Politics* article supporting Johnson, Michael was candid enough to note that both Johnson and Goldwater favored war in Vietnam, but argued that a Goldwater victory was worse because it would mean World War III. Considering the apocalyptic stakes of the election, Michael considered that Johnson was a lesser evil on both domestic and foreign issues.

Even though SDS was lukewarm when it came to Johnson, they still offered critical support, which was encapsulated in their slogan: "Part of the Way with LBJ." Many of the new recruits to SDS believed that even critically supporting Johnson went too far since the Democrats were a party of war. SDS

National Secretary C. Clark Kissinger antagonized pro-Johnson SDSers with a sign on his desk that read: "Support the War in Viet Nam – Register Voters for Johnson."

Kissinger was right that a vote for Johnson was a vote for war. In February 1965, Johnson announced the beginning of "Rolling Thunder," a sustained bombing campaign against North Vietnam. By the end of the year, the American military presence in Vietnam increased from 25,000 to 200,000. Johnson's escalation of the war caused an antiwar movement to spring up on campuses.

To capitalize on the ballooning antiwar sentiment, SDS supported calls for an antiwar march in Washington DC on April 21. The march promised to be a major event, which would attract opponents of the war from beyond leftist ranks. While Michael Harrington welcomed the march, he took issue with SDS's willingness to work with communists and Trotskyists. He believed that the involvement of communists in the antiwar movement was sure to alienate liberals and moderates. Michael also spoke to SDS organizers, expressing concern at pro-communist material they were publishing: "No strategic hamlets./No strategic hamlets,/No strategic hamlets around me./And before I'll be fenced in/I'll vote for Ho Chi Minh/And go home to the North and be free."[5] On the eve of the march, Michael's allies Bayard Rustin and Norman Thomas released a statement to the press warning people to stay away because of the participation of communists: "In an effort to register such concern with our government and people, we welcome the cooperation of all those groups and individuals who, like ourselves, believe in the need for an independent peace movement, not committed to any form of totalitarianism or drawing inspiration from the foreign policy of any government."[6] While worried about the war in Vietnam, Michael Harrington and his comrades believed there were definite limits on how to oppose it. Despite Michael Harrington's fears, the march proved to be a success and was the largest antiwar protest in American history. SDS had expected only 3000 people to come, but more than 25,000 showed up. The march and rally were quite moderate in both their slogans and tactics, eschewing any form of civil disobedience or confrontation with the government. Embarrassed that his fears proved unfounded, Norman Thomas apologized for the press release.

After the march, SDS became the focal point for resistance to the war and radicals flocked to it. Over the coming years, SDS was transformed. The new breed of SDSers came not from families with leftist backgrounds, but from working-class backgrounds in middle America. Paul Heideman observed: "For these students, the break with the mainstream of American politics was necessarily much harsher than it was for the earlier generation. At this point, however, this alienation expressed itself more organizationally than ideologically."[7] The Vietnam War and SDS's radicalization put it on a direct collision course with Michael Harrington's moderation.

Breakdown

A month before the April march, Michael Harrington suffered a nervous breakdown, causing him to retreat from playing an active role in the antiwar movement for the rest of the year. According to Michael's own account, the nervous breakdown occurred on March 14, 1965 before a routine speech in San Diego:

> As I reached the podium I suddenly felt faint and had to grip the sides of the lantern in order to keep my balance. Then the sense of being on the very edge of losing consciousness became so intense that I had to sit down and explain to the audience that I was indisposed and could only go on if I was seated. I did finish, mainly by pressing my legs into the chair to detract myself with a little pain from what seemed to be the imminence of kneeling over.[8]

After the speech, Michael feared that he was suffering from a heart ailment. However, his doctor found nothing physically wrong with him.

Michael turned to psychoanalysis to get an answer and he began therapy with Elizabeth Thorne. His therapy lasted for 4 years. What he told Thorne during those sessions remains a mystery, but Michael said that he did discuss, "the public causes of my private woes."[9] According to Harrington, the cause of his breakdown was due to his unexpected success as a writer with the publication of *The Other America*. He had great difficulty reconciling his new-found fame and wealth with his socialist commitments. Finally, the burden became too much to bear and he broke down:

> The itinerant radical agitator, the writer of articles with long titles for magazines of small circulation, the practitioner of a comfortable poverty on the margin of an affluent society, could not recognize the middle-aging participant in the discussions with men of power, who was married and received middle class fees for giving anti-capitalist speeches...Eventually that masquerade, and the furious pace it required, could not go on any longer. I came unstuck.[10]

After diagnosing the problem, it took Michael some time to develop a new speaking routine in order to avoid future anxiety attacks. He had to plan out all the details beforehand. He practiced all his speeches with his therapist, just to be sure they didn't contain any "psychic booby traps."[11] He became more attentive to his health and gave up smoking, but took up drinking before a speech to calm his nerves: "I also learned the therapeutic value – and destructiveness – of liquor."[12] Within a few months, his new coping mechanisms paid off and Michael was able to speak to large public audiences without any noticeable difficulty.

The Mystical Militants

As Michael recovered, he continued to follow the antiwar movement with growing apprehension at their softness on communism. In late 1965, he wrote a series of articles for the *Village Voice* on communism and the antiwar movement. He argued that the antiwar movement would only be effective if it "dissociates itself from any hint of being an apologist for the Vietcong."[13] In fact, Michael said that when radicals waved the flags of the communist-led South Vietnamese National Liberation Front (NLF) as a sign of solidarity, they were playing the role of agent provocateurs: "When I saw a [Viet Cong] flag introduced into the line of march, the nasty thought crossed my mind: Were I an agent provocateur for the CIA I would get a VC banner and join the demonstration. The more such flags, the more plausible the McCarthyite-Maoist thesis that the partisans of peace must also be apologists for Communism."[14] To Michael, the NLF was another species of totalitarianism and the antiwar movement could not afford to be agnostic "about the power structure that now rules one-third of the world. Is there not a colonialist aspect to demanding freedom now for every victim of Western injustice and not bothering to think about the victims of Communist injustice?"[15] Thus, the antiwar movement needed to uphold anticommunism or else they would give fuel to the right-wing belief "that peace mongering and Communism are one and the same thing."[16] Michael claimed that his anticommunism was not about adapting to popular moods, but something he considered duty-bound to defend: "But I don't want it to be thought that my attitude toward Communism is determined by an opportunistic desire to be popular at all costs. I am anti-Communist on principle – because I am pro-freedom."[17]

However, Michael's position was no longer welcomed by radicals in SDS and the antiwar movement. For one, SDS had already rejected anticommunism at Port Huron and Michael's arguments accepted the same anticommunism that justified

American involvement in Vietnam and the entire policy of the Cold War. Secondly, Michael's arguments that two sides were equally to blame for the Vietnam War completely misunderstood what was happening. To the radicals, it was self-evident that the most powerful country in the world was occupying and bombing a poor country, whose people were fighting back with the only means at their disposal.

Michael was also horrified that SDS was now willing to violate the law by burning draft cards and undertaking other militant action in order to halt the war effort. He claimed that the radicals wanted to "transform the protest into an apocalypse, a 'final conflict' in which extreme gestures of opposition will bring forth punitive retaliation from the authorities."[18] He sympathized with the young radicals, but argued that their militancy and hatred for American institutions were signs of voluntarism and ultra-leftism: "I can understand youthful impatience toward my insistence on democracy and democratic forms. The war is daily more monstrous and the political process seems so insensitive, slow and indifferent to basic moral issues... But an ugly tendency toward anti-libertarianism and elitism is developing among some of the resisters."[19]

Beyond SDS, Michael believed he could see a new Blanquism raising its head in the New Left:

> Among the college-educated and upper-middle-class Americans of the sixties and early seventies, I have glimpsed the wrath of the most proletarian of French revolutionaries, Auguste Blanqui. He, too, thought that the working class had been so stupefied by the capitalist system that it would have to be saved from itself by an elite conspiracy which could only permit democratic freedoms once the people had been properly educated.[20]

The new Blanquism caused these radicals to oppose

"corporate liberals" in the Democratic Party and the AFL-CIO officialdom as hopelessly "bought off." Instead of looking to the working class, the Blanquists looked for "substitute proletariats" among those untainted by prosperity and power such as the poor, blacks, alienated, rebellious young, hippies and outcasts.[21] Michael Harrington believed it was just a short step from the New Left's Blanquism to totalitarian communism, which was lying in the shadows. Michael was not alone in his criticism of the New Left. His friend Irving Howe was even more harsh on student radicalism in *Dissent*. In a 1965 essay, "New Styles in Leftism," Howe condemned the New Left for their hostility to American liberalism and Western Civilization. He said that the young radicals were unwilling to listen to the Old Left on the dangers of communism. As a result, they were led hopelessly astray and developed a "radical chic" for Third-World national liberation struggles and Marxism-Leninism.[22] SDS had grown tired of listening to the arguments of Harrington and Howe. Anticommunism made up one part of the Establishment that SDS wanted no part of. In the summer of 1965, they removed the last anticommunist exclusionary clauses from their constitution. LID was angered and warned SDS:

> The League for Industrial Democracy in its long history has stood firmly, as a matter of uncompromising principle, against totalitarianism of both the right and the left. We are therefore deeply troubled that the 1965 Convention of our student department, Students for a Democratic Society, removed from its Constitution and membership card the long-standing reference to Communism as an authoritarian movement.
>
> We urge the SDS to carry on in the coming year a thoroughgoing discussion of the nature and function of democracy in society. We pledge our support, through

> literature and speakers at the campus level, to aid SDS in these discussions.
>
> Toward this end, the Board seeks to continue and deepen the "dialogues" that have been initiated by the Student Activities Committee. We seek a reaffirmation of SDS's adherence to the traditional opposition of LID to totalitarianism of both the right and the left.[23]

Unlike the aftermath to Port Huron, SDS was no longer willing to make concessions. They ignored LID's summons to appear. Michael recognized that a split was imminent:

> ...[SDS's] whole style was increasingly one of screw-you. Their contempt for us was certainly coming through pretty loud and clear...They were not simply having a more militant tactic on the war, but their attitude toward trade unions, toward liberal change, toward change in the Democratic Party – a whole spectrum of tactical issues which had once united us – were in the process of changing. It was around the war that this whole constellation of things came to a head.[24]

The divide had become too much. On October 4, 1965, SDS formally severed ties with the League for Industrial Democracy and set out on its own. To the radicals in SDS, democratic socialists like Michael Harrington were no longer seen as allies, but were part of the Establishment they were fighting against.

1968 Election

Since 1968 was an election year, Michael once again supported the Democratic Party, at first backing the campaign of Minnesota Congressman Eugene McCarthy, who could appeal to the antiwar movement since he had voted against the Gulf of Tonkin Resolution and continued to speak out against the Vietnam War. To Michael Harrington, that was the most important issue of the 1968 election: "Ending the war in Vietnam must be the aim of any liberal or radical strategy for 1968."[25] Even though he condemned the war, he believed it was merely bad luck that had landed the United States in the Vietnam quagmire as opposed to anything deeper. Michael saw Johnson himself as "more tragic than malevolent."[26] As a result of Johnson's poor choices, money was taken away from the War on Poverty and funneled into the war. This represented a danger of conservative backlash against the welfare state and set back Realignment. The McCarthy campaign also attracted elements of the new class, particularly college students who were opposed to the war. To counter the image of college students as a bunch of dangerous, long-haired radicals, these volunteers went "Clean for Gene" by cutting their long hair and wearing nice clothes in order to reach ordinary people with an antiwar message. To Michael Harrington, McCarthy's campaign was exactly the type of movement he could get behind since it showed the potential of a new majority: "Senator Eugene McCarthy's campaign provides the most effective way of challenging administration policy."[27] For all that, Michael did not expect McCarthy to win the nomination, but rather supported him as a protest vote against the president. In the election itself, he was prepared to support Johnson as the lesser evil. He made no apology for that, stating that if the choice was between a "hawk" like Johnson and a "superhawk" like Nixon, then, "I would vote for Johnson on the grounds that he is clearly to be preferred on domestic questions."[28]

McCarthy became a serious contender in the race after the Tet Offensive. Now many Democrats viewed the Vietnam War as a lost cause and started looking for alternatives to Johnson. McCarthy's campaign gained momentum and he won an impressive showing against Johnson in the New Hampshire primary in March. At the end of the month, Johnson announced to a stunned nation that he would not seek reelection and was withdrawing from the race. Now the Democratic field was wide open.

Shortly after the New Hampshire primary, former Attorney General Robert F. Kennedy announced that he was running for the Democratic nomination. To Michael Harrington, RFK projected the mystique and liberal idealism of the Kennedy name and he offered "the better possibility of uniting the white working class and the black poor and of thus bringing middle-class liberals and radicals into a genuine majority coalition."[29] Perhaps feeling guilty about not supporting JFK, Michael wanted to campaign for RFK. He contacted Dick Goodwin, an aide to Kennedy, and expressed his willingness to volunteer. Goodwin took Harrington to meet Kennedy and it was agreed that he'd campaign in California.

That May, Michael traveled across California to spread Kennedy's message. At one campaign stop, he spoke alongside union leader Cesar Chavez and SNCC leader John Lewis. To Michael, a socialist together with organized labor and a civil rights activist was the realization of Realignment. SDS radicals did not share his enthusiasm for Kennedy or Realignment. At Berkeley, Harrington was booed by radicals when he defended RFK. Michael found this behavior inexplicable, since it felt like he was "speaking on behalf of the candidate of the Far Right. The prospect of a successful mainstream movement that would win real workers and blacks to the cause of peace and social change was not written in their sectarian scenarios and, in any event, a victory of the Left would destroy their righteous isolation."[30] His hopes soared on June 5 when Kennedy won the California primary. Just as quickly, though, Michael's heart sank when RFK was assassinated that very night. He attended Kennedy's funeral, where he embraced a weeping Tom Hayden.

After Kennedy's death, his hopes for Realignment lay in ruins:

> it took Robert Kennedy's death to make people realize how much they needed him...As the brother of the slain President, Robert Kennedy had touched millions; as the one white politician of stature who could communicate his passionate concern for blacks and Chicanos and the minorities, he had built up a new constituency...He was the one leader in America who could have led the nation out of the morass into which Vietnam had plunged it.[31]

Now Michael switched back to supporting McCarthy, but with far less enthusiasm than before.

McCarthy managed to win more votes than any other Democratic candidate; he garnered the support of only 23 percent of delegates at the 1968 Democratic National Convention. At the convention, the party regulars managed to push through the nomination of Hubert Humphrey. While Humphrey was a stalwart liberal, he was also Johnson's vice president and supported the Vietnam War. Michael Harrington acknowledged that Humphrey was not his ideal candidate and the only rationale he could offer for supporting him was simply "straight lesser-evilism."[32] Despite his misgivings about Humphrey, Harrington condemned radicals who refused to support him because they were "helping to condemn the American people – and particularly the black, the poor, and the young – to four years of Richard Nixon."[33] He argued that this election was not an example of Tweedledum/Tweedledee, but raised the specter of fascism "as the ghosts of the German Communists of 1932-33 can attest."[34] Virgil Vogel, a former writer for *New America*, said Michael's arguments for "straight lesser-evilism" were without merit: "Harrington has raised the specter of German CP policy 35 years ago when, despite the Hitler threat, they fought the Social Democrats. Their policy was of course stupid, but the analogy is not fitting, because Humphrey is not a Social Democrat and Nixon is not a Nazi."[35]

Despite the setbacks of the 1968 election campaign, Michael reaffirmed his support for Realignment. He noted that the new class, which was represented by the McCarthy-Kennedy wing of the Democrats, won a third of the primary vote. Michael hoped in the future that if these forces "eschew[ed] fourth-party adventures and self-righteous gestures and concentrates on assembling a new majority in the mainstream, I think it can transform American politics."[36] The Socialist Party also expressed its continued support for Realignment by electing Michael Harrington as chairman in July. Michael's election as chairman meant he was acknowledged as the heir-apparent to the ailing Norman Thomas and the new public face of socialism in America.

Chapter 8

The Tightrope

The Apparatus

Michael Harrington's election as chairman was the formal completion of Shachtmanite control of the Socialist Party. In fact the Shachtmanites had largely been running the party since 1958. Even though Max Shachtman preferred to play a background role in the Socialist Party, he remained just as visionary as ever. In line with the Realignment strategy, Shachtman hoped to transform the Democratic Party.

That meant his supporters needed to stop pressuring the Democrats from the outside and join the party in order to influence it from within. In 1961, Shachtman argued that it was time to join Democratic Party reform clubs to gain more clout among liberals, something Harrington had already done with the Village Independent Democrats. As Peter Drucker notes: "[The Shachtmanites] came to believe that they were creating a political force that would take over the Democratic Party and then the country. They kept making new contacts, new allies, new recruits."[1]

Shachtman also argued that the AFL-CIO with its powerful organization and millions of members was an indispensable tool for Realignment. He instructed his followers to take positions as staffers in the AFL-CIO, so they could influence its policy. Over the coming years, a number of Shachtmanites rose to prominence within the labor bureaucracy. For instance, Don Slaimon became head of the AFL-CIO's civil rights department, gaining the ear of Lane Kirkland (Meany's assistant and eventual successor). Shachtman's wife, Yetta Barsh, became the secretary of Al Shanker, President of the United Federation of Teachers (UFT). Tom Kahn worked as a speech writer and assistant for both

George Meany and Lane Kirkland. Shachtman's trusted protege, Bayard Rustin, founded the A. Philip Randolph Institute, which coordinated the AFL-CIO's work in the civil rights movement. This position enabled Rustin to act as a gatekeeper and bring more Shachtmanites into the AFL-CIO and keep the radicals in line at the 1964 Democratic Convention.

As the Shachtmanites rose higher in the labor bureaucracy, they no longer identified their interests with the rank-and-file, but with the union leadership. This meant the prerogatives of Realignment receded into the background since the Shachtmanites stopped backing reformers and reflexively followed the AFL-CIO leadership by endorsing the Democrats every election season. This did not matter to Shachtman. He saw the "AFL-CIO apparatus as the incarnation of the US working class"[2] and now he wanted its leaders to play the great and transformative roles he had envisioned.

Divergence

Shachtman's identification with the interests of the AFL-CIO bureaucracy meant he supported their anticommunist line on the Cold War. This produced resistance inside the Socialist Party to Shachtman's growing conservatism, particularly over Cuba. On April 18, 1961, the day after the failed Bay of Pigs invasion to overthrow Fidel Castro's revolutionary government, Shachtman was scheduled to give a speech to the YPSL's Berkeley branch. Both the local YPSL branch and the audience expected him to take a public stand and denounce the invasion. Instead, Shachtman denounced Castro's communist ties and supported the invasion:

> My sympathies – I don't even want to begin to conceal my sympathies – are primarily with these trade-union elements, the trade-union democrats, the trade-union revolutionists... were appalled by and then resisted the growth of the

> Communist influence there; because what that means, they know, and that I know too.[3]

The local Socialist Party and YPSL were outraged and they disinvited Shachtman. A prominent Berkeley socialist incensed at Shachtman's actions was Hal Draper. Draper had been with Shachtman since the split with the SWP in 1940, but he had worried for years at the growing right-wing tendency of the Socialist Party. Now Shachtman had betrayed the third camp position of "Neither Washington Nor Moscow" by siding with Washington. This was the last straw for Draper, who broke with Shachtman. Concurrently, opposition was developing to Shachtman inside the YPSL. Its chairman, Joel Geier, had originally been a firm supporter of Shachtman, but by 1962, he moved into opposition over Realignment. According to Peter Drucker, "[Geier's supporters] denied that Shachtman's forays into Democratic politics were compatible with any genuine independent politics. Being a little involved with the Democrats, they said, was like being 'a little bit pregnant.'"[4] As a result, YPSL was torn apart by factionalism between Geier and Shachtmanite loyalists. In 1964, Geier finally left the YPSL with 16 members to found the Independent Socialist Club with Hal Draper. That same year, YPSL, which was growing more radicalized and hostile to the parent party, was formally dissolved. When YPSL was reconstituted, its new leader was Penn Kimble, who was firmly loyal to Max Shachtman and Realignment. Through the 1960s, Michael Harrington remained Max Shachtman's loyal lieutenant. True, he differed with his mentor in condemning the Bay of Pigs invasion, but overall, they shared the same political perspective.[5] It was only with the Vietnam War that a divergence truly emerged between the two men. In 1965, the AFL-CIO's national convention adopted a resolution supporting American troops in Vietnam. Over the coming years, AFL-CIO president George Meany was one of the most consistent supporters of the Vietnam War and criticized others in the labor movement such as Walter Reuther who opposed it. Max Shachtman duly followed Meany's course, knowing that if socialists opposed the Vietnam War that they would lose their chance to influence the AFL-CIO leadership. Just like Meany, he supported victory over the communists.

In 1966, at Bayard Rustin's apartment, Michael Harrington argued with his teacher over Vietnam:

> The meeting rapidly became quite tense. Shachtman launched into a vigorous Marxist attack on pacifism and the moralistic approach to politics. For Max, condemning the Vietnam war primarily on the grounds that it was immoral was an excuse in phrasemongering which one could expect of students and professors who had no sense of political movements. Of course, he said, the war is horrible and the killing should be stopped as soon as possible; of course the United States is involved with dictators, scoundrels, and knaves; of course the bombing should cease. But the hard question, he continued, is the political basis on which the nation acts. Would there be a unilateral withdrawal of American troops leading to a Communist victory? A coalition government? Concessions from the North Vietnamese as well as from the South Vietnamese?[6]

While Michael thought there was a great deal of merit in Shachtman's arguments, he believed that such callous support for the Vietnam War reduced Marxism to a "kind of pragmatism without ideals."[7]

Despite their differences over Vietnam, the two continued to work together. In 1966, they formed a group called "Negotiations Now" which positioned itself as a moderate alternative to radical demands for a unilateral American withdrawal from Vietnam. Negotiations Now counted many distinguished names among its supporters such as Martin Luther King Jr, Arthur Schlesinger Jr and John Kenneth Galbraith. However, Negotiations Now lacked any teeth by design. According to Maurice Isserman, the purpose of Negotiations Now "was to serve as the SP's placeholder in the antiwar movement – something they could point to when challenged to show that they too were working to bring the war to an end. Negotiations Now also served as a convenient podium from which the Shachtmanites could criticize the rest of the antiwar movement as being, in contrast, extremist, misguided, and objectively pro-Communist. It was a sham."[8] Negotiations Now was committed to moderation ensuring that its antiwar position would not actually offend the sensibilities of Democratic Party liberals or anticommunists in the AFL-CIO. Negotiations Now allowed the Socialist Party to pose as antiwar, while they spent more time attacking the antiwar movement than the war makers in Washington. Whatever Michael Harrington's personal misgivings over the war, as a loyal comrade of Max Shachtman and leader of the Socialist Party, he was associated with their attacks on the antiwar movement.

The Shachtmanites opposed both the antiwar movement and the New Left since they were hostile to George Meany and the AFL-CIO. Shachtman believed that the New Left had no redeeming features and denounced them as "a wing of nuts – who aim not to hold things together, but to bust things apart."[9] Harrington shared Shachtman's hatred for New Left radicalism, but he wouldn't dismiss the movement *in toto*. He argued that the New Left was "articulating the authentic miseries of the poor while maintaining some of the attitudes of the middle class."[10] He believed that once the New Left's "substitute proletariats" and Blanquism failed, then they would return to realism and "come up with a strategy that offers real hope for the other America. And this means making a more sophisticated analysis of the coalition that supports the welfare state."[11] Eventually, the young militants of the New Left were going to lead the adult movements to change America and he wanted to win them over to moderate politics and Realignment. By contrast, Shachtman just completely dismissed them.

Michael also felt the AFL-CIO leadership was marked with divisions. In fact, he believed that Shachtman's identification with the most conservative layer of the labor bureaucracy was in the long run damaging to the alliance of the new majority at the heart of Realignment as evidenced by a series of New York City teacher strikes in 1968.[12] The catalyst for the strike came in the Brooklyn neighborhood of Ocean Hill-Brownsville. This community had a student population that was half black and Puerto Rican, but 90 percent of teachers were white and Jewish. In an effort to exercise community control, the school board summarily summarily dismissed 19 teachers and staff. The teachers turned to the UFT to demand their reinstatement, since they had been fired without due process. However, the school board defended their position causing the UFT to go on strike.

At its height, 54,000 out of 57,000 teachers in New York City were on strike for more than a month. The UFT, which had a reputation for left-wing politics and supporting racial equality, found itself opposed to the black community. As the strike dragged on, the conflict became bitter. UFT president Al Shanker claimed that the original firings were due to black antisemitism. Shanker further stoked the flames by printing half a million copies of an anonymous antisemitic letter to win public sympathy and support. The black population turned against the UFT, seeing the teachers as alien to their concerns, if not outright racist. Due to their close ties with Shanker and the UFT, the Shachtmanites were drawn into the strike. Michael Harrington and Tom Kahn worked as chairmen of "Ad Hoc Committee to Defend the Right to Teach" and took out advertisements in the *New York Times* supporting the UFT. Michael's support for Shanker led to attacks by longtime allies such as Dwight Macdonald in the *Village Voice*. According to Michael, he was caught in the middle between the two sides, "agreeing with the union on the specific issue, sympathetic to the local black school board, yet profoundly suspicious of some of the absurd claims made on its behalf."[13]

When the strike ended in November, the UFT had won almost all its demands. However, the victory was a Pyrrhic one since the teacher unions were alienated and detested by the black population. The alliance between progressive whites, Jews and blacks that had long characterized New York was replaced by hatred and bitterness. The Shachtmanite identification with the interests of the labor bureaucracy ended up undermining the larger strategy of Realignment and giving impetus to the right. According to Michael: "I suspect that this confrontation between two equal rights in 1968 was to prefigure the split in the liberal-labor-black movement, which was the precondition of Republican presidential power for the next two decades."[14] Instead of looking to conservative labor bureaucrats such as Al Shanker and George Meany as allies, Michael believed that progressive bureaucrats were the natural allies of Realignment: "Meany has made enormous strides in his social standing and has played a progressive role within the merged labor movement...But there are other tendencies in the movement too. Walter Reuther is the most obvious example, but there are still others...Shachtman and company did not see these things."[15] Despite his shared worldview with Shachtman, when it came to questions of strategy, they differed sharply: "Shachtman and his associates only saw the negatives; I was determined to build upon the positives."[16]

Split

The death of Norman Thomas in December 1968 removed the last unifying figure in the party, bringing latent tensions inside the Socialist Party to the surface. Michael was unprepared for this kind of fighting. Even though he was chairman, he had no organized support base of his own among the socialists. By contrast, Shachtmanites possessed their own disciplined machine inside the party that was ruthlessly efficient at factional warfare: "I was standing out in front singing the songs, and they were in the backroom running the whole operation."[17]

By 1969, the hostility between Shachtman and Harrington in the Socialist Party was boiling over. After Nixon's election, the fact that the Vietnam War was now being waged by Republicans instead of Democrats made it easier for him to oppose it. Michael spoke out more readily in favor of an American withdrawal from Vietnam without any prior negotiations, arguing that continued prosecution of the war was not only immoral, but "counterproductive from all points of view, including that of progressive anti-Communism."[18] This put him at odds with the Shachtmanites who were committed to relentless prosecution of the war until the communists were defeated.

The differing views on the war produced bitter internal fighting in the party between Michael and the Shachtmanites. In 1969, the Socialist Party passed a compromise resolution calling for an American withdrawal and the "democratization" of South Vietnam.[19] Before the 1970 Socialist Party Convention, the Shachtmanites submitted their own "Statement on Vietnam" among the delegates, that argued for fully supporting the war effort and the defeat of communism. It failed to pass and another compromise resolution was adopted stating that if peace and democracy were impossible in Vietnam, then the United States should pull out. These compromises satisfied no one on the left or right. David McReynolds felt they were toothless resolutions that failed to effectively oppose the war. McReynolds soon resigned from the party. Hawks like Shachtman did not even want to oppose the war on paper. Instead, they issued their own pro-war statement, differentiating themselves from the official

Socialist Party position.

Now that the Shachtmanites had issued a public statement, Harrington could no longer avoid a public confrontation with them on the issue. He bitterly attacked the Shachtmanite position:

> [The Statement on Vietnam] would commit the Party to a principled support of American foreign policy in any conflict with Communism; it endorses the unconscionable and self-defeating tactic of supporting reactionary anti-Communism as a lesser evil to Communism; it offers no hope in Vietnam for changing the regime or for peace.[20]

He argued that the war was unwinnable and the only sensible option was for the United States to leave: "I am ready, morally and politically, to accept the latter as an obvious lesser evil."[21] Shachtman felt completely betrayed by his disciple and never spoke to Michael again.

Still, Harrington and Shachtman belonged to the Socialist Party and neither of them were willing to leave without a fight. To strengthen their position, the Shachtmanites planned to fuse the Socialist Party with the Democratic Socialist Federation (DSF) who had more conservative politics. The DSF had left the Socialist Party in 1936 and was largely composed of Jewish social democrats who were hostile to Norman Thomas. Now that Thomas was dead, there were no major hurdles to them rejoining the Socialist Party. Michael objected to the planned fusion, knowing that it would strengthen his opponents. However, he was voted down and the two groups merged in March 1972. There was a shake-up in the party after the unification and Michael was no longer the sole chairman, but now alongside Bayard Rustin and Charles Zimmerman, one of three co-chairs. Michael Harrington was now outnumbered two to one. Despite his narrow support in the party, Harrington was determined to make a fight of it. He organized his own faction known as the "Coalition Caucus" and reached out to potential allies such as Bogdan Denitch, Carl Shrier and Irving Howe. He even contacted David McReynolds and the Debs Caucus for help, but they rebuffed him.

Factional warfare inside the Socialist Party reached a fever pitch with the 1972 election as Michael Harrington and the Shachtmanites took opposite positions. At first, the Shachtmanites backed Washington Senator Henry "Scoop" Jackson for the Democratic nomination. Jackson had a reputation for liberalism, support for labor and civil rights, but what really attracted the Shachtmanites was his hardline anticommunism and support for the Vietnam War. Shachtman loyalist Tom Kahn worked as a speech writer for Jackson. After Jackson dropped out of the race, the Shachtmanites switched their support to Hubert Humphrey.

Even though Michael had reluctantly supported Humphrey in 1968, this time he threw his support behind South Dakota Senator George McGovern. It was easy to see why McGovern appealed to Harrington. McGovern was the embodiment of liberalism, pro-labor reforms and support for the welfare state in the Democratic Party. In contrast to Humphrey, McGovern had been a critic of the war since the early 1960s and now supported an American withdrawal from Vietnam. His running mate was also Sargent Shriver, whom Michael had known from Johnson's anti-poverty task-force. Michael believed that the McGovern campaign would overcome the divisions in the Democratic Party and lay the foundations for a new majority: "I used to say that we had to unite the constituencies of the 'three Georges': the largely middle-class, antiwar forces of George McGovern; the blue-collar partisans of AFL-CIO President George Meany, a dedicated hawk; and the largely working-class and 'redneck' followers of George Wallace, people who were responding not simply to a very real racism, but to a phony populism as well."[22] Following the lead of George Meany and the AFL-CIO leadership, the Shachtmanites refused to support McGovern. Even though McGovern had a pro-union record, the AFL-CIO refused to formally endorse his campaign. For anticommunists like Meany and Shachtman, McGovern's position on Vietnam made him "soft on communism." According to Shachtman, McGovern would "turn...over all of Vietnam to the Stalinists."[23] While Michael Harrington believed that supporting the campaign was consistent with the Realignment strategy, Shachtman disagreed since the AFL-CIO refused to endorse McGovern. As Shachtman put it: "[McGovern's campaign ran] entirely against the grain of our realignment policy. He wants an anti-labor machine; I want the opposite."[24]

Despite the fact that the Socialist Party endorsed McGovern in September, this did not amount to much in practice. In the Socialist Party's endorsement, McGovern was condemned for the support he received from "radical leftists" and his "isolationist" and "conservative" foreign policy. Michael wrote later: "[the endorsement was] so reluctant and backhanded... that it committed the party to the anti-Nixon struggle only in the most formal sense...this shamefaced position was attacked by some of the most prestigious leaders of the party majority who refuse any support whatsoever to McGovern and look with enthusiasm upon a Nixon victory."[25] During the campaign itself, *New America*, now run by Shachtmanites, attacked the McGovern campaign with headlines such as "McGovern Underestimates the Communists" and "Jewish Voters Dissatisfied from Democratic Ticket."[26] Even though Shachtman had publicly stated: "I reject any sympathy or support for Nixon,"[27] *New America* published "An Open Letter to George McGovern" by Marxist philosopher turned anticommunist Sidney Hook arguing that Richard Nixon was the lesser evil in the election. In a cruel irony, all the "lesser evil" arguments that Michael Harrington had employed to support the Democrats in both 1964 and 1968 were now turned against him by his former comrades to back the Republicans.

The Socialist Party's timid support for McGovern caused their membership to hemorrhage. David Selden, a Socialist Party member and President of the American Federation of Teachers (soon to be replaced by Al Shanker) expressed the anger that many party members felt:

> George McGovern is the closest thing to a Socialist to run for President since Norman Thomas. Instead of trying to ape an inane official AFL-CIO policy, *New America* should fulfill its Socialist function by calling for a restructuring of the labor movement to make it more representative to the principles of progressive unionism.[28]

Michael agreed and wrote to others in the Coalition Caucus that the Socialist Party was "not simply objectively taking a pro-Nixon line; they are subjectively, consciously and enthusiastically working for McGovern's defeat."[29] To signal his opposition, Michael Harrington resigned as co-chairman of the Socialist Party on October 22. In his resignation letter, he charged that "the historic party of Eugene Victor Debs and Norman Thomas is today doing the work of Richard Nixon."[30] As if to prove his point, when Richard Nixon was reelected a month later, the Shachtmanites were exuberant.[31] Max Shachtman did not live to see the election, though, having died of a heart attack 3 days before.

In December, the Socialist Party held another convention to shed its linkage to socialism and renamed itself Social Democrats, USA (SDUSA). Michael was among the minority who objected: "I think the Socialist Party should forthrightly stand for socialism."[32] The change in name confirmed what Michael Harrington already knew: this was no longer his political home and it was time to leave. On June 21, 1973, he wrote a five-page letter resigning from SDUSA:

> The broad framework of my analysis of Communism – as a bureaucratic collectivist system that is both anti-capitalist and anti-socialist – is the same as that of the present leadership of SDUSA. But, as a Socialist, I believe that Communism must be countered by democratic alternatives, not by the dictatorial regimes America has backed in Saigon...Socialism in America as represented by the SD is completely isolated from the entire middle class reform movement as well as from the unions, representing well over five million workers and the most politically active sector of the labor movement, who broke with Meany over the war and McGovern... In presenting this resignation, then, I do not abandon the tradition of Debs and Thomas. On the contrary I take a step that will permit me – and those who agree with me – to extend and deepen that tradition among workers, reformers, the minorities, the women's movement and other partisans of social change. In the name of the future of the American Socialist movement, I resign from Social Democrats USA.[33]

In reflecting on the past, Michael Harrington noted that he shared the same underlying principles as his former comrades, but that it was tactical questions which divided them. He saw no reason to change his commitment to Realignment, reformism or anticommunism.

Reflecting on the political battles of the 1960s in his memoir, *Fragments of the Century*, Michael believed that socialists must walk a tightrope between staying true to their principles and realistic engagement in practical politics in order to reach the promised future:

> What conclusions does one draw from this sad little history? Many radicals would, I am sure, say it all goes to prove that when a socialist mixes in capitalist politics, he is selling out and has taken the first step down the slippery slope that

> leads to conservatism. Nonsense. The vocation of a radical is to walk a perilous tightrope. We must be true to the socialist vision of a new society and constantly develop and extend its content; and we must bring that vision into contact with the actual movements fighting not to transform the system, but to gain some little increment of dignity or even just a piece of bread.
>
> If the radical becomes totally obsessed with their vision, they will fall off that tightrope into a righteous irrelevance; if they adapt too well to the movement we hope to inspire, they will fall into a pragmatic irrelevance. Our task is to balance vision and practicality, to fight not simply for the next step, but for the next step in a voyage of ten thousand miles.[34]

When it came to Michael Harrington walking the tightrope between principles and pragmatism in the struggles in the Socialist Party, he chose pragmatism every time. The obligations of Realignment meant that liberals and the labor bureaucracy were allies and, therefore, socialists needed to keep open dialogue with them. If socialists were soft on communism or encouraged militancy, then they wouldn't be listened to by their potential allies. Thus, it was necessary for socialists to prove to liberals and labor officials that they were reasonable and moderate. While Michael Harrington differed from Max Shachtman on secondary details or tactics, at the end of the day, they shared the same fundamental strategic outlook.

Chapter 9

The Democratic Socialist Organizing Committee

Democratic Socialist Organizing Committee

Even before officially leaving SDUSA, Michael was laying the foundations for a new socialist organization. He began by reaching out to his supporters in the Coalition Caucus such as Irving Howe, Bogdan Denitch and Deborah Meier. To Michael Harrington, an "independent socialist" was a contradiction in terms. All his political training had convinced him that if socialists were going to have an impact, then they needed an organization of their own.

At Harrington's invitation, around a hundred socialists met at New York University in February 1973 to attend a weekend conference devoted to "The Future of the Democratic Left." By late Sunday, most of the attendees had left. The defeated remnant who remained continued their discussions in a rundown West Side hotel, where they resolved to create a new socialist organization. Having come to that decision, Michael Harrington and this faithful few ended their conference by singing *The Internationale*.[1]

This was a new Pascalian wager on Michael's part, like the one he made in the 1950s with Catholicism. After the break-up of the Socialist Party, he was passing through another crisis of faith, albeit one of a political nature. Whereas Michael's wager on Catholicism had only lasted a few years before he abandoned God, he was still betting on socialism in the long run:

> That is how the revolution goes forward sometimes, in such ridiculous settings, sometimes just a few people. The transformations of this century are not merely a matter of

> historic events; there is no day on which history will leap from necessity to freedom. There is rather a molecular process, composed of millions and even billions of personal decisions, whereby men and women assert their will and take control of their own destiny...But if we do not begin, who will?
>
> I do not romanticize, even though there is now a Pascalian cast to my Marxism. I am excruciatingly aware of the socialist failures of the past and of our woeful inadequacies in the present. But precisely because the social classes wearing their economic masks did not act as they were supposed to and the struggle therefore became the more complex and ambiguous than Marx ever imagined, the individual decision has become more important. That is not to say that the socialist ideal is merely a matter of private wish. Socialism is today the dream of the majority of mankind... And yet, after more than a century, it is still beginning, a task to be accomplished, not a destiny to be awaited.[2]

The next step of "the great task to be accomplished" occurred a few months later when Michael presided over the foundation of the Democratic Socialist Organizing Committee (DSOC). The founding congress was attended by 500 and held at both New York University and the McAlpin Hotel. Michael's opening speech declared: "Today we shall begin the work of building the seventies left."[3] This was a slight paraphrase of Lenin's proclamation on the morrow of the Bolshevik Revolution that "we shall now proceed to construct the socialist order!" Michael Harrington's ambitions for DSOC were far more modest: "We, on the contrary, hunkered down for a long miserable stay in the trenches."[4] The long struggle that Michael envisioned meant not going into the streets or manning the barricades, but realigning the Democratic Party. In his address, Michael said it was time to "let bygones be bygones" and for the left to leave behind the fights of the sixties. Now that SDS was gone and nothing had arisen to take its place, he envisioned DSOC acting as a rallying center for socialists. This struck a chord with the large number of attendees who were under 30, including large student contingents from Harvard, Yale and Columbia.[5]

The conference itself was attended not only by students and former members of the Socialist Party; the labor bureaucracy was represented as well, along with: American Federation of Teachers president David Selden; Ralph Helstein, who was president emeritus of the Amalgamated Meat Cutters and Butchers Workmen, and Victor Reuther (Walter's brother), the retired international affairs director of the UAW. Greetings were sent to DSOC's founding convention from William Dobbs and Douglas Fraser of the UAW; from Murray Finley, President of the Amalgamated Clothing Workers; Patrick Gorman, secretary-treasurer of the Amalgamated Meat Cutters and Butchers Workmen; Moe Fraser, executive secretary of District 1199, National Union of Hospital and Health Care Employers; Edward Sadlowski, director of District 31 of the United Steelworkers; Dolores Huerta, vice president of the United Farm Workers; Victor Gotbaum, executive director of the American Federation of State, County and Municipal Employees (AFSCME) for New York, and Jerry Wurf, president of AFSCME.[6]

While organized labor was well represented at DSOC's founding, Harrington admitted that there "were practically no blacks or Hispanics present."[7] Considering Michael Harrington's hostility to revolutionary black nationalism in the 1960s, there was not much hope that working-class blacks would be interested in DSOC's white and moderate politics. Instead of seeking to remedy that, DSOC make a conscious decision to reach out to progressives in the black elite such as Julian Bond, Jim Farmer, David Dinkins, Mike Conyers, Ron Dellums and John Lewis.[8]

Furthermore, the convention had the atmosphere of an "old

boys' club."[9] In fact, there was not a single woman speaker at the convention, angering many DSOC women who felt the organization was alienated from the concerns of women. This was far from Michael's mind, who felt triumphant in rescuing American socialism. After the convention, he wanted to celebrate and headed with his wife to a party at Debbie Meier's apartment with other DSOC members. As soon as Michael entered, he was confronted by angry women: "When I walked in the door, I was hustled into a bedroom where about ten people were already deeply involved in an intense, even tearful, acrimonious discussion of our insensitivity to women. I emerged 5 hours later; the party was, of course, over."[10] Michael was shocked by how he was treated, despite his professed feminism. Later he admitted those women were right: "We were profoundly insensitive to the demands of women wanting to play a major role in the organization as women, as feminists. We were more than willing to acknowledge and respect those women who had achieved leadership under the old, male-dominated rules of the game."[11] To rectify their practice, DSOC changed its structure in 1979, mandating that 50 percent of national committee members must be women. The convention was not strictly an American affair, but attended by members of socialist organizations from abroad. The keynote speaker on the opening day of the conference was David Lewis, one of the leaders of the Canadian New Democratic Party, and fraternal greetings to DSOC came from the British Labour Party, French Socialist Party and Swedish Social Democrats.[12] Michael hoped for the new organization to take the Socialist Party's place in the Socialist International and after several years, he succeeded when DSOC was admitted to membership in 1976.

On the final day of the convention, DSOC adopted a constitution and elected a governing national board. To the surprise of no one, Michael Harrington was elected chairman. The two vice chairs were Ralph Helstein and Victor Reuther. On the national board of DSOC aside from Helstein and Reuther were Leslie Nulty and Carl Shrier, both members of the UAW. Also at Michael's side in DSOC were his longtime friends Debbie Meier, Bogdan Denitch and Irving Howe. The membership of Irving Howe was a welcome surprise to Michael, given that he had remained organizationally independent since the 1950s: "Over the years our lives and opinions increasingly converged, but Irving remained 'unorganized' on principle. So when he signed up and committed his considerable reputation and unquestionable integrity to our enterprise, it was a significant morale lift for us all."[13]

At its beginning, DSOC had a solid 250 members with ties to the Democratic Party, labor unions and the campuses. Like many leftist groups, DSOC had only a shoestring budget in its early days. Their first paid staffer was a 23-year-old named Jack Clark, who got by on $50 a month and lived in Debbie Meier's spare bedroom and was nicknamed "Smolny" (after the Bolshevik headquarters that planned the October Revolution). Eventually finances improved and DSOC was able to move into a larger office in New York's Union Square. DSOC managed to grow steadily throughout the seventies, creating a youth wing in 1975, which grew to a thousand members by 1980.

Even though Michael had much to be proud of, he knew that the odds were stacked against DSOC. DSOC was a minor and insignificant player in American politics and socialism itself remained a distant horizon.

The Professor

While Michael was engaged in the world of politics, major changes occurred in his personal life. He learned the joys of fatherhood when he became the parent to two young boys: Alex (1968) and Teddy (1971). After the birth of their second son, Stephanie decided to leave her job at the *Village Voice* to spend more time with the children. Since Stephanie's job had provided health insurance for the children, the Harringtons needed a new way to gain insurance. After spending his adult years avoiding a normal work routine, Michael was determined to get a full-time job to provide for his family.

Even though he lacked the formal qualifications, Michael began seriously looking for a job teaching the social sciences at a local university.[14] He was helped by his friends, particularly Irving Howe, who reached out to Joseph Murphy, the new president of Queens College. By the early 1970s, the rapidly-expanding Queens College was the third largest college in New York State. Many of the 35,000 Queens College students were from Jewish, Italian and Irish working-class backgrounds. Murphy believed that these students deserved the same kind of education as elite institutions like Harvard and Yale: "His reasoning for wanting me to teach there? He felt it would enrich the students to have contact with an extramural political intellectual who did not fit into any of the standard academic categories. I immodestly think he turned out to be right."[15]

In 1972, Michael was hired as a visiting professor in the political science department at Queens. A year later he became a full member of the department and was given tenure in 1974. Michael was pleasantly surprised at his new career. Not only did it provide him with financial security, union membership in the American Federation of Teachers, but he was good at it: "I never dreamed that the need for health insurance would turn into such an enriching experience."[16]

The Democratic Agenda

DSOC picked up where the Socialist Party had left off by supporting reforms and working to realign the Democratic Party. In 1974, Michael ran for a delegate seat for New York City's Seventeenth Congressional District to the Democratic Party's mid-term conference held in Kansas City to make changes to the party platform. The Kansas City conference had grown out of the McGovern campaign. At the conference, party activists were supposed to discuss the platform and "make the Democratic Party into something vaguely resembling a party."[17] Michael advocated that the Democrats prioritize economic and social issues, but he considered issues such as gay rights to be a distraction:

> I explained that I would vote for a gay rights resolution because I believed in it, but that I felt my role at the convention should be to unite the trade union, minority, and middle-class segments of the Left around a common economic program. Given that definition of my function, I said, I could not pledge to become a major leader of the gay rights fight. I would speak and vote for it, but if I were to take the lead on any issue, I thought it should be that of economic policy. The gays were not in the least persuaded and opposed me.[18]

Still, Michael would "not urge the Democratic Party to embrace democratic socialism in 1976. That proposal is premature given the current political realities and the views of most Americans."[19] He ended up winning the election and was ready to fight for his ideas at the conference.

The Democratic Party leadership wasn't enthusiastic about the conference and planned to hold it with a "minimum of publicity and a maximum of gracelessness."[20] By contrast, Michael and DSOC took the conference seriously. He believed that the Democrats expected easy electoral victories after Nixon's resignation. Rather, Michael believed the Democrats needed to motivate regular people to get involved in the political process by attacking the Republican economic agenda. He hoped that this would be the foundation to creating a permanent left-liberal bloc within the Democratic Party.

Instead, the conference showed just how isolated DSOC was from its purported liberal and labor allies. Nothing symbolized this more than a planned socialist breakfast for delegates when no one showed up. In reflecting on the experience, Michael noted "[DSOC] had become part of the mainstream Democratic Party, just as our theory said we should, and had even won the approval of voters in one congressional district in the process. Our only problem was, we didn't know what to do."[21]

Michael was undeterred and vowed that DSOC would do better next time. The following year, he developed plans with Marjorie Phyfe Gellerman and Jack Clark to influence the Democratic Party platform for the 1976 presidential race. He hoped that this program, known as the "Democratic Agenda," would advance a progressive social and economic agenda along the lines of the War on Poverty.[22] This would not only help the Democrats to win the election, but show that DSOC was a force to be reckoned with inside the party.

Throughout 1975-1976, Michael Harrington and DSOC aggressively pushed the Democratic Agenda. They were helped by their supporters in organized labor, notably in AFSCME, UAW and the International Association of Machinists (IAM), whose vice president Bill Winpisinger was a member of DSOC.[23] As Michael recalled: "With the aid of our trade union allies we got the support that made it possible to turn our theories about building coalitions in the Democratic party into some kind of reality."[24] At the Democratic Agenda's inaugural meeting held in Washington in February 1976, Michael denounced prominent Democrats such as Jerry Brown and Michael Dukakis "as deserters from the liberal Democrats...who compete with their old enemies in avowing their lack of faith in the capacity of this society to deal with the crises which are all but overwhelming it."[25] Michael wanted a liberal nominee and supported Arizona congressman Morris Udall. After Udall dropped out, Michael threw his support behind Jimmy Carter, who became the nominee.

Michael's main focus was the platform that the Democratic Party would adopt at the convention. During Carter's acceptance speech, he proudly invoked the tradition of FDR, Truman, JFK and LBJ. Carter even selected a Humphrey-style liberal – Senator Walter Mondale of Minnesota – as his running mate. The convention adopted a progressive program calling for full employment, national health insurance and cuts in defense spending. It appeared that the Democratic Agenda was now the program of the Democratic Party. This was all music to Michael Harrington's ears: "So it was that the 1976 platform was probably the most liberal in the history of the Democratic party."[26]

It was only natural that Harrington campaigned for the Carter-Mondale ticket. The day before the election, he debated Peter Camejo from the SWP. Michael believed that leftists who argued that socialism could only come through "cataclysmic changes" needed to give up their fantasies and go among the "real workers."[27] He argued that revolutionaries who refused to support Carter were sectarian since "they are counterposing themselves to the actual working class."[28] Michael claimed that while Carter was not perfect, this was a reality that socialists had to accept:

> Corporate big business is not voting for Ford because they like his smile. They are voting for Ford because they know he will represent them. Second, the labor movement in this country is supporting Carter...They are thinking politically on an organized class basis. Tomorrow, class organizations of the workers, organizations you can join only by virtue of your membership in a union, are going to be mobilizing voters. If Carter wins, he will owe his victory in considerable measure to the working class politically organized as a class. That is a reality. One may not like this working class. One may wish it had other politics. I certainly do. But there is a working class in America. It is politically organized. It is for Carter. There is a corporate class. It is politically organized. It is for Ford.[29]

Michael's case for Carter was based not just on lesser-evilism, but on implementing the progressive planks of the Democratic Party platform adopted at the convention: "Carter is in favor of a bill guaranteeing the right to work to every worker in the United States. That bill's not half good enough. Carter is not half good enough for it. But he is for it and Ford is against it."[30]

Finally, Michael declared that if Carter won, it would open the way for the Realignment of the Democrats by its progressive constituency:

> If we get Carter, there is the possibility, an infinitely greater possibility, they can be involved. They can be brought back into politics.
>
> Which is why the Democratic Socialist Organizing Committee, those of us in it, have participated in the Democratic party. We've gone in with "socialist" very clear on our sweatshirt. We're not "boring from within." We're not conspirators. That's why I testified at the national platform hearing. That's why we were the organizers of the, I think, the best left-wing meeting at the Democratic party convention.
>
> We do not accept the Democratic party as it is. We seek to transform it. But we go with the real live workers and minority groups and women where they are. We do not make our conditions to them. We only want to work with them to transform the society.[31]

In arguing against Michael Harrington, Peter Camejo defended the traditional Marxist position that the working class needed their own independent party since the Democrats and Republicans represented the interests of the capitalist class:

> The corporations run this country. The oil industry gets the secretary of state no matter who wins, Democrat or Republican, every time. The undersecretaries and the cabinet

> posts, the people who really write the laws, are the people who will continue to run the country no matter who gets elected. Both these parties represent the same class. The rich have two parties. We have none. That's the problem. That's what we must go out and tell people.
>
> We must go out and tell people the truth about the Democratic party. It's a war party; it's a racist party; it's a sexist party; and it's antilabor. And the minute you start telling people to join such a party, you've undermined your entire ability to have a strategy for social change.[32]

Camejo maintained that socialism could never be built through an anti-socialist party like the Democrats. In fact, he claimed that socialists like Harrington who supported the Democrats were not working to create socialism, but to defend capitalism:

> I think Mr Harrington, who's a Democrat, who votes Democrat, supports the Democratic party, should call himself what he is: a Democrat.
>
> And that means to defend capitalism. I know he doesn't want to do that. I know that in his ideology he would like to see socialism. We will never get socialism by supporting capitalism. You will never win equal rights for women by supporting sexists. You will never win the end of racism by supporting racists - even if there are worse racists and worse sexists. We mustn't fall into the trap of the ballot box myth: You pull the curtain, no one can see what you're doing, then you vote for one of them or you vote for another of them. Then they announce they won again, and you think you decided something.
>
> That is a myth. The decisions are made by much broader social forces, and the key to it is that the workers movement must be independent. We must favor that the unions break

> from the Democratic and Republican parties and form their own party. That's what Mr Harrington won't do. And I wish he would. I wish we could join together on that, as we have on other things.[33]

Michael Harrington saw no reason to break with the Democrats since Carter won the election the following day. The Democrats controlled not only the White House for the first time since 1968, but had large majorities in both houses of congress. Now Michael believed that the Democratic victory would turn into law the progressive promises contained in their 1976 party platform, leading to the "greatest forward strides since the days of Kennedy and the early Johnson."[34]

The Progressive Alliance

The record of the Carter administration was not one of a New Deal reformer, but cutbacks and austerity. In 1978, the Democratic-controlled congress instituted what later became known as "Reaganomics" by freezing social spending, deregulating the transport and phone industries, and supporting high interest rates to fight inflation.[35] The Carter presidency also ended the unwritten social contract with unions, angering Michael Harrington's allies in the labor bureaucracy. In 1976, the AFL-CIO supported the Labor Law Reform bill to stop the decline of union membership by making it easier for them to use the National Labor Relations Board to sign up new members with a top-down approach with little regard for rank-and-file members. According to Mike Davis, "the AFL-CIO's strategy was not to take the offensive nor even to lead a legislative battle against business; the reform legislation had been purposively moderated to solicit corporate cooperation."[36] Even these compromises were not enough and the bill didn't pass. According to UAW President Doug Fraser:

> I believe leaders of the business community, with few exceptions, have chosen to wage a onesided class war in this country – a war against working people, the unemployed, the poor, the minorities, the very young and the very old, and even many in the middle class of our society. The leaders of industry, commerce and finance in the United States have broken and discarded the fragile, unwritten compact previously existing during a period of growth and progress.[37]

Even though Fraser was not willing to break with the Democrats (his remarks were carefully chosen to say they were not as bad as Republicans), the UAW still wanted to put pressure on them. Before the 1978 mid-term elections, the UAW International Executive Board held a conference "to consider the formation of a new alliance aimed at transforming the American political system by making it more accountable, responsible and democratic."[38] On October 17, 1978 the UAW sponsored a meeting that included representatives of 30 unions including the IAM, AFSCME, United Farm Workers and other organizations such as the NAACP, the National Farmers' Union, the National Women's Political Caucus, and the National Organization for Women.[39] Michael Harrington was among those in attendance. In January 1979, this coalition was organized as the Progressive Alliance. The Progressive Alliance made no explicit mention of socialism or social democracy, instead they spoke a populist language demanding "social and economic justice" and "America first."[40] In line with Harrington's Realignment strategy, the Progressive Alliance also supported reforming the Democratic Party.

For all its tough talk, the Progressive Alliance didn't amount to much. They focused on lobbying Democrats and refused to transform the Progressive Alliance into a membership organization. Not only did the Progressive Alliance lack any real political direction, but they offered no alternative to labor-capital collaboration. When Chrysler was threatened with bankruptcy, the federal government bailed them out while Fraser and the UAW supported "shared sacrifice" and accepted wage cuts and the loss of 50,000 jobs. In return, Douglas Fraser himself was later named to the Chrysler Board of Directors.[41] The Progressive Alliance's Realignment and business unionism perspective meant they refused to act outside of the Democratic Party or to use the organizational power of unions to advance their own demands. The Progressive Alliance accepted the Democratic Party as the only vehicle to advance its politics and simply wanted to pressure the party machine to listen to them. When the Democrats ignored the demands of the Progressive Alliance, the latter crumbled like a house of cards. During the 1980 election, the Progressive Alliance supported Ted Kennedy as a primary challenge, but ended up backing Carter in the end. According to Kim Moody, the Progressive Alliance got nothing in exchange for supporting Carter: "This alliance was on Carter's terms: more austerity."[42]

Pyrrhic Victories

The Democrats were holding another convention in Memphis for 1978 and Michael Harrington planned to attend and protest Carter's betrayal of the party's progressive platform. Anticipating a fight, the Democratic Party tightened up the convention rules to make sure that no controversial resolutions reached the floor. The Democratic National Committee decided that a quarter of the delegates needed to sign an appeal 3 days before the convention in order for a resolution to be presented on the floor. Considering how difficult it was to contact 25 percent of the delegates before the convention, the party leadership was sure these rules would ensure an orderly event. However, the Democratic Agenda and DSOC successfully used their networks to collect the needed signatures and file their resolutions before the convention started.[43]

At the convention, Michael Harrington and Doug Fraser co-chaired the liberal caucus of the Democratic Agenda and Americans for Democratic Action. Their resolutions challenged the Carter administration's domestic agenda, especially his retreat from the Humphrey-Hawkins bill guaranteeing full employment. The liberal caucus also supported national health insurance and government-run gas and oil corporations modeled on the Tennessee Valley Authority.[44] The Democratic Agenda purposely avoided "fringe" issues such as gay rights since this would cost them support among black delegates. When the gay and lesbian caucus asked the Democratic Agenda to support their resolutions, Michael refused. The liberal caucus' resolutions were all defeated since they were opposed by not only the party machine, but by most of the black delegates who backed Carter. Still, the Democratic Agenda managed to win 40 percent of the vote. According to UAW staffer Don Stillman: "It was an electric moment. A sitting Democratic President had come quite close to a humiliating rebuff at the hands of his own party."[45]

There was a formidable liberal opposition in the Democratic Party who were angry at Carter. This was shown not only by the votes on the convention floor, but by how liberals such as Massachusetts Senator Ted Kennedy were viewed by the delegates. When Kennedy spoke in support of national health care, he received a standing ovation. According to the polls, Kennedy was more popular among Democrats than Carter. In 1979, Kennedy announced his intention to run for president and Michael Harrington didn't hesitate to support him.

However, Kennedy's campaign was bogged down by mismanagement, scandal and lacked direction. By contrast, Carter had the support of a more efficient campaign machine and benefited from the nationalist fervor over the hostage crisis in Iran. While Carter managed to secure re-nomination in 1980, he had difficulty winning back Kennedy supporters.

Michael refused to support Carter in the general election, but he didn't give up on Realignment. After the Democratic Agenda's experience in 1978, he believed that a left-liberal bloc could still capture the apparatus: "If Carter wins in November, he will be a lame duck president in 1982, unable to dominate the mid-term conventions as he did in 1978 at Memphis; if Carter loses, the internal structure of the Democratic Party will be wide open. In any case, if the Party's Left will take the 1982 meeting seriously, it should be able to win there and write its own program."[46] Events proved Michael Harrington to be terribly wrong.

DSA

Despite the disappointments of the Carter years, DSOC continued growing throughout the 1970s and reached approximately 4000 members in 1982.[47] The democratic socialists had strong links with the labor bureaucracy and links to prominent liberal politicians inside the Democratic Party. The bulk of DSOC was composed of members who were either over 40 or under 25. The missing demographic contingent in DSOC were those radicalized in the 1960s who remembered Michael Harrington's role in SDS. Michael and DSOC believed that the old divisions were not insurmountable because now that the times had changed, many of those radicals had grown up and come around to his way of thinking: "A solid majority of the people who had been really committed to the movement in the sixties became trade union staffers, community activists and organizers, radical academics, and the like, in the seventies. The founding cadre of DSOC understood that fact well. Which was one of the many reasons we wanted to reach out to this group."[48]

One group that Michael Harrington and DSOC believed had "matured" was the New American Movement (NAM). NAM was originally in 1971 formed by former members of SDS and the New Left such as Michael Lerner, James Weinstein and Staughton Lynd. According to Michael Lerner:

> My goal when creating NAM was gathering people who wanted precisely what I started in Seattle – namely an organization that spoke to the majority of Americans whose needs were being shortchanged by the government and society, and who were growing increasingly angry at a government that was spending their taxes for war and for the interests of the ruling elites of the society. I argued that NAM should appeal and speak to the interests of working people, that it should advocate a different kind of society, one no longer privileging the interests of capital, and that the movements advocating such a society should be explicit in its democratic socialist vision as well as anti-imperialist and anti-racist in its analysis.[49]

While NAM believed that building a Marxist-Leninist organization was inappropriate in the United States, they were not explicitly anticommunist. In fact, NAM supported revolutionary Marxist groups in Vietnam and Palestine and looked to the ideas of the Italian communist Antonio Gramsci for inspiration. Unlike DSOC, NAM was comfortable in mass demonstrations and community activism as opposed to convention floor fights in the Democratic Party.

In its early days, NAM still believed that the radical energies of the sixties would lead to a revolution. As the radical wave ebbed with the end of the Vietnam War, NAM adopted more pragmatic tactics. Throughout the seventies, NAM also recruited former members of the Communist Party such as Dorothy Healey. The ex-communists accelerated NAM's rightward moves with their support for the CPUSA's popular front strategy and Eurocommunism, with its explicit embrace of a "democratic road to socialism."[50] NAM inched closer to DSOC, but the two groups still kept their distance from each other: "We came together – and in many cases, we discovered how distant we were from each other."[51]

While NAM may have pulled away from socialist revolution, they still believed that DSOC was hopelessly compromised by its work within the Democratic Party. Roberta Lynch, who was elected to NAM's leadership in 1977, wrote a critical report after speaking at DSOC's convention, where she criticized them for ties to the Democratic Party and the union bureaucracy. Furthermore, Michael believed that NAM's support for the Third-World Marxists and the Palestinian Liberation Movement was incompatible with DSOC's anticommunism and Zionism. If the two groups were going to work together, then that distance would have to be bridged.

Slowly, the gap between NAM and DSOC narrowed as the former moved closer to the latter. Roberta Lynch, who had been scathing in her criticism of DSOC, now found herself backing Chicago Democrats in 1978. She believed that NAM's refusal to back the Democrats meant they were out of touch with the needs of ordinary people. NAM's change of perspective meant that they began working closely with DSOC, first in Chicago and then elsewhere.[52]

Cooperation between DSOC and NAM led to talks for a merger, which became serious. However, divisions still remained. Some of NAM's members were suspicious of DSOC's anticommunism and reformism. In DSOC, there were some fears about the influence of former communists in NAM, but not from Michael Harrington or Irving Howe who believed the legacy of the popular front was compatible with the aims of democratic socialism. According to Howe: "If we are ever to see a resurgent democratic left in America, it will have to learn tactically from the Popular Front initiated by the Stalinists than from those political ancestors whose integrity we admire."[53]

The main disagreement between NAM and DSOC lay over Israel. In contrast to the revolutionary left, Michael Harrington proudly defended Israel: "I support Israel as an internationalist. Israel is a democratic country whose people are passionately defending its self-determination."[54] DSOC shared Harrington's liberal Zionism and in one of the organization's earliest acts, they supported the American government sending military aid to Israel during the Yom Kippur War.[55] In 1979, a Committee Against Merger with NAM was formed by Ben Ross and Alex Spinrad, which criticized NAM for their anti-Zionism along with their focus on community activism. As merger talks proceeded, Michael Harrington recalled that the debates on Israel were the most contentious: "We worked out a 'two-state' position in which every word and comma was subjected to careful scrutiny."[56] After a great deal of heated negotiations, it was agreed to support a two-state solution and continued American aid to Israel.

Finally in 1981, NAM and DSOC had hashed out all the details and planned to hold a unity convention the following year. A majority of NAM voted for merger and a left-wing minority broke away. DSOC voted 80 percent in favor of the merger with none against and 20 percent abstaining, but the minority remained: "Our opponents wanted to indicate that they were unhappy – and that they were staying."[57] Michael Harrington had every reason to be satisfied with the results.

On March 20-21, 1982 the Democratic Socialists of America was founded. As its most important member, Michael Harrington was elected chairman. Serving on DSA's national board were former DSOC stalwarts such as Irving Howe, William Winpisinger, Mike Rotkin and Harry Britt. Ex-NAM members in the new leadership included feminist author Barbara Ehrenreich, Roberta Lynch, Manning Marable and Richard Healey with Dorothy Healey as national vice chair.[58] DSA numbered 6000 members (bringing in 4000 from DSOC and 800-2500 from NAM),[59] making it the largest democratic socialist organization in the United States since the Socialist Party in the 1930s. Michael Harrington had every reason to be satisfied with the results: "I had finally expiated my stupidity with SDS."[60]

Chapter 10

The Realist

Professional Air Traffic Controllers

Four years after Ronald Reagan's victory, Michael Harrington observed that he was an "authentic radical."[1] This was not meant as praise, but Michael's recognition that Reagan's agenda of unbridled capitalism was genuine and threatened to roll back the gains of the labor movement. Nothing symbolized this more than the Professional Air Traffic Controllers (PATCO) strike of 1981. On August 3, 1981, twelve thousand PATCO members went on strike over unsafe working conditions. Air traffic controllers were employed by the federal government and due to their vital role in maintaining air traffic safety, they were bound by a no-strike pledge in their contract. Ironically, PATCO was one of the few unions which had endorsed Reagan and now found themselves the main target of the White House. Reagan went on national television and gave PATCO an ultimatum: either return to work within 2 days or be fired. When the air traffic controllers refused, Reagan promptly fired them. Reagan was perfectly able to carry through his threat since he relied on contingency plans developed by the Carter administration to run air traffic without the controllers if they went on strike.[2]

Conservative AFL-CIO president Lane Kirkland said Reagan's response was "harsh and vindictive."[3] With the exception of a few individual unions, though, the AFL-CIO did nothing to build solidarity with the air traffic controllers. According to Kirkland: "I personally do not think that the trade union movement should undertake anything that would represent punishing or inconveniencing the public at large for the sins and transgressions of the Reagan administration."[4] Among the unions that refused to help PATCO was IAM under

William Winpisinger. IAM represented airline machinists who were strategically placed and could have shut down the airports. Winpisinger refused to take any action: "It should be recognized that the IAM has a no-strike clause with the airlines."[5] If IAM had honored PATCO's picket lines, it could have galvanized the rest of the labor movement into action. Instead, PATCO was left alone and the strike was crushed. It was now open season on organized labor in Reagan's America.

The PATCO strike showed that the AFL-CIO leadership was so fearful of mobilizing rank-and-file members and so tied to business unionism dogmas that they couldn't even organize basic solidarity. The labor bureaucracy believed it was imperative to preserve the union apparatus at all costs and feared any actions from below that could threaten it. Instead, the only "action" they advocated was playing it safe and voting for the Democrats. For the AFL-CIO, it was better to prevent workers from fighting back, since that could lead to escape from their control, even if it meant total defeat. Even left-leaning union leaders like William Winpisinger were unable to escape this dilemma, something that Michael Harrington recognized:

> If you say to me, is it possible that someone who is now a member of DSOC in the union movement will be so fixed and anchored in the bureaucracy that they will be appalled by the rank and file movement and try to put it down? I guess, sure, it's happened before and I suppose it will happen in the future. What will we do then? I hope we will go with the rank and file...but I'm sure that some of us might fail the test. There's no way you can anticipate.[6]

Michael Harrington had no solution to offer except reliance on the labor bureaucracy's good intentions and as the PATCO strike proved, that was not good enough.

Foreign Policy

The Reagan administration's hardline anticommunism also meant an escalation of the Cold War. The White House announced plans to station nuclear weapons in Europe and to increase the defense budget in order to achieve military superiority over the Soviet Union and triumph in a nuclear war. In order to halt "communist expansion," the Reagan administration provided aid to right-wing death squads in Central America and Islamic fundamentalists fighting Soviet troops in Afghanistan.

Michael Harrington believed that Ronald Reagan's bellicose anticommunism was irresponsible and the wrong way to defeat the Soviet Union: "To advocate a new Cold War is to advocate the crushing of the dissident movement in every country in Eastern Europe and in the Soviet Union itself."[7] Michael believed that drastically increasing the military budget was wasteful; instead, he advocated a leaner budget that would enable the United States to maintain American technological superiority in the Cold War:

> We should not act stupidly merely for the sake of acting... We should not advocate increasing military spending by two or three or five percent – on what? on wasteful projects? on escalating projects? On projects which threaten the peace'?...I am for increased military spending to maintain the necessary cadre in the US Army, not to reinstitute the draft. The problem of our defense forces is not the need for masses, but the need for specialists.[8]

Michael also criticized the Reagan administration's approach to Central America as a wrongheaded one: "When I criticize American foreign policy, our intervention in Central America, the MX, I do that in the name of the national security of the United States...Our critique is that President Reagan's policy with regard to Nicaragua does not promote the national security, it hurts it."[9] Instead of Reagan's crude anticommunism, Michael Harrington preferred liberalism's softer approach, which he considered not only more intelligent, but believed would enable the United States to defeat communism.

Jesse Jackson

In the 1980s, Michael Harrington believed that the main task of the socialists was ousting Reagan by supporting the electoral campaigns of the Democratic Party: "And by now practically everyone on the left agrees that the Democratic Party, with all its flaws, must be our main political arena."[10] In practice, Michael's strategy followed in the footsteps of Shachtman by uncritically supporting the leadership of the AFL-CIO, who ended up backing conservative presidential candidates such as Walter Mondale and Michael Dukakis as opposed to more progressive Democrats such as Jesse Jackson's Rainbow Coalition. In 1984, former civil rights leader Jesse Jackson mounted a primary campaign that had all the hallmarks of Realignment with a social-democratic program and support from labor unions, blacks and progressives. In line with Realignment, Jackson's program envisioned not only defending the welfare state, but expanding it. Compared to other Democrats, the Rainbow Coalition supported a pro-labor program and managed to gain enthusiastic support from progressive sections of the AFL-CIO. However, the Rainbow Coalition had its strongest base within the black community with support from reform-minded black mayors such as Richard Hatcher of Gary Indiana and Harold Washington of Chicago. Jackson also offered an alternative to Reagan's foreign policy; he supported non-intervention in Central America and broke anticommunist taboos by meeting Nicaraguan leader Daniel Ortega and Cuban president Fidel Castro. Jackson even flouted the longstanding Zionist consensus in American politics by supporting the formation of an independent Palestinian state. Over the course of the 1984 primary season, Jesse Jackson managed to win an impressive 3 million votes and finished third. As Mike Davis observed: "In contrast to Mondale's warmed over corporatism or [Gary] Hart's yuppie conservatism, Jackson's domestic program was arguably the first social-democratic alternative seriously offered to the American electorate in a presidential campaign."[11]

Even though Jesse Jackson was everything that Michael Harrington expected from a Realignment campaign, he willfully ignored it. At the height of the primary in June 1984, Michael Harrington and Irving Howe gave an 8000-word interview in the *New York Times* on the current state of the American left. Not once did Jesse Jackson or the Rainbow Coalition come up. On the whole, DSA was absent from the Jackson campaign.[12] There was a minority view inside DSA represented by Manning Marable, that supported the campaign, believing it represented a new (black) social democracy. Marable argued that the Rainbow Coalition was a continuation of the black movement of the sixties and would unite a progressive bloc of labor, blacks, the poor and other minorities that would push the Democrats to the left.[13] Jackson ended up losing the nomination to Minnesota senator Walter Mondale. He offered nothing in exchange for Jackson's endorsement. During the presidential campaign, Mondale clothed himself in fiscal conservatism and attempted to outflank Reagan on the right when it came to the Cold War. The demands of blacks and labor unions were viewed as liabilities by Mondale. As Mondale moved rightward, DSA attempted to "transform the election from an ordinary campaign into a bold progressive crusade."[14] It didn't work and Reagan swept the election in 49 states (Mondale won only his home state of Minnesota). Mondale won over 90 percent of the black vote, but only a slim majority of organized labor. The AFL-CIO and DSA's entire lesser evil strategy of "Anybody But Reagan" had failed. In a postmortem of the democratic socialist 1984 electoral strategy, Alexander Cockburn concluded:

> They must now be foot soldiers in a campaign whose captains are implacably antagonistic to the principles of their constituencies...So in control are the Democratic "pragmatists" as the pollsters and pundits call them, the ones who argue for party unity at the expense of movement and who propose that the way to beat Reaganism is to denounce its excesses while accepting its premises. The pathos of their opportunism lies in its shortsightedness. As every tactician can attest, the key to defeating Reagan is turnout. But turnout has political content and context. People will not simply vote for Anybody But Reagan; they want somebody who speaks to their interests, who promises them more than they've got and who offers them hope.[15]

Just a scant 4 years before, Michael Harrington had predicted that a Reagan victory would open the Democratic Party to the left. Now the opposite was occurring as the party swung to the right and ditched its commitment to New Deal liberalism. Following the Carter debacle, the corporate lawyer Charles Manatt organized the Democratic Business Council (DBC) to develop a pro-business Democratic Party alternative to Reagan: "[Manatt's] program was perfectly straightforward. Like most other business Democrats, Manatt wanted to strengthen the party's ties with the business community, rather than those with blacks, community organizations or the poor. To that end, he and his allies deliberately sought out millionaires and other wealthy figures to run as candidates."[16] By 1985, the DBC was touted by Democratic National Committee chair Paul Kirk as the "backbone of the Democratic Party's finances and its intellectual resources."[17] Reagan's second victory only accelerated these trends. Immediately after Mondale's defeat, the Coalition for a Democratic Majority, which was comprised of prominent Democrats, blamed the party's failure on pandering to "special interest groups" such as blacks and labor unions. They argued that if the Democrats wanted to make a political comeback, then they must become the "party of business leaders, doctors, pharmacists, stockbrokers, and professionals."[18] The *New Republic, Dissent, In These Times*, all respectable journals of liberal and social democrat opinion, echoed these sentiments. They blamed Jackson and the Rainbow Coalition for the Democratic loss to Reagan. Four years later, Jesse Jackson ran another primary campaign in the Democratic Party. To win the support of rich donors and business, Jackson presented himself as a more mainstream liberal and distanced himself from "extreme" positions such as support for Palestine.[19] It worked and the Jackson campaign won more business support this time around. Many of the same progressive activists and labor unions who had backed Jackson in 1984 found themselves canvassing for him once again. Included in their number was DSA and Michael Harrington, who supported the Rainbow Coalition's program: "Jackson has won a real 'rainbow' campaign in 1988, much more than in 1984. He is not relying on events but actively building an interracial coalition. It is a long, long shot – but no more ridiculous than an aging second-rate actor becoming President in 1980."[20] Michael did not expect Jackson to win, but argued that by breaking racial barriers, his campaign could act as the forerunner to a future progressive presidential campaign. However, Michael Harrington and DSA feared that public support for Jackson would be a political liability, so they quietly approached the campaign before endorsing him: "[Jackson] made it very clear he ain't shunning nobody. He wants our support and he was upset that people might get the impression that he was turning his back on any part of his coalition...We raised the problem with Jackson that we want to support you but we don't want to support you in a way that would harm you."[21] Eventually, Jackson agreed to accept DSA's support and he discreetly asked for Michael Harrington's help in writing some speeches.

Jesse Jackson performed better in 1988 with seven million votes (nearly 30 percent), but still lost the primary to the dull and wooden technocratic Massachusetts governor Michael Dukakis. Michael Harrington himself hailed the Dukakis nomination:

> I'm assuming the election of Michael Dukakis. That's the first step. I supported Jesse Jackson in the primaries, but I'm very much for Dukakis. Reagan created a mythic interlude, and the new President will have to confront the problems he neglected. There will be new possibilities for talking to the people and changing things and creating another America. A Democratic administration always opens up a space for those who stand on the left.[22]

As Michael Harrington uttered those words, space for the Rainbow Coalition was being closed off in the Democratic Party. At the convention, Jackson withdrew or watered down all his platform planks for the sake of party unity. In exchange for Jackson's support, several of his advisors were now represented in the Democratic National Committee and the Dukakis campaign. One Jackson staffer, Robert Borosage, summed up the results of all the horse-trading: "We could come in to sack and ruin, particularly with the number of delegates we have. But we're not doing that. We've agreed to disagree [with Dukakis], but that in itself is a form of agreement."[23] In the end, the compromises were for nothing, since Dukakis ended up being decisively defeated by George H. W. Bush in November.

Jesse Jackson's Rainbow Coalition was one of the most serious election campaigns in line with Michael Harrington's Realignment strategy, but it still ended up being co-opted by the Democratic Party. As we discussed in Chapter Three, the Rainbow Coalition's strategy was built on a fundamental misunderstanding about the structure of the Democratic Party. The Democratic Party was seen as composed of different interest groups such as big business, labor, media, blacks, etc and it was only a matter of increasing the strength of one bloc in order to realign the party. In fact, the Democrats are not composed of equal interest blocs, but are controlled by liberal capitalists who determine its political agenda. Campaigns like the Rainbow Coalition perpetuate the myth that the Democrats are the "party of the people" and allow the party to elicit support from labor, blacks, etc that provide popular "legitimacy" for carrying out a pro-business agenda. In absorbing progressive campaigns like the Rainbow Coalition, the Democrats are not only able to co-opt any potential opposition, but they block the emergence of independent political parties committed to a left-wing or socialist program.

Secondly, the Rainbow Coalition like other Realignment campaigns was not a social movement, but managed from the top down and committed to winning elections at any cost. The logic of electoralism meant that the Rainbow Coalition's goals were watered down to being compelled to voting blue no matter who. As Robert Brenner observed:

> Winning an election is entirely different: it demands two basic things: 1) appealing somehow to 50% plus one of the voters; 2) getting potential supporters to the polls. Nothing else matters. Money and bodies, and little else, are required. It follows that the way to win is to adapt one's program to the existing consciousness of the electorate. The right has to move left; the left has to move right...To win an election, one must essentially accept consciousness as it is and try to adapt.
>
> Naturally, there are limits beyond which candidates cannot go without turning off their core supporters; but

> these supporters are often quite flexible. In the first place, where else can they go? They are not going to support the opposition (to the right), for this would be self-defeating. At the same time, and equally important in this context, the supporters of the reform candidate almost always freely accept the necessity of moderating the candidate's image and program, for they, too, understand that this is required to win. Winning, moreover, is everything, for unless the candidate takes office, absolutely nothing can be gained. There is, for the overwhelming majority of leaders and followers in the campaign of progressive Democrats, no other payoff.[24]

This ensured the Rainbow Coalition's activists were bound to the business interests who really controlled the Democratic Party. It meant their marginalization and defeat.

Realignment had led Michael Harrington and DSA to the same end as Max Shachtman by unconditionally following the cues of the AFL-CIO leadership. The AFL-CIO believed they could cooperate with liberal capitalists and influence the Democratic Party, but since the party is beholden to the interests of business, the scales were always stacked against labor. The labor bureaucracy further handicapped themselves by accepting the logic of business unionism and refusing to consider independent politics. Since the AFL-CIO saw no alternative to the Democrats, they were compelled to endorse Mondale and Dukakis with no strings attached – and without consulting their memberships – losing any chance to advance their own demands. As a result, the AFL-CIO failed to advance a liberal, let alone a social-democratic, agenda in the Democratic Party and ended up using their resources to canvass for right-wing Democrats.

If the AFL-CIO was, at best, a secondary player in the Democratic Party, then DSA was a lilliputian unable to influence anything. As shown by DSA's struggle to endorse Jackson, the logic of Realignment meant that explicitly socialist politics always took a back seat to getting out the vote for the Democrats. As Lance Selfa observed: "Instead of DSA influencing the Democrats, the Democrats influenced the DSA."[25] This was the natural end result of Realignment and Michael Harrington's democratic socialism – the transformation of leftists into the most loyal servants for the Democratic Party.

Chapter 11

The Long-Distance Runner

In 1984, the 56-year-old Michael Harrington had the energy of a man half his age. He was as busy as ever running DSA, traveling across the world, feverishly writing and lecturing. He enjoyed his reputation as the most well-known democratic socialist in America, something William F. Buckley smugly mocked: "Being called America's foremost socialist is like being the tallest building in Topeka, Kansas."[1] Despite everything, Michael Harrington remained as optimistic as ever about the victory of democratic socialism.

Four days after Reagan's re-election, he drove to Princeton University to participate in a conference honoring the hundredth birthday of his mentor, Norman Thomas. When stopped at a traffic light, he absentmindedly felt the left side of his neck and discovered a bump. He thought it was nothing more than a swollen glad, but just as a precaution, he went to see his doctor after returning to New York. The doctor agreed with Michael that the bump was nothing to get worried about.

A few months later in January 1985, Michael returned to the doctor for his annual physical. The doctor discovered that the bump was still there. Now he became worried and told Michael that he was sending a sample to the lab for testing. The doctor assured him that it was not cancerous, but he just wanted to be sure. Michael hoped that in just a few days, he would be given a clean bill of health. Instead, he learned a week later that he had cancer. Further tests revealed that the cancer was located at the base of his tongue, which was likely caused by his heavy drinking and smoking that he had given up 2 decades before.

When Michael heard the news about his cancer, he spontaneously thought of a polemic by Leon Trotsky against his former mentor, Max Shachtman, with the title: "From a Scratch to the Danger of a Gangrene." He became fixated on that phrase: "Now that phrase echoed in my mind as a way of describing an insane causality, from a bump on the neck to a metastatic carcinoma."[2]

The doctors prescribed 7 weeks of radiation treatment and surgery. After completing the radiation treatment, he felt well enough to travel to Stockholm for a meeting of the Socialist International. In Sweden, he was joyously welcomed by Willy Brandt and other delegates.

While the trip abroad had a positive effect on his health, he anxiously awaited his surgery. Before his procedure, Michael met with his cousin, Peggy Fitzgibbon, who was a nun. He confessed to Fitzgibbon that his cancer had caused him to briefly reconsider his atheism and that he still missed the Catholic Church: "I was never one of those militant ex-Catholics who had to kill their one time God over and over, since I found the Church, in its highest expressions, profound and beautiful. My only problem was that I did not believe in any of it."[3] This was no death bed conversion on Michael Harrington's part. He told Peggy that if he went to heaven, then he'd angrily confront God.

The operation was a success and Michael was told that he was cancer free. After recovering from surgery, he went back to his hectic schedule. Everything was fine until November 1987 when Michael suddenly had difficulty swallowing. He went back to the doctor and received the terrible news that he now had esophageal cancer with an inoperable tumor. Michael was given 2 years at most to live. Over the coming months, Michael underwent monthly treatments of chemotherapy, which caused him to lose 40 pounds and left him too weak to do much beyond writing. He was determined not to waste the time remaining to him, but to keep working. He planned to write a final book, *Socialism: Past and Future,* as his political testament. News of Michael Harrington's terminal illness quickly spread and he received well-wishes from friends and comrades throughout the world. Even William F. Buckley wrote a moving letter to him:

> I saw you briefly on tv yesterday (you were making a brief appearance on behalf of socialism), and I rejoiced both that your appearance was brief and that you looked so well...I have said a special prayer for your recovery...Meanwhile, take care of yourself: You are a brave and admirable man, the daemons to one side.[4]

In June 1988, a "Celebration of Michael Harrington" was held in the Roseland Dance Hall in New York to mark his sixtieth birthday and the publication of his memoir, *The Long-Distance Runner*. Among the 600 guests were many friends and well-wishers such as William Winpisinger, Irving Howe, Cesar Chavez and Senator Ted Kennedy. Senator Kennedy offered a glowing tribute to Michael Harrington:

> In our lifetime, it is Mike Harrington who has come the closest to fulfilling the vision of America that my brother Robert Kennedy had, when he said, "Some men see things as they are and say 'Why?' But I dream things that never were and say 'Why Not?'"...Some call it socialism; I call it the Sermon on the Mount.[5]

Michael was moved by Kennedy's words and expressed his own undiminished optimism in the final triumph of democratic socialism.

That fall, Michael felt well enough to travel and speak again. Knowing that his time was short, he took advantage of the opportunity. Michael made his first trip to his ancestral home of Ireland, where he delivered the annual James Larkin Memorial Lecture on behalf of the Federated Workers' Union of Ireland.

That winter, he attended a gathering of a hundred activists of DSA's youth section at Columbia University. Michael seemed to know that this would be his last time addressing the young cohort of democratic socialists, so he made his closing remarks count:

> Some of you, God bless you, will pay your dues, you'll be around for a while, and then you'll leave. You will be enriched somewhat and when you get older, you'll say, "Oh, I was a socialist when I was a youth...but I got older, I got smarter, I gave up all that stuff." But you'll probably remain, at least, a good liberal. You'll go to a reproductive rights march, you'll campaign against aid to the contras. You'll do fine things, and I just wish that there were more of you.
>
> But I'm really addressing others, in a sense, because some of you, I hope, will see these ideas as affecting the way you lead your life, and not simply how you think about society, or how you act in society. But to do that, to have a social commitment that lasts with the ups and downs – and in America, from experience in forty years of the movement, I've got to tell you that the downs tend to predominate over the ups.
>
> To hang in there, you have to know why you're there. That is to say, it's not simply a question of understanding why you play a role. You must realize that the battle for trade union rights, and the battle for racial justice, and the battle for gender justice, and the battle for a decency in the Third World are all part of a whole, are all interconnected. What we are dealing with is not simply an economic transition, or a political transition. What we are dealing with is the emergence of a new civilization. What we are dealing with are new ways of life for all people of the Earth. By the end of the twenty-first century, existence will nowhere, in any way, look like it looks now.

> And if you know that and even though you know in your lifetime there will be no answer, but you understand that if there is the least possibility of freedom being the answer, it is worth a lifetime commitment. That's what holds you together.
>
> This movement should enrich you, this movement should allow you to lead a different kind of life. This is not a burden. At its best this is a movement of joy...You will have an opportunity to make these ideas come alive. You are lucky to be part of Democratic Socialists of America.[6]

Michael kept traveling and speaking throughout the spring of 1988, but his health continued to deteriorate. He was forced to skip a meeting of the Socialist International in Vienna, but assured Willy Brandt that he would be attending the next meeting in Stockholm that June. As it turned out, Michael never made it to Stockholm, but in honor of his long service to the movement, the delegates elected him honorary president of the Socialist International. Michael was able to celebrate May Day, but his health worsened so much that he had to be hospitalized. As Michael Harrington entered his last days, he managed to finish his book, which was dedicated to Willy Brandt and the Socialist International. Finally, on July 31, 1989, Michael Harrington quietly passed away.

Across America and the world, tributes flowed in celebrating Michael Harrington as a tireless social activist and the man who had discovered poverty. Among his comrades, he was remembered for keeping democratic socialism alive in the United States and being the rightful heir to the legacy of Eugene Debs and Norman Thomas.[7]

Conclusion: The Legacy

Nadir

The death of Michael Harrington coincided with the collapse of Soviet-aligned communism, which altered the entire political landscape. Even though DSA had no illusions about the Soviet Union and welcomed its downfall, they were still placed on the political defensive. The end of the USSR and the wave of capitalist triumphalism spread demoralization across the left, even among democratic socialists who argued it had nothing in common with socialism. Despite this, in the minds of most people, the Soviet Union had represented socialism and its ignominious end dealt a major blow to the entire left, including DSA.

In this new environment, DSA abandoned the strategy of Realignment on paper without replacing it with any new vision. DSA recognized that the decline of organized labor's strength and the rise of the conservative Democratic Leadership Council to a commanding position inside the Democratic Party weakened the social base for Realignment: "If we once positioned ourselves as the left wing of the possible, there is now no 'possible' to be the left wing of."[1] While DSA was now pessimistic about the prospects of transforming the Democratic Party, this did not lead to a break. Instead, democratic socialists needed to keep one foot inside the Democrats and another on the outside:

> Democratic socialists reject an either-or approach to electoral coalition building, focused solely on a new party or on realignment within the Democratic Party. The growth of PAC-driven, candidate-based, entrepreneurial politics in the last 25 years leaves little hope for an immediate, principled electoral response to the rightward, pro-corporate social

> movements capable of winning reforms that empower people. Since such social movements seek to influence state policy, they will intervene in electoral politics, whether through Democratic primaries, non-partisan local elections, or third party efforts. Our electoral work aims at building majoritarian coalitions capable of not only electing public officials on the anticorporate program of these movements, but also of holding officials accountable after they are elected.[2]

The recognition that democratic socialists needed to build "anti-corporate social movements" allowed for some political experimentation and they were now willing to consider third-party efforts.

Still, the new orientation only went so far. In the 2000 election, DSA's National Political Committee was divided between supporters of Green Party candidate Ralph Nader, Socialist Party candidate David McReynolds and Al Gore for the Democrats. This political division prevented DSA from making an official endorsement in 2000. The organization remained fixated on the Democratic Party as the main site for political action. Four years later, DSA backed the Democratic standard-bearer John Kerry with a statement that could easily have been written by Michael Harrington:

> While we have no illusions about how a Kerry administration would govern – absent mass pressure from below – and are not impressed with his delayed criticism of the war and his earlier commitments in favor of "free trade," we also realize that the Bush administration is as reactionary as Reagan's. A Kerry defeat would be taken not as a defeat of the US political center, which Kerry represents, but of the mainstream Left. As a result, it would embolden the Right and demoralize the Left (as well as trade unionists and people of color) as much

> as Reagan's 1984 defeat of Mondale did. On the other hand, a Kerry victory will let us press onward, with progressives aggressively pressuring an administration that owed its victory to democratic mobilization from below.[3]

When DSA endorsed Barack Obama in the presidential race, the rationales echoed those of Realignment. DSA claimed that they supported Obama "without illusions" and that a Democratic victory would not bring any significant reforms. However, they claimed that an Obama presidency would be amendable to "consistent pressure from below" since the Democrats in power would provide more space for the left to organize.[4] Once in office, Obama proved himself to be a loyal champion of business interests. Despite Obama's record, DSA's talk of holding his feet to the fire amounted to nothing when they endorsed him again in 2012.

The Jacobins

During these difficult years, DSA maintained a presence on college campuses and managed to attract many dedicated and intelligent young people, including a precocious Bhaskar Sunkara. Barely out of high school when he joined DSA, Sunkara believed it was time for democratic socialist ideas to come out of the margins and become more mainstream. In September 2010, at the age of 21, Sunkara launched *Jacobin*, a new type of magazine to embody these ideas. Sunkara distinguished *Jacobin* from similar journals such as *Socialist Worker, In These Times* or *Dissent* as "representing a politics that was neither Leninist nor the kind of broad liberal-left opinion...I wanted to stake out a vision that was uncompromisingly socialist, but that married some of the accessibility of *The Nation* with the political seriousness of publications further to the left."[5] While Sunkara intended for *Jacobin* to be a "big-tent" journal, he acknowledged that Michael Harrington's ideas played a major role in shaping its politics:

> One of them would definitely be Michael Harrington, even though we disagree with him politically. Those of us who are on the left wing of DSA often fight against a lot of Harringtonite ideas, like his softness towards the trade union bureaucracy and the Democratic Party. We're much more comfortable with independent political action, and I'd hope for a break with the Democrats much more than Harrington did. But intellectually, I think he's very underrated as a popularizer of Marxist thought.[6]

Even though *Jacobin* was born at a time when print media was declining, it has managed to steadily grow and publishes a wide range of contributors ranging from prominent intellectuals such as Noam Chomsky and Slavoj Žižek, moderate social democrats and revolutionary Trotskyists. *Jacobin*'s real take off came in 2016 when it published glowing coverage of the Democratic primary campaign of the self-described "democratic socialist" Bernie Sanders, attracting a whole new audience.

The 2016 Bernie Sanders campaign breathed new life into DSA after years of stagnation. According to DSA NPC member Joseph Schwartz, DSA's "number one priority" was supporting Vermont Senator Bernie Sanders' primary run.[7] Despite Sanders' embrace of "democratic socialism," Schwartz acknowledged that Sanders' program, which called for a "political revolution against the billionaire class," had more in line with liberal Keynesianism and fell short of DSA's conception of socialism: "Bernie's New Deal or social-democratic program did not fulfill the socialist aim of establishing worker and social ownership of the economy. But in the context of 40 years of oligarchic rule, Sanders' program proved sufficiently radical and inspiring."[8] While Bernie Sanders did not win the nomination, he did win over 13 million votes showing that his message had fallen on fertile ground. DSA tapped into the enthusiasm and energy of the Sanders' campaign and grew from 6500 in fall 2014 to 8500 members on election day 2016.[9] No doubt DSA's support for Bernie Sanders would have met with Michael Harrington's approval.

While the Sanders campaign brought a new layer of activists to DSA, this was nothing compared to the surge in membership that occurred after the election of Donald Trump to the presidency. DSA's membership explosion transformed it from an organization of elderly trade union bureaucrats with a median age of 68 to one made up overwhelmingly of younger people with a median age of 33.[10] By early 2017, DSA jumped to more than 28,000 and at the end of 2019, it was approaching 60,000 members, making it the largest self-proclaimed socialist organization since the heyday of the Communist Party USA in the late 1950s.

DSA has flexed its new-found strength by running or endorsing 42 "democratic socialist" Democratic candidates in local, state and federal office elections in 20 states.[11] The most high-profile DSA candidate was the 29-year-old Alexandria Ocasio-Cortez, a former bartender, who defeated the entrenched incumbent Democratic Congressman Joe Crowley in a major political upset in 2018. Since her successful election to congress, Alexandria Ocasio-Cortez has effectively become the face of the new DSA: youthful, energetic and idealistic.

The following year, Ocasio-Cortez along with DSA enthusiastically endorsed Bernie Sanders' second bid to become the Democratic presidential nominee.[12] DSA went all in for Bernie Sanders and its members zealously volunteered in droves for the campaign. *Jacobin* became the unofficial press release office for the Sanders campaign, publishing 340 articles devoted to him in 2019. These articles offered no criticisms of Sanders, but simply argued why he would win or defended his positions on every issue.[13] Now that the campaign is over,

DSA is at a crossroads. On the one hand, they have seen a spike in membership, reaching 66,000.[14] While DSA remains officially uncommitted in November's general election, there is mounting pressure from many democratic socialists for the organization to formally endorse Joe Biden.[15] Even those like Bhaskar Sunkara, who support the Green Party's presidential candidate Howie Hawkins, remain committed to Realignment and the Democratic Party in the long term.[16]

The Harringtonites

It stands to reason that Michael Harrington would be pleased with DSA's growth, but would he have still recognized it? In some symbolic ways, DSA moved away from his legacy in ways that would have horrified him. There are now Marxist study groups in DSA that openly talk about Lenin and Trotsky. At its 2017 convention, DSA severed its longstanding ties to the Socialist International and endorsed the Boycott, Divestment and Sanctions Movement to end international support for Israel's oppression of Palestinians.[17] Support at the convention for breaking with the Democrats attracted a substantial minority inside DSA. Does all this mean that DSA is abandoning the politics of Michael Harrington and embarking on a new course?

In fact, the legacy of Michael Harrington casts a long shadow over DSA. Even though DSA prides itself on being a "big-tent" organization, there remains a formal ban on members from "democratic-centralist" (revolutionary Marxist) groups joining. When it comes to an orientation to the Democratic Party and "democratic socialist" reformism, Michael Harrington's politics remain the "common sense" of DSA.

Harringtonites such as Maurice Isserman argued that DSA is growing precisely by supporting Democratic candidates such as Alexandria Ocasio-Cortez and Cynthia Nixon: "The two of them did immeasurably more to popularize democratic socialism by acting as the left wing of the possible than any number of purist third-party campaigns, or electoral abstinence, could ever have accomplished."[18] Isserman claims that those who propose breaking with the Democratic Party are "left sectarians" who embrace "whatever policy and doctrine seems to promise the greatest personal sense of moral purity."[19]

Isserman himself is a member of the North Star Caucus, one of the many caucuses that have sprouted up in DSA. Many of the signatories of the North Star Caucus represent the Harringtonite "Old Guard," who were active in either DSOC and NAM along with various social and labor movements. The North Star Caucus believes the main goal of DSA is to defeat the Republicans:

> We believe that the defeat of Trumpism and the Republicans in the 2018 and 2020 elections is a strategic imperative, the most important political task of our time. At stake in these elections is the future of the United States: we risk our democracy if we lose and anticipate a political terrain far friendlier to progressive and democratic socialist organizing if we win. DSA must focus on this task and should play a constructive role in organizing a broad coalition to achieve victory.[20]

The inevitable logic of this position means that the North Star Caucus is committed to supporting the Democratic Party as a matter of strategy. To accomplish that, the North Star Caucus believes that the Democratic Party needs to be Realigned:

> To defeat Trumpism and the Republicans, we must recognize that the Democratic Party's decades-long acquiescence to neoliberal policies – austerity, privatization, deregulation and corporate-dominated globalization – has played a role in the rise of racist, far-right populism. The Democratic Party has been too passive as these neoliberal policies

> have led to the decimation of unions in the United States and to the socioeconomic devastation of large swaths of its working class. As democratic socialists, we believe that a clear, unequivocal break with neoliberal policies is needed to defeat Trumpism and the authoritarian politics of today's Republican Party.[21]

Supporters of the North Star Caucus such as George Fish draw inspiration from Michael Harrington on their political vision and understanding of socialism. According to Fish, "Harringtonism is the guiding ideology of democratic socialism in the US" which is characterized by a socialism that "fights for free, honest and open elections for achieving socialism based on democratic self-determination and for transformative change for the here and now" as opposed to totalitarian Marxism-Leninism and Trotskyism.[22] Secondly, Fish says Michael Harrington was "correct in seeing the locus for socialist struggle within the Democratic Party, and constituting DSA as the left wing of the Democratic Party," which he believes was vindicated by DSA's growth after their involvement in the Bernie Sanders campaign in 2016.[23]

While the North Star Caucus are champions of a Realignment strategy in almost identical terms to Michael Harrington, others such as Seth Ackerman have attempted to update the strategy for the twenty-first century. Like Harrington and the North Star, Ackerman acknowledges that the Democratic Party is undemocratic, lacks a coherent program and its leadership is unaccountable to the membership. Instead of simply uncritically supporting all Democrats like the North Star, Ackerman proposes that DSA utilize the Democratic Party by running their own candidates on its ballot line. For Ackerman, supporting the Democratic Party ballot line is not a question of principle, but a "secondary issue" and should be utilized "on a case-by-case basis and on pragmatic grounds."[24] In order for a DSA member to run as a Democrat, Ackerman says they would have to adhere to a "democratic socialist" program and be accountable to DSA. In effect, DSA Democrats would function as "a party within a party." According to Ackerman, his proposal would enable:

> the Left to organize to the point that it can strategically and consciously exploit the gaps in the coherence of the system in order to create the equivalent of a political party in the key respects: a membership-run organization with its own name, its own logo, its own identity and therefore its own platform, and its own ideology.[25]

For all its sophistication, Ackerman's updated Realignment strategy comes up against the same roadblocks as Harrington's original strategy and, as the 2020 election shows, offers no solutions to overcome them.

All the factions in DSA are formally committed to the democratic socialist road to power that Michael Harrington would have felt quite comfortable with. For instance, Bhaskar Sunkara and Joseph Schwartz are in favor of an expanded welfare state on the Nordic model, but recognize that "social democracy is good, but not good enough."[26] Like Harrington, they argue that capitalism undermines social democracy in the long run:

> Even if we wanted to stop at socialism within capitalism, it's not clear that we could.
>
> Since the early 1970s, the height of Western social democracy, corporate elites have abandoned the postwar "class compromise" and sought to radically restrict the scope of economic regulation. What capitalists grudgingly accepted during an exceptional period of postwar growth and rising profits, they would no longer.[27]

In line with Michael Harrington's strategy, they advocate building a new majority where socialists "must be both tribunes for socialism and [its] best organizers" along the model of the Communist Party's Popular Front:

> Of course, there are also negative lessons to be learned from the Communist growth during the Popular Front period. They hid their socialist identity in an attempt to appeal to the broadest swath of Americans possible. When forced to reveal it, they referred to an authoritarian Soviet Union as their model. And by following Moscow's line on the Hitler-Stalin Pact and then the no-strike pledge during World War II, the party abandoned the most militant sectors of the working class. Thus, the Communists put themselves in a position that prevented them from ever winning hegemony within the US working-class movement from liberal forces.
>
> Still, the Popular Front was the last time socialism had any mass presence in the United States – in part because, in its own way, the Communists rooted their struggles for democracy within US political culture while trying to build a truly multiracial working-class movement.[28]

According to Sunkara and Schwartz, a new popular front would have the broad base of support necessary to implement "non-reformist reforms" to weaken capitalism and increase the power of the working class, and in due course lead to socialism. The exact mechanisms of Sunkara and Schwartz's socialist transition remain unclear.

A much more developed strategy of the "democratic road to socialism" was developed by the sociologist Vivek Chibber. Strangely, Chibber says that democratic socialists should look to the early years of the Bolshevik Party as an example of "a mass cadre-based party with a centralized leadership and internal coherence" that is rooted in working-class communities.[29]

However, Chibber does not advocate a revolutionary insurrection on the Bolshevik model since that is no longer viable due to the overwhelming armed power of the state. Like Sunkara and Schwartz, Chibber argues that the left needs to pursue a strategy of "non-reformist reforms" that "should have the dual effect of making future organizing easier, and also constraining the power of capital to undermine them down the road."[30] In the distant future, Chibber believes that socialism requires a "final break" with capitalism, but what that means is left unspecified. For now, Chibber advocates the creation of a reformist Bolshevik Party with a gradualist strategy, which is a fundamentally contradictory and untenable proposal to say the least.

While Michael Harrington is unknown to most of DSA's new members, his ideas continue to shape the contours of the current debates whether on Realignment, reforms or democratic socialism. Some such as the North Star remain unreconstructed Harringtonites while Sunkara, Schwartz, Ackerman and Chibber have attempted to make those ideas relevant to the present. In light of the 2016 and 2020 elections, none of the latter-day Harringtonites have seriously confronted the limitations of Realignment. The growth of DSA's membership, the futility of operating inside the Democratic Party and mounting crises of capitalism open up the possibility that the organization may break with Realignment. Ultimately, if the American left wants socialism, then it must abandon the entirety of Michael Harrington's politics for those of revolutionary communism.

Appendix: The Meaning of Democratic Marxism

Introduction

From the 1960s until the end of his life, Michael Harrington developed a sophisticated theory of "Democratic Marxism" that covered everything from philosophy to imperialism to the transition to socialism. Michael Harrington made no claim to originality in Democratic Marxism, but hoped that it would serve as both the ideology and political strategy for democratic socialists and the American labor bureaucracy. In contrast to both the communists and anticommunists, who made Marx the champion of anti-democratic and totalitarian communism, Michael Harrington wanted to "remove the mountain of rubbish from his tomb" and present the "real" Karl Marx who was "the foe of every dogma, champion of human freedom and [a] democratic socialist."[1]

God's Funeral

According to Michael Harrington, Marxism was unique because it could provide coherent understanding to the modern world. This used to be the role of religion, but due to the advance of science and the Enlightenment, that was no longer the case. The decline of religion was rooted in the development of capitalism, which was "the first agnostic economic-social formation in the history of the West."[2] Capitalism was marked by a "cold decadence" and its continual advance brought about an expansion of the productive forces alongside moral decay: "the civilization of capitalism, its ethics, its morality, its philosophy, was being destroyed by the practice of capitalism."[3] Contemporary capitalism was dominated by "anonymous collectivities" that erased human individuality. Now the corporations were making undemocratic decisions that placed profit ahead of the common good. The pursuit of profit and secularization meant that the old social roles of God and religion were dead, causing the traditional social fabric to become undone with nothing left to take its place. As a result, people searched for a "substitute deity to take over the social functions of the dying God of tradition."[4]

Michael Harrington lamented the decline of religion and sympathized with those who looked back to the "good old days" where the Church could provide all the necessary answers. However, he believed that it was impossible to turn back the clock and that religion could not provide a solution to the problems of capitalism:

> If the empty heavens signal a failure to find larger meanings in a society hoist on its own ingenuity, then the death of God is indeed a decadence. The mindless, and self-destructive, hedonism which would result from such an eventuality might make us nostalgic for the old absolutes – for some this has already happened – but absolutes cannot be brought back from the grave we have dug for them.[5]

In explaining the loss of meaning caused by the death of God, Michael Harrington admitted that there were a thousand schools of thought looking for answers: "In other words, the fact of our empirically rich bewilderment is not in doubt. Every thoughtful person for several hundred years has known about that. But the reason for it is a matter of great contention."[6] Those answers ranged from fundamentalism to fascism to socialism to conservatism to liberalism to bourgeois political economy.

Michael Harrington argued that it was Marxism that best filled the gap left by religion and explained the pressing issues of the modern world.

> In a society whose fundamental principle was an antiprinciple

> of free market atomism and which, furthermore, did not understand that its own exuberant individualism was the result of the most intricately socialized organization of production in the history of the race, there could be no overarching cohesion. Moreover, Marx argued...that such a system produced not merely goods and services, but a characteristic way of seeing reality as well.[7]

Thus, Marxism not only provided a methodology to investigate society, but it offered the best means of changing the world.

Spiritual Materialism

In reconstructing Marx's methodology, Michael Harrington begins by challenging a common view of Marxism as a crude form of economic determinism with rigid scientific laws:

> [Marx] knows "the economic reasons for our acts." In the vision of this familiar Marx, history develops according to laws as inexorable as those discovered by the physical sciences. The dynamic principle of this process is an economic base, the means of production, which determines a political and cultural superstructure. Thus, the laws and art of an age, and particularly its political conflicts, are to be understood as masquerade in which the real actors are the economic forces.[8]

For Michael, this conception of Marxism is either a half-truth at best or a caricature and falsification at worst. Yet this "pseudo-Marxism" was the dominant one "that has taken hold in the minds of millions and helped to change reality."[9]

According to Michael Harrington, one reason why "pseudo-Marxism" was so influential is due to Frederick Engels, who seriously misrepresented Marx's theories. He argues that Marx tolerated Engels' distortion of his ideas for pragmatic reasons because the latter was a skilled popularizer, who could reach a wider audience. In the process of popularization, Engels developed Marxism into a systematic worldview, particularly with the codification of dialectical materialism: "Engels did much more consistent harm to his mentor's theory although he sometimes was its shrewdest interpreter. He was the inventor of an omniscient theory of society and nature, called dialectical materialism, which is not to be found, even as a momentary indiscretion, in the writings of Marx."[10] In advancing dialectical materialism and drawing upon Hegel, Harrington believed that Engels created a determinist worldview and a quasi-religion among socialists that promised an inevitable victory. The Marxist Weltanschauung was put into practice by Lenin, and was later implemented with disastrous consequences under Stalin:

> ...Lenin himself was the proponent of an integralist brand of Marxism, borrowed in considerable measure from Engels, which was to provide the anti-theology for Stalin's atheist church...Lenin was an activist, the organizer of an underground party of committed revolutionaries rather than a mass electoral party like that of the German socialists. Under such circumstances, the party's ideology had to be an all-consuming faith which would provide the cadres with a reason to risk their freedom and their lives...
>
> Lenin proceeded to make a supreme virtue out of this alleged necessity – and unintentionally to prepare the way for a state cult of atheism under Stalin which would be every bit as orthodox as the Orthodox Church he wanted to smash...
>
> The Party's infallibility was no longer an opinion; it was a dogma enforced by the secret police.[11]

As a result, Engel's promotion of dialectical materialism led to the creation of Stalinist totalitarianism.

While Engels was the chief culprit for the falsification of Marxism, Michael Harrington did not let Marx himself off the hook. Marx's 1859 *Preface to A Contribution to the Critique of Political Economy* may have provided a succinct introduction to the basics of historical materialism, but it was a poor introduction to Marxism: "In fact, it is either so compressed as to guarantee that most readers will miss its subtleties, or else, when it is straightforward and clear, it gives an inaccurate – and unMarxist – description of social reality."[12] The *Preface's* formulations present society as a simplistic model where the economic base determines the superstructure and the iron laws of history inevitably

lead to socialism. Thus, Marx's formulations in the *Preface* provide an ideological foundation for Stalinist dogmatism. Michael Harrington argued that Marx's claim that "the mode of production in material life determines the general character of the social, political, and spiritual processes of life" was simplistic. For one, he said that the term "material relations of life" was not clearly defined. Did material refer to just "inanimate" matter such as the economic base? Michael Harrington interpreted "material relations of life" much more broadly, saying that it encompassed what Hegel defined as civil society: "Civil society, then, defined the whole world of laissez faire, its pleasures and poverty, its human interrelationships and its needs, as well as its material goods and machines. It was, even in its greed, suffused with a specific humanity, with precisely that which made man greater than the animals."[13] This allowed Harrington to claim that "material relations of life" are not just the economic base, but include social classes, culture, consciousness and human interrelationships.[14]

From this, he concluded that historical materialism was not the crude form presented in the *Preface* where the base determines the superstructure, Instead, he viewed society as an organic totality "of many determinations and relationships"[15] where the economic, political and social parts interact reciprocally upon each other. In an organic totality, all the parts are defined by their relation to the whole:

> The relationships arising out of production are dominant in the very simple sense that they are the primordial precondition of the life of the species and in the complex sense that they provide a society with its pervasive lighting, its special atmosphere. These production relationships are not economic in the technological or material meaning of the term; they are, rather, human relationships which have been turned into things. Moreover, the production relationships do not infuse every aspect of cultural and political life with a single, underlying content. They bathe the superstructure in that pervasive light, they touch and color the totality, but that leaves room for relative autonomies. Art, science and politics all have their own rhythms.[16]

Drawing from Erich Fromm, Harrington defined this as "spiritual materialism" which he differentiated from "pseudo-Marxism" with its "crass, sordid materialism."[17] According to Michael Harrington, spiritual materialism took into account the spiritual side of people by giving the utmost attention to ideas, culture and collective consciousness. However, Harrington admits that spiritual materialism is not a scientific theory: "As a tool of social and economic analysis, the concept of man as a spiritual materialist is almost empty of meaning."[18] Instead, spiritual materialism offers "some very broad and basic guidelines."[19]

Michael Harrington claims that there are eight essential parts to spiritual materialism. First: "The Marxist paradigm is critical about its own definitions and data. Marxism, then, is a "critical" theory in the Kantian sense of the term – it probes its own concepts and terms as well as those of its opponents; it seeks to articulate the unstated assumptions of an era and regards their unstatedness as eloquent clues to what a society really means."[20] The second is that Marxism is not "value-free," but seeks to be rigorously scientific. Third: people are made by and create society. While human actions are understood in terms of conscious intentions, they are limited by what can be done in a particular moment. As Marx said: "Men make their own history, but they do not make it as they please; they do not make it under self-selected circumstances, but under circumstances existing already, given and transmitted from the past."[21] Fourth: economics is the "essential determinacy in the structure of society," but economics includes a series of reciprocal interactions with other elements such as politics, culture and the social. Fifth: contradictions are a key element in social change and history, but contrary to the claims of dialectical materialism, there are no universal contradictions in either society or nature. Sixth: class is essential to any Marxist analysis. Seventh: technology is an important variable, but it does not determine an entire social system. Last: crises are inherent to capitalism, so it is necessary to know their origin and this "requires scrupulous attention to the actual workings of the system at a given moment, not generalities about its structural (and undoubted) iniquity."[22]

For all its apparent sophistication, Michael Harrington's "spiritual materialism" makes no attempt to reconcile theory and practice. Rather, it follows Lukács in claiming that Marx's method can be separated from its results: "there is no necessary relationship between Marxist theory and political positions (that is, that those who agree as to methodology can utilize that method to reach contradictory political judgments)."[23] This leads Michael Harrington to endorse Lukács' conclusion that one could be an Orthodox Marxist "as long as one asserts that the Marxist method offers the best way of proceeding and that it can only be deepened in the spirit of its founder."[24]

It is certainly true that people are often very inconsistent and that their actions are in contradiction to their principles. Instead of exposing the social roots of that inconsistency, however, Harrington offers a rationalization for it. By separating theory from practice, he allows for opportunism. If Democratic Marxism attempted to reconcile Marxist theory and practice, then Michael Harrington could not justify supporting the Democratic Party or opposing proletarian revolution. In 1939, Trotsky criticized a similar celebration of theoretical inconsistency and eclecticism in Michael Harrington's mentor, Max Shachtman:

> Appealing to "inconsistency" as justification for an unprincipled theoretical bloc, signifies giving oneself bad credentials as a Marxist. Inconsistency is not accidental, and in politics it does not appear solely as an individual symptom. Inconsistency usually serves a social function. There are social groupings which cannot be consistent. Petty-bourgeois elements who have not rid themselves of hoary petty-bourgeois tendencies are systematically compelled within a workers' party to make theoretical compromises with their own conscience.[25]

Spiritual materialism does not simply provide a theoretical rationale for opportunism, but involves a wholesale revision and abandonment of the core conceptions of Marxism, particularly its "crass, sordid materialism." In place of materialism, Harrington adopts a subjectivist theory of knowledge that "the senses do not, in the Marxist view, 'reflect' an external reality that is independent of the subject."[26] According to George Novack, this subjectivism means that Michael Harrington abandons the Marxist theory of knowledge:

> This is not the Marxist view. Every materialist theory

> of knowledge has held that sensory experience is the primary source of our knowledge about the world, which exists independently of human activity and individual consciousness. If sensory reflection did not provide relatively accurate and reliable information about the things and events in the environment the human species would not have survived or developed. Without the checks upon our mind and imagination imposed by objective reality we would have no way to distinguish fact from fantasy, truth from error.
>
> A sensation is a subjective image with an objective content referring and corresponding to some aspect of the material world. To deny any internal connection of our sensations with what exists outside ourselves is to make a mystery of knowledge, since whatever we know comes in the first place from evidence supplied by the senses. Let Harrington put his finger on a red-hot stove and then cry out that the painful sensation he reacts to does not "reflect" an external reality.[27]

Harrington resorts to subjectivism and denies materialism, but Marx and Engels argued that philosophical materialism was integral to their revolutionary politics:

> There is no need for any great penetration to see from the teaching of materialism on the original-goodness and equal intellectual endowment of men, the omnipotence of experience, habit and education, and the influence of environment on man, the great significance of industry, the justification of enjoyment, etc., how necessarily materialism is connected with communism and socialism. If man draws all his knowledge, sensation, etc., from the world of the senses and the experience gained in it, then what has to be done is to arrange the empirical world in such a way that man experiences and becomes accustomed to what is truly human

> in it and that he becomes aware of himself as man. If correctly understood interest is the principle of all morality, man's private interest must be made to coincide with the interest of humanity. If man is unfree in the materialistic sense, i.e., is free not through the negative power to avoid this or that, but through the positive power to assert his true individuality, crime must not be punished in the individual, but the anti-social sources of crime must be destroyed, and each man must be given social scope for the vital manifestation of his being. If man is shaped by environment, his environment must be made human. If man is social by nature, he will develop his true nature only in society, and the power of his nature must be measured not by the power of the separate individual but by the power of society.[28]

Thus, if one accepts Harrington's "spiritual materialism," then, ironically, this leads to a complete abandonment of Marx's own materialism.

Michael Harrington makes a major error in ascribing to Marx and Engels a mechanical and vulgar theory where the base wholly determines the superstructure. Neither Marx nor Engels ever made such claims, even if their views were interpreted that way by many, including by Michael Harrington. In fact, Engels specifically said economic reductionism was a misrepresentation of historical materialism:

> According to the materialist view of history, the determining factor in history is, in the final analysis, the production and reproduction of actual life. More than that was never maintained either by Marx or myself. Now if someone distorts this by declaring the economic moment to be the only determining factor, he changes that proposition into a meaningless, abstract, ridiculous piece of jargon. The economic situation is the basis, but the various factors of the

> superstructure – political forms of the class struggle and its consequences, namely constitutions set up by the ruling class after a victorious battle, etc., forms of law and the reflections of all these real struggles in the minds of the participants, i.e. political, philosophical and legal theories, religious views and the expansion of the same into dogmatic systems – all these factors also have a bearing on the course of the historical struggles of which, in many cases, they largely determine the form. It is in the interaction of all these factors and amidst an unending multitude of fortuities (i.e. of things and events whose intrinsic interconnections are so remote or so incapable of proof that we can regard them as non-existent and ignore them) that the economic trend ultimately asserts itself as something inevitable. Otherwise the application of the theory to any particular period of history would, after all, be easier than solving a simple equation of the first degree.[29]

Thus, if anyone was countering the falsification of Marxism it was that great "distorter" himself, Frederick Engels!

Finally, the eight guidelines of spiritual materialism are nothing more than a rehashing of the theory of multiple factors. The theory of multiple factors disassembles a social formation like capitalism into different pieces of politics, economics, culture, etc with each one possessing equal weight. Since none of the factors outweigh any other, one factor can be dominant today and another tomorrow. In the last instance, this means that there is no way to explain social change. Still, Harrington claims the opposite, that "production predominates within the organic whole...Yet, even so, it exists in a reciprocal relationship with all the other elements."[30] This statement would not have met with any objection from Marx and Engels. What leads Michael Harrington to the theory of multiple factors is that he remains unclear on the question of what element plays the decisive part in the process of historical change, sometimes it is economics and sometimes it is politics. Michael Harrington can't answer that question because he denies that there are universal social laws, so he has no theoretical foundation to understand what factor plays the determining role in history. As a result, understanding history remains a mystery to spiritual materialism.

Marx and the Dictatorship of the Proletariat

At the heart of Democratic Marxism is a rejection of both violent revolution and the dictatorship of the proletariat. Michael Harrington envisioned the transition to socialism as a gradual and peaceful process. Therefore, it was essential to the ideological and political claims of Democratic Marxism to present Marx not as an irreconcilable revolutionary opponent of capitalism, but as someone who could be appropriated by democratic socialists.

Michael Harrington does not deny that Marx supported the violent overthrow of capitalism, notably in the *Communist Manifesto*, but claims that was a youthful phase of ultra-leftism and Blanquism because revolution appeared imminent in 1848.[31] During that youthful phase of his life, Marx did use the phrase "dictatorship of the proletariat," but Harrington claims this was an unfortunate error on Marx's part because "[he] did not mean dictatorship when he said dictatorship."[32] What Marx meant by the term dictatorship was not necessarily authoritarianism and tyranny, but rather that dictatorship "defined the class basis of a society, not its political forms, and it did not necessarily imply the repression of civil liberties."[33] This meant that both a democratic republic and a fascist junta were class dictatorships considering that the bourgeoisie was the dominant class. Therefore, the dictatorship of the proletariat did not mean the rule of the elite minority, but the rule of the entire working class over the bourgeoisie. Still, Harrington said that after the failure of the 1848 revolutions, Marx's ultra-leftist phase ended and he recoiled from the tragic error of the "dictatorship of the proletariat" which hid "the depth of his democratic commitment."[34] Increasingly, Marx's perspective matured over the coming decades and "[he] increasingly envisioned the nonviolent and electoral conquest of power."[35]

Harrington's claims that Marx abandoned advocacy of violent revolution need to be reconciled with support for the 1871 Paris Commune as an example of the "dictatorship of the proletariat." Michael Harrington acknowledges that Marx did view the Commune as a proletarian dictatorship, but says he later revised that view.[36] Rather, the blame for viewing the Paris Commune as a dictatorship of the proletariat lies not with Marx, but with Lenin who used that "myth" as a "crucial precedent for his seizure of power in October 1917, so that every state and party that venerates his memory must also acquiesce to his version of what happened in Paris in 1871."[37]

If Marx's rejection of violent revolution was true in the nineteenth century, then Michael Harrington believed it was even more true in the present. He argued that socialists must "transcend the sterile debate of reform versus revolution" and to rid themselves of "that old Jacobin – or more exactly, Babouvist – notion that there will be a 'day' of revolution when all the reforms culminate and history turns a corner. Given the complexity of modern society, this is not going to take place."[38] The modern age meant that there was no revolutionary class that would liberate humanity: "The united, revolutionary working class which would act as History's right arm for the creation of socialism did not, and does not, exist."[39]

This Karl Marx bears little relation to the actual one since his revolutionary vision is effaced and he is transformed into a mild-mannered reformer who is strikingly similar to Michael Harrington himself. Nowhere is this more true than when it comes to questions of revolutionary violence and the dictatorship of the proletariat.

It is certainly true that Marx did advocate the use of the elections by the working class (independently of bourgeois political parties) and that it was even possible for them to win a majority and form a government. Marx even granted the theoretical possibility of a peaceful transition to socialism: "We do not deny the existence of countries like America, England, and if I knew your institutions better I might add Holland, where the workers may achieve their aims by peaceful means."[40] However, Michael Harrington takes as an article of faith what Marx offered as a remote possibility. Marx knew that if a socialist majority was elected into office that the bourgeoisie would not peacefully surrender their privileges and power: "The English middle class has always shown itself willing enough to accept the verdict of the majority so long as it enjoyed the monopoly of the voting power. But mark me, as soon as it finds itself outvoted on what it considers vital questions we shall see here a new slave-owner's war."[41] In the face of bourgeoisie resistance, Marx considered violence to be both necessary and legitimate: "Reaction exists throughout the Continent, it is general and permanent – and even in the United States and in England in another form – We must tell them – we know that you are the armed force opposing the proletariat – we shall act against you peacefully wherever possible – and take up arms when that is necessary..."[42] On the whole, Marx did consider the peaceful transfer of power to be possible, but emphasized "that in most countries on the Continent it is force which must be the lever of our revolution."[43]

For Marx, the overthrow of the bourgeoisie required the utilization of force and the institution of the dictatorship of the proletariat: "Between capitalist and communist society there lies the period of the revolutionary transformation of the one into the other. Corresponding to this is also a political transition period in which the state can be nothing but the revolutionary dictatorship of the proletariat."[44] Marx wrote this in 1875, long after Michael Harrington claimed he had abandoned all forms of "ultra-leftism." Similarly, both Marx and Engels hailed the Paris Commune as an example of the dictatorship of the proletariat, a position they consistently defended throughout their lives.[45]

Michael Harrington is correct that the phrase "dictatorship of the proletariat" does mean an expansion of democracy for the working class as evidenced by the Paris Commune. However, he forgets that Marx and Engels' criticized the Paris Commune because it did not act swiftly to crush the bourgeoisie: "If they are defeated only their 'decency' will be to blame."[46] Michael Harrington would be loath to admit it, but in their defense of the dictatorship of the proletariat, Marx and Engels were "Proletarian Jacobins." They learned from the French Revolution and the Jacobins that it was necessary for the working class to forcibly expropriate and suppress the class enemy. True, Marx and Engels were always critical of Jacobin elitism, voluntarism and romanticism, but they assimilated its essential truths that the working class needed leadership, organization, discipline and terror in order to prevail. Michael Harrington is incapable of admitting this since it would mean he could not appropriate Marx's legacy for democratic socialism. It seems that the German revisionist socialist Eduard Bernstein (whose politics closely resemble those of Harrington) was correct that Marx's legacy does not belong to democratic socialists, but to communists: "The Bolsheviks are not unjustified in claiming Marx as their own. Do you know? Marx had a strong Bolshevik streak in him!"[47]

The Transition to Socialism

Instead of a violent revolution and the dictatorship of the proletariat, Michael Harrington believed that socialism could be achieved peacefully through an electoral majority. In formulating a democratic strategy, he drew upon the work of Antonio Gramsci, whom he called "one of the most fascinating thinkers in the history of Marxism."[48] Michael Harrington believed that socialists needed to create a counter-hegemonic bloc that composed a majority of the population, who had a vested interest in a new order. Michael Harrington believed that a counter-hegemonic bloc would win support by promoting a "practical program in a language of sincere and genuine idealism. A politics without poetry will simply not be able to bring together all the different, and sometimes antagonistic, forces essential to a new majority for a new program."[49] Harrington argued that the Marxist Weltanschauung was insufficient to build a new majority since "such theoretical commitment narrowed the movement by excluding many."[50] A "genuine" Marxism will mobilize the power of morality and values that "transcend material interest." Thus, a new majority "would have to be united on the basis of ethical values and not simply in terms of the material interests of a single class."[51] By uniting around greater values, atheists would be able to join forces with religious believers, since they spoke about the same underlying social problems of capitalism: "serious atheists and agnostics now share a common cause with serious believers: a concern for values as such, for a vision of individual and social meaningfulness which goes beyond the latest consumer or cultural fad."[52]

The Gramscian "intellectual and moral reform" that socialists needed to undertake involved building on American traditions, particular Jeffersonian republicanism with its ideals of moral virtue and citizenship. According to Michael Harrington, Jeffersonian republicanism was something that the socialist left needed to reclaim: "But I do not think that the Left can afford to leave the civic emotions to the Right. In a profound sense, that is our heritage more than theirs."[53] The promotion of a new republican ethic would not only Americanize socialism, but enlighten people and mobilize them for social change.

For a democratic transition to socialism to be possible, then, socialists must be able to capture the existing state apparatus from the bourgeoisie. Building on the work of the Greek Marxist Nicos Poulantzas, Michael Harrington said that the capitalist state was "relatively autonomous" and was not an instrument of a single class.[54] Michael Harrington said that the classical Marxist position on the state – that it was a machinery of repression in the hands of the dominant class, designed to preserve capitalist rule and existing property relations – was false since it was "tied to a base-superstructure model of society and is flawed for that reason. It metaphorically imagines the government as an inert thing that has no life of its own and is wielded by the 'real' powers residing in the economic base."[55] This led him to conclude that in the capitalist society, there was no ruling class, just competing blocs of classes.[56] Due to the great wealth of the bourgeoisie, they naturally exercised greater power in the state than the working class. On the other hand, if socialists could mobilize their new majority bloc, then they could win concessions from the state and gradually tilt the state to favor working-class interests.

The strategy he proposed for socialists to tilt the balance of forces was utilizing the state bureaucracy for progressive ends and a transitional program of structural reforms. Harrington argued that socialists could not dispense with bureaucracy since it was essential to the functioning of a modern economy. The problem lay not with bureaucracy per se, but bad bureaucrats. To serve as a check against bad bureaucrats, he envisioned some form of grassroots control alongside more responsible bureaucrats: "bureaucracy is itself a weapon to be used against bureaucracy."[57] The structural reforms that Harrington advocated were the socialization of investment; the progressive socialization of corporate property; and, later, the socialization of private property itself; and finally the use of taxes as an instrument of socialist change.[58] Michael Harrington believed that this transitional program could be enacted without any cataclysmic changes, since he did not expect violent resistance from the bourgeoisie. Looking to the example of Sweden, he argued that "it is now possible to have a relatively painless transition to socialization if socialists will only learn how to encourage the 'euthanasia of the rentiers.'"[59]

In advocating a positive model for his strategy, Michael Harrington defended the Communist Party's popular front. As he said in his 1976 debate with Peter Camejo:

> My policy is very much like the Communist policy in the 1930s. You bet your life it is. I'm an opponent of communist dictatorship and totalitarianism. But while the Socialist party and the Socialist Workers party were getting absolutely nowhere because they counterposed themselves to the workers who wanted to vote for Roosevelt, the Communist party of the 1930s was building the biggest, largest movement calling itself socialist in the United States since the days of Gene Debs, and winning leadership in a third of the unions of the CIO.[60]

In other words, he believed in a popular front without Stalinism (as he sometimes put it).[61]

It is true that the CPUSA did have a visible presence in unions, black freedom struggles and anti-fascist coalitions, but this did not come about due to the popular front strategy. The major success of the CPUSA in organizing workers occurred before the popular front was implemented in 1935-1936, when the party experimented with militant united front tactics and still maintained a revolutionary identity. After adopting the popular front strategy, the CPUSA retreated from its militant tactics. In the interests of Moscow, the communists ceased all criticism of the labor bureaucracy, the Roosevelt administration and liberal organizations. Over the course of the 1930s, the class character of the CPUSA changed as its members took up positions within the labor bureaucracy to discipline working-class militancy and act in the interests of the Democratic Party. According to Charlie Post:

> Popular Frontism transformed the CP from the main current promoting self-organization, militant action and political independence among workers, African Americans and other oppressed groups into the emerging CIO's bureaucracy's "point men" in their drive to "tame" worker and popular militancy and to cement their partnership with the Roosevelt administration.[62]

Accordingly, the CPUSA retreated from its advocacy of communist revolution and ended up as the "left-wing" of the Democrats and the New Deal.

The "hidden secret" of why the anticommunist Michael Harrington supported the CPUSA's popular front was not because socialism had mass influence or spoke the language of ordinary people. Rather, it was when the communists ceased to be revolutionary by giving up militant action, self-organization of the working class, and "sectarian" political independence and became loyal allies of the labor bureaucracy and liberals. In other words, it was when the communists were ready to act like Michael Harrington's democratic socialists that he admired them. Like his usage of Marx and Gramsci, Harrington's appropriation of Poulantzas' theory was for the purposes of promoting evolutionary socialism and ignoring ideas to the contrary. In *Political Power and Social Classes*, Poulantzas explicitly attacks the theoretical foundations of social democracy, which claimed that the state was a neutral instrument that can easily change hands.[63] Poulantzas' argument on the state's relative autonomy is not in contradiction to the state acting in the interests of the bourgeoisie, but fully in line with it. For capitalism to exist, the state cannot simply rely upon force, but must act in the long-term interests of the bourgeoisie by being flexible enough to grant reforms to the working class. When using the terms "relative autonomy" we should be careful to note that both terms are equally important. Perhaps the best analogy to explain the "relative autonomy" of the state is that of a tether for a dog. The tether can be either long or short, giving the dog room for maneuver, but ultimately it is firmly implanted in the ground. The same is true of the state. The state remains a class state, but needs its own room to move and cannot be tied to the momentary passions or the interests of a small group of capitalists. If it is to rule for the interests of the ruling class as a whole, then it has to be able to maneuver against any group or individual capitalists that get out of line and thereby threaten its long-term interests.[64] An example of the state's adaptability that Michael Harrington should have been familiar with was the New Deal where FDR granted concessions to the labor movement in the face of resistance from certain sections of the capitalist class. The New Deal did not change the class character of the state and in the long run, it helped to bolster the political stability of American capitalism.

While the early Poulantzas was working in fidelity to the Leninist and revolutionary tradition, it was not without reason that Harrington was able to push his ideas to reformist conclusions. In fact, Harrington was anticipating Poulantzas himself in that regard, who argued that point in his later work, *State, Power and Socialism*: "some of my earlier formulations may now be made more precise. The (capitalist) state should not be regarded as an intrinsic entity: like 'capital', it is rather a relationship of forces, or more precisely the material condensation of such a relationship among classes and class fractions, such as this is expressed within the State in a necessarily specific form."[65] Poulantzas' lack of clarity on this question enabled Harrington to argue that the welfare state was not tied to any single class, but open to capture by any class, and was the theoretical justification for democratic socialism's political strategy. In the end, Michael Harrington's Poulantzasian and popular frontist strategy depends on a profound misunderstanding of the state. He is unable to recognize the realities of the state's dependency on both the existing bureaucracy and profitability. The ability of socialist governments to deliver reforms such as higher wages and an expanded welfare state depends on higher taxes on capital, which ultimately depend upon profitability. If a socialist government pursued serious structural reforms, this would threaten the flow of profits and spark resistance from the existing bureaucracy. That means there are definite limits on the ability of the capitalist state – even if its governing personnel are dedicated socialists – to implement reforms.[66]

Michael Harrington forgets that a socialist majority in parliament does not equal state power. Rather, real power resides in its unelected institutions – the military, state bureaucracy, courts – all of which will resist structural reforms and the democratic road to socialism with whatever means are at their disposal. This was shown when Spain's popular front government and Salvador Allende's socialist government in Chile were overthrown in military coups wholeheartedly supported by the bourgeoisie. The reality that no ruling class willingly surrenders its privileges and power was precisely why Marx and Engels said a violent revolution and the dictatorship of the proletariat was necessary. This is something that Harrington refused to acknowledge. All he can offer are moral appeals to the ruling class and hope. But this is an ahistorical picture that will always lead to a dead end.

Imperialism and the Leninist Temptation

Michael Harrington's analysis of capitalism and democratic socialist strategy was predicated on a rejection of Lenin's theory of imperialism. His main objection lay in Lenin's claim that imperialism was a necessary stage of capitalism. If Lenin was right and imperialism was a stage of capitalism, then war and underdevelopment were both structured into the system itself with the entire bourgeoisie taking part. Harrington argued to the contrary that Lenin's theory of imperialism led to "a militant-sounding passivity" because "if America is inevitably fated to act imperialistically as long as it is capitalist, and if there is no imminent prospect of America ceasing to be capitalist, then a 'radical' analysis proves that there is not much point to doing anything."[67] Instead, he argued that socialists must act on the assumption that imperialism was not a necessary stage of capitalism, where imperialist policies were the fault of a small clique of reactionary capitalists against which the broad strata of the bourgeoisie can take a sharp stand. If imperialism was just policy, then socialists had the opportunity of working with enlightened capitalists to achieve major domestic and international reforms: "[if the] Leninist analysis fails and it's no longer bourgeois sentimentality to suggest that a capitalist system under the political control of democratic socialists could behave with a modicum of decency within the international economy. For it is no longer fated to do evil."[68]

While Michael Harrington readily acknowledged the horrors of colonialism and imperial plunder, he argued that, "it is precisely the emergence of the welfare state that significantly altered this pattern. With managed economies and an unprecedented expansion of production, it became possible for the advanced capitalisms to profiteer off one another."[69] For him, nowhere was this more true than in the United States where, aside from oil, the country did not depend upon exploiting the Third World. Harrington did admit that the reactionary policies of the American government did widen the gap between rich and poor across the world, but they are "not the inexorable expressions of economic and social structure. They are reasonable, businesslike but unnecessary evils perpetuated according to the rules of this world which was so carefully made for us. But these rules could be changed. And this possibility is something that is not to be found in the philosophy of V. I. Lenin and his followers."[70] Still, Harrington admitted that "capitalism...requires international inequality as a precondition for its contradictory existence"[71] and that no country has impeded the economic growth of the Third World more than the United States.[72]

Yet Harrington claimed the American role in maintaining global inequality was not the result of anything intrinsic to capitalism or even bad intentions. In fact, he accepted the claims of the American government that its international policies were motivated by noble ideals. Michael Harrington believed those who ran the United States were basically good men. The problem was that tragic results like the Vietnam War resulted despite the best of intentions. This was evidenced by Robert McNamara, one of the Vietnam War's architects: "I think McNamara is a man of enormous sincerity, decent values and genuine moral passion. So his participation in our international wrongdoing, like that of the nation itself, is unwitting and even dedicated to effecting results that are nearly the exact opposite of those that are in fact achieved."[73] The United States had no principled reasons to reject Third-World modernization plans and other measures designed to alleviate global poverty. He believed that the problem with many American politicians was their ignorance of the Third World and that by appealing to their good will, this would compel them to act. Michael Harrington also argued that appeals to moral values were not enough for capitalists to support a global New Deal, but they also should do so "on the basis of sophisticated capitalist self-interest"[74] since this would make it easier for them to continue doing business. Michael Harrington's entire understanding of imperialism leaves him unable to explain the systematic reasons that caused "enlightened" capitalists like FDR, Truman, JFK, LBJ and Carter to carry out imperialist policies. All he can say is that their imperialism was the result of good intentions gone awry. This failure of analysis stems from Harrington's claim that imperialism rests on the misguided policy of reactionaries, which the broad strata of the bourgeoisie can be mobilized against. If Michael Harrington is wrong and imperialism is a *necessary* stage of capitalism, then it is the only possible *policy* for the entire bourgeoisie in the current era. That means there is not and can be no "anti-imperialist" sections of the bourgeoisie. Since this leads to the inevitable conclusion of the need for a revolutionary strategy against imperialism, Michael Harrington refuses to consider it. As a result, his whole theory of imperialism is a confused mess that cannot understand its causes and effects and, thus, his strategy consists of little more than empty moral appeals to a non-existent "anti-imperialist" bourgeoisie. Michael Harrington was forced to admit that while Lenin's theory of imperialism was "simplistic and overgeneralized," its staying power "is still quite substantial" because imperialism for a majority of the Third World was "an overwhelming fact of life."[75] Even though Harrington advocated a global New Deal to alleviate poverty, he considered these to be just modest "first steps" and that something else was needed for the long term because "for most of the countries of Asia, Africa and Latin America, capitalist modernization is now impossible."[76] This meant that democratic socialism and classical capitalism were not viable options, leaving open only the path of a socialist revolution for the Third World. Considering the bleak conditions in the Third World, he sympathized with Julius Nyerere's socialism in Tanzania and the Sandinistas in Nicaragua to find alternative paths to development.[77] Still, Harrington feared that any alternative form of development in the Third World led to a potentially Stalinist outcome; for instance he was always on guard lest his sympathy for the Sandinistas' struggle led him to accepting their socialist claims: "It was impossible not to be sympathetic to [the Nicaraguan people]. Yet I had to remind myself of how often 'revolutionary tourists' had been seduced by those they had casually – and not always accidentally – met in the Soviet Russia of the twenties and thirties or Mao's China of the fifties and sixties. The naked eye, alas, can never 'see' a society."[78]

Still, he warned the Third World against the "Leninist-Stalinist temptation" because they lacked necessary preconditions of socialism such as modern industry and an educated working class. In light of their unfavorable material conditions, Third-World revolutionaries could only rely upon "substitute proletariats" such as army officers, radical intellectuals, the lumpenproletariat and the peasantry. These would be looked upon as agents of socialist transformation, acting against the legacy of imperialism.[79] However, due to the backward conditions, the "substitute proletariats" could not create socialism, but only "[organize] their own totalitarian subjugation as a means to freedom."[80]

Despite Harrington's background in Trotskyism, he seemed oblivious to Trotsky's theory of permanent revolution that argued precisely in favor of the possibility of a socialist revolution in backward countries. Trotsky rejected theories of stagism where the bourgeois revolution must necessarily precede the socialist one:

> The perspective of permanent revolution in no case signifies that the backward countries must await the signal from the advanced ones, or that the colonial peoples should patiently wait for the proletariat of the metropolitan centres to free them. Help comes to him who helps himself. Workers must develop the revolutionary struggle in every country, colonial or imperialist, where favourable conditions have been established, and through this set an example for the workers of other countries. Only initiative and activity, resoluteness and boldness can really materialize the slogan "Workers of the world, unite!"[81]

The theory of permanent revolution bases itself on the combined and uneven development of global capitalism. According to this theory, capitalism was not a consciously directed system following a single path of development. Rather, there was no plan at all. While capitalism's development tended to overcome feudalism, this is not a linear process. According to Trotsky's analysis of Russia, capitalism had developed later there than in England and France. In order to overcome backwardness, Russia did not pass through the same stages already traversed in the advanced countries, but telescoped or even skipped them. For instance, Russian industry adopted the most modern technology with higher rates of productivity along with a greater concentration of workers (who were militant and potentially stronger than the bourgeoisie). However, advanced industry was combined with feudal survivals – absolutism and primitive agriculture – which limited the growth of the internal market and acted as a brake on further industrialization. The consequence was that the bourgeoisie was both incapable and unwilling to carry out a bourgeois-democratic revolution. This task fell to the proletariat, who were not only compelled to eliminate feudalism, but wouldn't stop by handing power over to the capitalists. As Trotsky said: "The political domination of the proletariat is incompatible with its economic enslavement. No matter under what political flag the proletariat has come to power, it is obliged to take the path of socialist policy."[82] Rather the democratic revolution would spill over into a socialist revolution – becoming a permanent revolution. However, a socialist revolution in Russia could not be consummated in a single backward country, but would spark revolutions in the advanced countries:

> The conquest of power by the proletariat does not complete the revolution, but only opens it. Socialist construction is conceivable only on the foundation of the class struggle, on

> a national and international scale. This struggle, under the conditions of an overwhelming predominance of capitalist relationships on the world arena, must inevitably lead to explosions, that is, internally to civil wars and externally to revolutionary wars...The socialist revolution begins on the national arena, it unfolds on the international arena, and is completed on the world arena. Thus, the socialist revolution becomes a permanent revolution in a newer and broader sense of the word; it attains completion only in the final victory of the new society on our entire planet.[83]

According to Trotsky, for the working class to establish its leadership in the Third-World revolutions, they must accomplish three main tasks: 1) eliminate the vestiges of feudalism, slavery and pre-capitalist forms of exploitation by expropriating the landlords and giving the land to the peasantry; 2) free the nation from imperialist domination and create a unified national market and control key strategic resources; 3) achieve democracy by establishing institutions that allow participation and the exercise of power by the working class.[84] Trotsky argues that imperialism may have created a new working class and increased the productive forces, but a "normal" bourgeois revolution like those in France and England was barred to the Third World. It is precisely the theory of permanent revolution that explains how revolutions were possible not only in Russia, but in China, Cuba, Vietnam and elsewhere.

By contrast, if we accept Michael Harrington's premises, then we arrive at a diametrically opposed position where revolution is forever barred to the Third World due to the weaknesses of the working class and the productive forces. And any revolutionary strategy that seeks to mobilize poor peasants or intellectuals is condemned in advance as leading to "totalitarian subjugation." In the end, Michael Harrington's theory of imperialism condemns the people of the Third World to endure poverty forever while they sit patiently with folded arms waiting for socialism to arrive in the remote future.

Bureaucratic Collectivism

The theoretical basis of Michael Harrington's anticommunism was his characterization of the Soviet Union as a bureaucratic collectivist society, where:

> the state owns the means of production, and the elite Party bureaucracy owns the state. By totalitarian means it is able to extract a surplus from the direct producers and to invest it in industrial modernization and its own class privileges. It does these things in the name of "socialism," and yet it is based on the continuing expropriation of the political power of the workers and peasants.[85]

Bureaucratic collectivism triumphed in Russia mainly due to backward conditions, since the country was not ripe enough for socialism without the revolution spreading to advanced countries like Germany. Once hopes for an international revolution receded, Russia was left isolated and the development of a bureaucratic collectivist regime was inevitable.

Michael Harrington borrowed this theory from Max Shachtman, who argued that the Soviet Union ceased to be a workers' state, but a new form of class society. According to Shachtman, a counter-revolution occurred under Stalin who politically expropriated the working class:

> The comparative one-sidedness of the civil war attending the Stalinist counter-revolution was determined by the oft-noted passivity of the masses, their weariness, their failure to receive international support. In spite of this, Stalin's road to power lay through rivers of blood and over a mountain of skulls. Neither the Stalinist counter-revolution nor the

> Bolshevik revolution was effected by Fabian gradualist reforms.
>
> The conquest of state power by the bureaucracy spelled the destruction of the property relations established by the Bolshevik revolution.[86]

After the Stalinist counter-revolution, the ruling bureaucracy:

> has acquired a degree and type of independence from its social basis without parallel, at least in modern times... the interests of the bureaucracy conflict with the interests of maintaining nationalized economy as the basis for the transition to socialism – the nationalized economy which is all we can defend in the Soviet Union. Now, it is not the nationalized economy that goes to war; it is not the economy that decides when the war should be declared or started, or against whom it should be directed, or how it should be conducted. Nor does the working class make these decisions – either directly or indirectly – for it is gagged and fettered and straitjacketed. The decisions and direction of the war are entirely in the hands of the bureaucracy, which "is endowed with its own movement," that is, with its own social, economic and political interests, which are reactionary through and through.[87]

The implication of Shachtman's argument was that the Soviet Union was now an imperialist power "seeking new territories, new wealth, new privileges, new power, new sources of raw material, new trade facilities, new sources of labour power."[88] After World War II, the Soviet bureaucratic collectivist model served as a template for similar states in the Eastern European People's Democracies.[89] In Third World countries such as China, Cuba and Vietnam, bureaucratic collectivism served the historic function of "totalitarian accumulation." Wherever bureaucratic collectivism spread meant not the triumph of socialism, but a totalitarian nightmare.

While Max Shachtman said that Lenin and Trotsky were not responsible for the emergence of bureaucratic collectivism and blamed it on conditions of Russian backwardness, Harrington argued that the anti-democratic choices of the Bolsheviks after they took power contributed to the triumph of Stalinism. In 1917, Lenin proved himself to be "a man of substance, of daring political imagination, and...he won political power by persuading masses of people to rally to his cause."[90] Once the Bolsheviks won, they proceeded to abolish civil liberties and democratic elections, crush all dissent and monopolize power in their own hands to create a new dictatorship over the proletariat: "There is a classic name in Marxist literature for this tactic of using a minority dictatorship to reeducate the majority and to clear their minds of the corruptions of capitalism: Blanquism."[91] The tragedy of the Bolsheviks was that they inadvertently paved the road for the triumph of Stalinist totalitarianism in Russia. The Bolshevik complicity in Stalinism was shared by all its major leaders, including Leon Trotsky. Trotsky was a brilliant polemicist, literary critic and historian, and prophetic on many events, but he was also a "tragic hero" who failed to understand what Stalinism represented until it was too late. Since Trotsky was partly responsible for Stalinism, he was unable to confront the truth that the revolution he led "had not only been betrayed but destroyed."[92] For Michael Harrington, Trotsky does not represent an alternative to Stalinism, but rather his fate serves as a warning about the dangers of revolutionary zeal because he helped lay the foundations for totalitarianism.[93]

The Shachtman-Harrington bureaucratic collectivist thesis fails on a number of grounds. Firstly, if the Soviet bureaucracy was indeed a ruling class, then it lacked the characteristic features of other ruling classes throughout history. Under capitalism, the ruling class played the necessary historical role in developing the productive forces. Furthermore, the bourgeoisie possesses its own class consciousness, specific unifying ideology and can maintain stability as a class by transmitting its property to the succeeding generation. By contrast, the Soviet bureaucracy lacked these traits. While the power and privileges of the Soviet bureaucracy were tied to the nationalized industries like other ruling classes, they could not accumulate wealth from that property or transmit ownership onto their children. Instead, the Soviet bureaucracy was not bound up with the planned economy, but merely acted as a parasitic element upon it.[94] What we are left with in Shachtman-Harrington's bureaucratic collectivist thesis is a new ruling class that is just floating disembodied in the air and motivated by a lust for power. This leaves the theory completely arbitrary and unable to understand the internal contradictions of the USSR and similar states.

Secondly, bureaucratic collectivism sees a harmony existing between the planned economy and the bureaucracy. What is missing are the contradictions that exist between them. The revolutions in Russia, China, Cuba, etc did abolish capitalist property relations and replace them with state ownership and a planned economy. Due to the exceptional challenges faced by these workers' states (backwardness, imperialist attacks, etc), a contradiction exists between their nationalized and planned economy and rule by a bureaucratic caste. The planned economy represents a conquest of the revolution that must be defended, while the bureaucracy is a hindrance to the development of socialism. Therefore, the ruling bureaucracy must be overthrown by the working class in order to bring the political superstructure into harmony with the economic base.[95] For Michael Harrington, no such contradiction exists and the entire system is simply regressive with no redeeming features about it. Thus, there is no reason to defend the conquests of the revolution such as the planned economy. As a result, even with Michael Harrington's support for the Hungarian Revolution of

1956 and the Prague Spring of 1968, he ignores the desires of its participants to defend the nationalized economy.

Lastly, bureaucratic collectivism is based on a profound historical pessimism about the prospects of socialism. For one, the theory claims that after the overthrow of capitalism, the next stage may not be socialism, but the continuation of class society in a totalitarian form. If the Soviet bureaucracy is viewed as a new ruling class, then it leads to the conclusion that all communist parties out of power are future bureaucratic ruling classes in embryo. This not only flies in the face of twentieth-century history, but calls into question the mere idea of working-class emancipation. Socialism is transformed from a historical necessity into a distant Kantian moral imperative.

If socialism is no longer on the historical agenda, then this has profound political implications. Leaving aside the option of a third camp, there remains only the choice between two evils: imperialism or bureaucratic collectivism. If the bureaucratic collectivist ruling classes are viewed as progressive when compared to capitalism, then it is possible to offer them "critical support." The price of that is to identify with Soviet tanks against the anti-bureaucratic struggles of the working class whether in Hungary 1956 or Czechoslovakia 1968. The second option is to view the bureaucratic collectivist ruling class as a greater evil and to offer various forms of "critical support" to "democratic" capitalist states.

This is the option that Michael Harrington ultimately chose:

> Indeed, if one were asked to choose in the abstract between the reactionary policies of bourgeois democratic America and those of totalitarian Communism, the former are infinitely preferable, for they are much less destructive of freedom and human dignity. In Spain and Greece, and even in South Vietnam, there is a greater possibility that the underground opposition will survive as an underground force than in

> Russia, China, or North Vietnam. French imperialism never knew how to kill the Trotskyist revolutionaries in Indochina; Ho Chi Minh did. Our despots tend to be corrupt and inefficient; theirs are honest and murderously effective.[96]

Following the implications of bureaucratic collectivism, it was only natural that Michael Harrington became a "critical" supporter of American democracy against the greater evil of communism.

Socialist International

Michael Harrington had no hope of ascending to high office in America, but he achieved great international prominence within the Socialist International. Michael took an active role in the affairs of the Socialist International writing manifestos, resolutions and programs. In the Socialist International, Michael Harrington counted presidents and prime ministers such as Willy Brandt, Olof Palme, François Mitterrand, Mário Soares, Felipe González and Simon Peres to be his friends. According to the Swedish Social Democrat Pierre Schori, "If Mike had been a European politician, he would have been prime minister."[97] His loyalty to the Socialist International was based on shared politics and the conviction that if there was "any hope for the renewal of the socialist ideal...in Europe it is located in the mass socialist parties."[98] This is not to say that Michael Harrington was uncritical of the Socialist International. He was dismayed that most of the European socialist parties had given up their commitment to the socialist transformation of society. He also lamented that before the 1970s, the Socialist International functioned "primarily as an 'old boy's' reunion of European left politicians with an ideology shaped in the coldest days of the Cold War."[99] However, Michael Harrington believed that the International was capable of change and renewal. For instance, European socialists were successfully able to attract and assimilate many of the demands of the new social movements of the sixties into their programs, allowing them to keep up with the times.

The main example of hope in the Socialist International for Harrington was Willy Brandt's initiatives in the 1970s. Brandt wanted to revive the International by addressing environmental concerns, global poverty and détente with the USSR. Michael Harrington believed that Brandt's vision of bringing the Global North and South together was "the key to any possibility of a serious and new international world order."[100] Still, Michael Harrington was apprehensive about Brandt's desire to open dialogue with the Palestinian Liberation Organization (PLO), even if this was premised on their acceptance of a two-state solution. When Brandt met with PLO leader Yassir Arafat in 1982, he objected: "I was all in favor of his having dialogue with Arafat, but not under conditions that gave a kind of diplomatic recognition to the PLO before it publicly accepted the right of Israel to exist."[101] To Michael Harrington, this was proof that the Socialist International's engagement with the Third World was fraught with moral and political ambiguities. For Michael Harrington, another instance fraught with difficulty and shades of gray for the Socialist International occurred in Peru. The Peruvian president Alan García was a member of the Socialist International and hailed as a Latin American JFK. During García's administration, his government was fighting a bloody counterinsurgency war against the Maoist guerrillas of the Communist Party of Peru (aka Sendero Luminoso/Shining Path).[102] During the Socialist International's 1986 congress held in Lima, Sendero prisoners rioted in at least three prisons and García sent in the army, who proceeded to massacre at least 124 inmates.[103] In response, the Socialist International passed a resolution which condemned the massacre, but they did not expel García or his party from their ranks. To Michael Harrington, this proved that "the

International had acted decently in an impossible situation."[104] Even though Michael Harrington had immense faith in the Socialist International as a force for socialism, it was misplaced. To paraphrase Voltaire, the Socialist International was neither socialist nor internationalist. Most of the European socialist parties supported the creation of NATO as a bulwark against the Soviet Union. As critical as the Socialist International's parties and men like Brandt, Soares or Peres could be of America at times, they still considered themselves part of the capitalist west.[105] The parties of the Socialist International were not committed to socialism, but they aspired to be managers of capitalism and the welfare state, who opposed the revolutionary transformation of society.[106]

Conclusion

What then is the meaning of Democratic Marxism? The real Karl Marx, who welcomed revolutionary struggles of the oppressed against capitalism and its defenders, is erased by Michael Harrington. In order to appropriate Marxism for democratic socialism, Michael Harrington is forced to cut away its revolutionary parts wherever he may find them. In place of the revolutionary heart and soul of Marxism, Democratic Marxism turns moderation, compromise and opportunism into principles. This is a Marxism suited to the needs of the "progressive" leaders in the labor bureaucracy, who want an alliance with "enlightened" sections of the bourgeoisie in order to deliver reforms and a welfare state. It is a Marxism committed to the defense of capitalism, not the struggle for socialism. Michael Harrington's Democratic Marxism is a Marxism stripped of everything save its name. In the last analysis, it is a failure of vision.

Endnotes

Introduction

1. Information on the 2019 DSA convention was gathered from the following sources: Dan La Botz, "DSA Convention 2019 – Overcoming Divisions – Votes to Maintain Strong National Organization," *Medium*, August 6, 2019. https://medium.com/@danlabotz/dsa-convention-2019-overcoming-divisions-votes-to-maintain-strong-national-organization-takes-c3243517e792; Tatiana Cozzarelli, "DSA Convention 2019: Sanderism and the Tyranny of the Procedural," *Left Voice*.
https://www.leftvoice.org/dsa-convention-2019-sanderism-and-the-tyranny-of-the-procedural; Lauren Gambino, "'We're here to win': US democratic socialists move to center stage"; *The Guardian*, August 6, 2019. https://www.theguardian.com/politics/2019/aug/06/democratic-socialists-us-alexandria-ocasio-cortez-bernie-sanders; Harold Meyerson, "What the Socialists Just Did – and Why," *American Prospect*, August 9, 2019. https://prospect.org/article/what-socialists-just-did-and-why; Andrew Sernatinger, "DSA Is Leading the Charge," *Jacobin Magazine*, August 11, 2019.
https://jacobinmag.com/2019/08/democratic-socialists-for-america-dsa-convention-2019-atlanta; Andrew Sernatinger, "DSA 2019 Convention Breakdown," *New Politics*, July 6, 2019. https://newpol.org/dsa-2019-convention-breakdown/; Andrew Sernatinger, "Moving Targets: DSA's 2019 Convention," *New Politics*, August 21, 2019. https://newpol.org/moving-targets-dsas-2019-convention/; Eric Blanc, "Democratic Socialists of America Seize the Day," *The Nation*, August 7, 2019. https://www.thenation.com/article/dsa-convention-sanders-atlanta-socialism/; Nathan

J. Robinson, "A Gathering of Comrades," *Current Affairs*, August 7, 2019. https://www.currentaffairs.org/2019/08/a-gathering-of-comrades; Tatiana Cozzarelli, "DSA Convention 2019: This is Not What Democracy Looks Like," *Left Voice*. https://www.leftvoice.org/dsa-convention-2019-this-is-not-what-democracy-looks-like; Kurt Stand, "Looking Backward to Look Forward: DSA's Past, Present, Future," *Medium*, July 30, 2019. https://medium.com/@kurtstand/looking-backward-to-look-forward-dsas-past-present-future-47350c014840

2. Michael Harrington, "Out Beyond Liberalism," *New York Times*, March 3, 1973. https://www.nytimes.com/1973/03/03/archives/out-beyond-liberalism.html and Michael Harrington, "The Left Wing of Realism," *Democratic Left* Vol. 1, No. 1 (March 1973): 5.
3. Dustin Guastella and Connor Kilpatrick, "After the Nevada Blowout, It's Bernie's Party Now," *Jacobin Magazine*, February 22, 2020. https://jacobinmag.com/2020/02/bernie-sanders-nevada-caucus-democratic-primary-win

Chapter 1

1. Michael Harrington, *Fragments of the Century: A Social Autobiography* (New York: Saturday Review Press, 1973), 1.
2. Maurice Isserman, *The Other American: The Life of Michael Harrington* (New York: Public Affairs, 2000), 14.
3. Harrington 1973, 4.
4. Ibid. 5.
5. Isserman 2000, 17.
6. Harrington 1973, 8-9.
7. Ibid. 13.
8. Ibid. 21.
9. Ibid. 23.
10. Ibid. 30.
11. Ibid. 64.

12. Ibid.
13. Ibid.
14. Ibid. 65.
15. Ibid. 35.
16. Ibid. 36.
17. Ibid. 65.
18. Ibid. 36-37.
19. Ibid. 39.
20. Ibid. 16-17.
21. Ibid. 66.
22. Ibid. 41.
23. Isserman 2000, 60 and Harrington 1973, 41.
24. Harrington 1973, 41.
25. Ibid. 44.
26. Ibid.
27. Ibid. 46.
28. Quoted in Isserman 2000, 63.
29. Harrington 1973, 23.
30. Ibid. 23-25.
31. Harrington 1973, 17. Italics in the original.
32. Ibid. 18.
33. Michael Harrington, "Existential Saint," *New York Times*, June 13, 1982. https://www.nytimes.com/1982/06/13/books/existential-saint.html
34. Terrence C. Wright, *Dorothy Day: An Introduction to Her Life and Thought* (San Francisco: Ignatius Press, 2018), 19.
35. Dorothy Day, *The Long Loneliness: The Autobiography of Dorothy Day* (San Francisco: Harper & Row, 1981), 165–166.
36. The Catholic Worker Movement, "The Aims and Means of the Catholic Worker." *The Catholic Worker.* http://www.catholicworker.org/cw-aims-and-means.html
37. Harrington, "Existential Saint." See also Michael Harrington, "Michael Harrington on the Uniquely Orthodox

Radicalism of Dorothy Day," *In These Times*, September 25, 2015.
inthesetimes.com/article/18451/pope-francis-dorothy-day-michael-harrington

38. Harrington 1973, 22.
39. Michael Harrington, *The Other America: Poverty in the United States* (Baltimore: Penguin Books, 1962), 88-96.
40. Harrington 1973, 68-69.
41. Quoted in Isserman 2000, 80.
42. Myrna Oliver, "Michael Harrington, Socialist Activist and Author, Dies at 61," *Los Angeles Times*, August 2, 1989. http://articles.latimes.com/1989-08-02/news/mn-565_1_michael-harrington/2
43. Harrington 1973, 23.
44. Quoted in Isserman 2000, 80.
45. Quoted in ibid. 88.
46. Harrington 1973, 37.
47. Ibid. 65.
48. Quoted in Isserman 2000, 97-98.
49. Ibid. 100-102.
50. Maurice Isserman, *If I Had a Hammer...The Death of the Old Left and the Birth of the New Left* (New York: Basic Books, 1987), 61.
51. Isserman 2000, 102.
52. Michael Harrington, *The Long-Distance Runner: An Autobiography* (New York: Henry Holt and Company, 1988), 22.
53. Harrington 1973, 25.

Chapter 2

1. Isserman 2000, 106.
2. Jack Ross, *The Socialist Party of America: A Complete History* (Potomac Books, 2015), 459.
3. Isserman 2000, 122.
4. Richard Seymour, *The Liberal Defense of Murder* (New York:

Verso, 2008), 120.

5. Ibid. 134.
6. Gary Dorrien, *The Neoconservative Mind: Politics, Culture, and the War of Ideology* (Temple University Press, 1993), 79–84; Daniel Kelley, *James Burnham and the Struggle for the World: A Life* (Wilmington, ISI Books, 2002), 149-181 and 188-191; Alexander Bloom, *Prodigal Sons: The New York Intellectuals and Their World* (Oxford: Oxford University Press, 1986), 259-273; Frances Stonor Saunders, *The Cultural Cold War: The CIA and the World of Arts and Letters* (New York: New Press, 1999), 230.
7. Quoted Isserman 2000, 121.
8. Quoted in ibid. 123.
9. Harrington 1973, 71.
10. Ibid. 62-63.
11. Michael Harrington, *Socialism* (New York: Sunday Review Press, 1970), vii.
12. Harrington 1970, 169; Michael Harrington, *Socialism: Past and Future* (New York: Arcade Publishing, 1989), 67-89; Michael Harrington, *The Twilight of Capitalism* (New York: Simon and Schuster, 1976), 174-175; Michael Harrington, "Marxism and Democracy," *Palinurus.* http://anselmocarranco.tripod.com/id25.html
13. Harrington 1973, 72. See also Peter Drucker, *Max Shachtman and his Left: A Socialist's Odyssey through the "American Century"* (Atlantic Highlands: Humanities Press International, Inc., 1994), 41-44; Alan Wald, *The New York Intellectuals: The Rise and Decline of the Anti-Stalinist Left from the 1930s to the 1980s* (Chapel Hill: University of North Carolina Press, 1987), 172-175; Isserman 1987, 39-42.
14. Isaac Deutscher, *The Prophet Outcast: Trotsky 1929-1940* (New York: Verso, 2003), 219-221.
15. See Leon Trotsky, *The Crisis of the French Section [1936-36]* (New York: Pathfinder Press, 1977) and James P. Cannon,

The History of American Trotskyism (New York: Pathfinder Press, 1972), 216-255.

16. Wald 1987, 165.
17. On the SWP split see: Deutscher 2003, 381-386; Wald 182-192; James P. Cannon, *The Struggle for a Proletarian Party* (New York: Pathfinder Press, 1970); Leon Trotsky, *In Defense of Marxism* (New York: Pathfinder Press, 1973); Drucker 1994, 108-132; Sean Matgamna, ed., The Fate of the Russian Revolution: Lost Texts of Critical Marxism, *Volume 1* (Phoenix Press, London, 1998). Although written before the split, Shachtman and Burnham prophetically anticipate the social dynamics leading middle-class intellectuals (including themselves and later Harrington) from revolutionary Marxism to social democracy. See James Burnham and Max Shachtman, "Intellectuals in Retreat," *Marxists Internet Archive.* https://www.marxists.org/history/etol/writers/burnham/1939/intellectuals/index.htm
18. See the Appendix for a longer discussion on the Shachtman/Harrington thesis of bureaucratic collectivism.
19. Max Shachtman, "'Defend the Soviet Union"?" *Marxists Internet Archive.* https://www.marxists.org/archive/shachtma/1941/08/letter.html
20. Max Shachtman, "Is Russia a Workers' State?"
21. Max Shachtman, "Against Both War Camps – For The Camp Of World Labor!" *Marxists Internet Archive.* https://www.marxists.org/archive/shachtma/1940/05/mayday.htm; see also Alan Johnson, ""Neither Washington Nor Moscow": The Third Camp as History and a Living Legacy," *Nova.* http://nova.wpunj.edu/newpolitics/issue27/johnso27.htm
22. Drucker 1994, 145.
23. Isserman 1987, 46.
24. Drucker 1994, 154.
25. Ibid. 155 and Martin Glaberman, *Wartime Strikes: The Strug-*

gle Against the No Strike Pledge in the UAW During World War II (Detroit: Bewick, 1980).

26. Drucker 1994, 156.
27. The New International, "Notes of the Month: A National Service Act," *The New International* Vol. XI, No. 1 (January 1945): 3–7. https://www.marxists.org/history/etol/newspape/ni/vol11/no01/notm.htm
28. Max Shachtman, "The Victories of the 'Red' Army and the Struggle for Socialism," *Marxists Internet Archive.* https://www.marxists.org/archive/shachtma/1943/03/stalinism.htm; Max Shachtman, "Left Wing of the Labor Movement?" *Marxists Internet Archive.* https://www.marxists.org/archive/shachtma/1949/09/stalinism.html
29. Ibid. See also Victor G. Devinatz, "A Cold War at International Harvester: The Shachtmanites and the Farm Equipment Workers Union's Demise, 1946-1955," *Science and Society* 72, no. 2 (April 2008): 189.
30. Drucker 1994, 190 and 204.
31. "For Socialist Democracy! Independent Socialist League Launched on May Day," *Labor Action*, April 25, 1949. https://www.marxists.org/history/etol/newspape/laboraction-ny/1949/v13n17-apr-25-1949-LA.pdf
32. Quoted in Drucker 1994, 243.
33. Max Shachtman, "Why Labor Supports Democrats," *The New International* Vol. XVIII, No. 4 (July-August 1952): 186. https://www.marxists.org/history/etol/newspape/ni/vol18/no04/v18n04-w155-jul-aug-1952-new-int.pdf
34. See Drucker 1994, 244-249.
35. Max Shachtman, "Socialist Policy and the War: A Discussion of Position on the Third World War – Part II," *The New International* Vol. XVII, No. 4 (July-August 1951): 204-205. https://www.marxists.org/history/etol/newspape/ni/vol17/no04/v17n04-w149-jul-aug-1951-new-int.pdf

36. Harrington 1988, 6. Strictly speaking, Harrington is correct since the Shachtmanites had broken with Trotskyism several years before he joined.
37. Harrington 1973, 72-73.
38. Ibid. 63.
39. Tim Wohlforth, *The Prophet's Children: Travels on the American Left* (Atlantic Highlands: Humanities Press, 1994), 29.
40. Michael Harrington, introduction to "What is Orthodox Marxism?" by Georg Lukács, *New International* 23, No. 3 (summer 1957): 179-180. https://www.marxists.org/history/etol/newspape/ni/vol23/no04/v23n4-w177-fall-1957-new-int.pdf
41. Isserman 2000, 125.
42. Harrington 1973, 80.
43. Gerald Sorin, *Irving Howe: A Life of Passionate Dissent* (New York: New York University Press, 2002), 82. Howe colorfully describes his time as a Shachtmanite in "Life in a Sect," *Grand Street* vol. 2, no. 1 (Autumn, 1982): 73-93. See also John Rodden, ed., *Irving Howe and the Critics: Celebrations and Attacks* (Lincoln: University of Nebraska Press, 2005).
44. Ibid. 155-156.
45. Ibid. 153.
46. Isserman 2000, 65.
47. Michael Harrington, *Taking Sides: The Education of a Militant Mind* (New York: Holt, Rinehart and Winston, 1985), 22.
48. Harrington 1973, 85-86.
49. Ibid. 87-88.
50. Peter Fryer, *The Hungarian Tragedy* (London: Index Books, 1997). See also *Labor Action*'s coverage of the Hungarian Revolution in their 1956 and 1957 issues. https://www.marxists.org/history/etol/newspape/laboraction-ny/
51. Isserman 1987, 32.

52. Quoted Isserman 2000, 163.
53. Ibid.
54. Isserman 1987, 33.
55. Max Shachtman, "American Communism: A Re-Examination of the Past," *New International* Vol. XXIII, No. 4 (Fall 1957): 244. https://www.marxists.org/history/etol/newspape/ni/vol23/no04/v23n4-w177-fall-1957-new-int.pdf
56. Ibid. 243. See also "Socialist Regroupment: A Discussion," *Labor Action*, May 27, 1957, 5. https://www.marxists.org/history/etol/newspape/laboraction-ny/1957/v21n21-may-27-1957-LA.pdf
57. ISL Political Committee, "Independent Socialist League's Statement of Dissolution," *New International* Vol. XXIV, No. 2-3 (Spring-Summer 1958): 75. https://www.marxists.org/history/etol/newspape/ni/vol24/no02/v24n2-w179-spr-sum-1958-new-int.pdf
58. Quoted in Isserman 2000, 167.
59. Harrington 1973, 89.

Chapter 3

1. Harrington 1973, 88.
2. Ibid. 91.
3. Ibid. 92.
4. Harrington 1988, 70.
5. Ibid. 71.
6. Ibid. 73.
7. Harrington 1973, 91.
8. Ibid. 178-179.
9. Ibid. 179.
10. Ibid. 139.
11. Ibid.
12. Ibid. 140.
13. Ibid. 96.
14. James Forman, *The Making of Black Revolutionaries* (Seattle:

University of Washington Press, 1997), 220.
15. Harrington 1973, 106.
16. Ibid. 107.
17. Ibid. 114.
18. Quoted in Isserman 2000, 188.
19. Quoted in Robert Gorman, *Michael Harrington: Speaking American* (New York: Routledge, 1995), 142.
20. Michael Harrington, *Decade of Decision: The Crisis of the American System* (New York: Simon and Schuster, 1980), 291.
21. Michael Harrington, *Toward a Democratic Left* (New York: The Macmillan Company, 1968), 290. For a succinct summary of the new class see Harrington 1968, 282-291 and Harrington 1970, 361.
22. Michael Harrington, "The New Class and the Left," in B. Bruce-Biggs, ed., *The New Class?* (New Brunswick: Transaction Books, 1979), 24.
23. Ibid.
24. Harrington 1973, 75-76.
25. Michael Harrington, *The Accidental Century* (New York: Penguin Books, 1965), 40.
26. Harrington 1968, 290.
27. Ibid. 287-288.
28. Ibid. 289.
29. Harrington 1973, 132.
30. Harrington 1968, 274.
31. Socialist Party-Social Democratic Federation, "To Build a Democratic Left, 1968 Platform: Socialist Party, USA," *Archive.org.* https://archive.org/details/ToBuildADemocraticLeft1968PlatformSocialistPartyU.s.a/page/n0
32. Harrington 1968, 294.
33. Michael Harrington, "Out Beyond Liberalism."
34. Harrington 1970, 250.

35. Ibid. 260.
36. Ibid. 263.
37. Ibid. 269.
38. Ibid. 267.
39. Harrington 1980, 321. See also Michael Harrington, "Socialists examine the two souls of liberalism," *Democratic Left* Vol. V, No. 3 (March 1977): 1, 5-7.
40. See Lance Selfa, *The Democrats: A Critical History* (Chicago: Haymarket Books, 2008).
41. Kim Moody, *On New Terrain: How Capital is Reshaping the Battleground of Class War* (Chicago: Haymarket Books, 2017), 111-112.
42. Socialist Party-Social Democratic Federation, "A way forward; political realignment in America. political declaration of the 1960 national convention." and see also Ross 2015, 476-477.
43. Christopher Lasch, *The Agony of the American Left* (New York: Alfred A. Knopf, Inc., 1969), 198-199.
44. V. I. Lenin, "One Step Forward, Two Steps Back," *Marxists Internet Archive.* https://www.marxists.org/archive/lenin/works/1904/onestep/r.htm
45. George Novack, "The Politics of Michael Harrington," *International Socialist Review* Vol. 34, No. 1 (January 1973): 20. http://www.themilitant.com/NI/ISR73/ISR73_01.PDF

Chapter 4

1. Harrington 1973, 129.
2. Ibid. 172.
3. Michael Harrington, *The New American Poverty* (New York: Holt, Rinehart and Winston, 1984), 8.
4. Harrington 1962, 24.
5. Ibid. 9.
6. Ibid. 24.

7. Ibid. 22.
8. Ibid. 158-159.
9. For more on debates around the culture of poverty, see Paul Heideman and Jonah Birch, "The Poverty of Culture," *Jacobin Magazine*, September 16, 2014. https://www.jacobinmag.com/2014/09/the-poverty-of-culture/
10. Harrington 1962, 151.
11. Ibid. 16.
12. Ibid. 22.
13. Harrington 1985, 80-81.
14. Harrington 1962, 156.
15. Harrington 1973, 179.
16. Dwight Macdonald, "Our Invisible Poor," *The New Yorker*, January 19, 1963. https://www.newyorker.com/magazine/1963/01/19/our-invisible-poor
17. Harrington 1973, 173.
18. Quoted in Gorman 1995, 53.
19. Quoted in Isserman 2000, 208.
20. Lyndon Baines Johnson, "1964 State of the Union Address," *American Rhetoric*. https://www.americanrhetoric.com/speeches/lbj1964stateoftheunion.htm
21. Harrington 1973, 177.
22. Harrington 1968, 11.
23. Harrington 1973, 175.
24. Isserman 2000, 212.
25. Quoted in ibid.
26. Michael Harrington, "Should the Left Support Johnson?" *New Politics* (Summer 1964): 6. http://www.unz.com/print/NewPolitics-1964q3-00006/
27. Ibid. 8.
28. Ibid. 10.
29. Ibid. 8-9.

30. Isserman 2000, 268. For more on the Freedom Budget and Michael Harrington see Paul Le Blanc and Michael D. Yates, *A Freedom Budget for All Americans: Recapturing the Promise of the Civil Rights Movement in the Struggle for Economic Justice Today* (New York: Monthly Review Press, 2013).
31. Harrington 1973, 130.
32. Michael Harrington, "Big Lie about the Sixties," *The New Republic,* November 29, 1975, 15-19 and Michael Harrington, "Welfare Capitalism in Crisis," *The Nation*, December 28, 1974, 688-689.
33. Harrington 1968, 82. With the experience of the New Deal and Great Society in mind, Harrington stated in 1979 that Keynesianism was no longer a viable strategy: "The Keynesian answers of the last generation will not work." See Michael Harrington and Jack Kemp, "Tax Policy and the Economy: a debate between Michael Harrington and Representative Jack Kemp, April 25, 1979," *Archive.org*. https://archive.org/details/TaxPolicyAndTheEconomyADebateBetweenMichaelHarringtonAnd/mode/2up
34. Harrington 1968, 11.
35. Harrington 1980, 111.
36. Michael Harrington, *The Next Left: The History of the Future* (New York: Henry Holt and Company, 1986), 57.
37. Harrington 1970, 199.
38. Harrington 1976, 321.

Chapter 5

1. Isserman 1987, 185.
2. Quoted in ibid. 186.
3. Isserman 2000, 224.
4. Harrington 1973, 137.
5. Isserman 2000, 225.
6. Ibid. 226.
7. Ibid.

8. Harrington 1985, 63.
9. Ibid. 64-65.
10. Ibid. 65.
11. Kirkpatrick Sale, *SDS* (New York: Random House, 1973), 690.
12. Ibid. 691.
13. Ibid.
14. Ibid. 16-17.
15. Harrington 1973, 141.
16. Ibid. 143.
17. Sale 1973, 53-54.
18. See Jim Creegan, "Left wing of the permissible," *Weekly Worker*.
    https://weeklyworker.co.uk/worker/1169/left-wing-of-the-permissible/
19. Students for a Democratic Society, *Port Huron Statement* (Chicago: Charles H. Kerr Publishing Company, 1999), 71.
20. Ibid. 74.
21. Ibid. 74-75.
22. Ibid. 40-41.
23. Ibid. 69-70.
24. Harrington 1988, 58.
25. Students for a Democratic Society 1999, 39.
26. Ibid. 37.
27. Harrington 1973, 144.
28. Sale 1973, 56-57.
29. Ibid. 61.
30. Ibid.
31. Ibid. 62.
32. Ibid.
33. Ibid. 62-63.
34. Ibid. 65.
35. Ibid. 66-67.
36. Harrington 1973, 148.

37. Sale 1973, 67.
38. Harrington 1973, 149.
39. Ibid.
40. Ibid.

Chapter 6

1. Information for this section was drawn from Aaron Hess and Elizabeth Wrigley-Field, "Civil Rights Betrayed: How the Democratic Party Shut Out the Mississippi Freedom Democratic Party," *International Socialist Review.* http://www.isreview.org/issues/38/MFDP.shtml
2. Quoted in Peter B. Levy, *The New Left and Labor in the 1960s* (Urbana: University of Illinois Press, 1994), 29.
3. Ibid. 22-23.
4. Quoted in Elizabeth Sutherland, *Letters from Mississippi* (New York: McGraw Hill, 1965), 83-84.
5. Quoted in Juan Williams, *Eyes on the Prize: America's Civil Rights Years, 1954-1965* (New York: Viking Penguin Inc., 1987), 241.
6. Quoted in Isserman 2000, 245.
7. John Dittmer, *Local People: The Struggle for Civil Rights in Mississippi* (Champaign: University of Illinois Press, 1995), 290.
8. Kay Mills, *This Little Light of Mine: The Life of Fannie Lou Hamer* (New York: Plume, 1994), 5.
9. Levy 1994, 29-40.
10. Forman 1997, 392. Rustin expanded on these arguments the following year. See Bayard Rustin, "From Protest to Politics: The Future of the Civil Rights Movement," *Commentary* (February 1965). https://www.commentarymagazine.com/articles/from-protest-to-politics-the-future-of-the-civil-rights-movement/; Bayard Rustin, "The Failure of Black Separatism," *Harpers* (January 1970): 25-34.
11. Forman 1997, 392.

12. Harrington 1973, 124.
13. Forman 1997, 295-296.
14. Harrington 1973, 130.

Chapter 7

1. Editorial, "Colonial World in Ferment," *The New International* Vol. XI, No. 8 (November 1945): 229. https://www.marxists.org/history/etol/newspape/ni/vol11/no08/cd-comm.html
2. Arthur Stein, "Indo-Chinese Leader Seeks Deal with French Cabinet," *Labor Action,* March 10, 1947, 7. https://www.marxists.org/history/etol/newspape/laboraction-ny/1947/v11n10-mar-10-1947-LA.pdf See also Harrington 1973, 201.
3. "Power of the Third Camp," *The New International* Vol. XX, No.4 (July-August 1954): 196. https://www.marxists.org/history/etol/newspape/ni/vol20/no04/v20n4-w166-jul-aug-1954-new-int.pdf
4. Harrington 1973, 63 and 207-209.
5. Sale 1973, 178.
6. Ibid. 179 and Isserman 2000, 258.
7. Paul Heideman, "Half the Way with Mao Zedong," *Jacobin Magazine,* May 23, 2018. https://jacobinmag.com/2018/05/half-the-way-with-mao-zedong/
8. Harrington 1973, 166.
9. Ibid. 170.
10. Ibid. 183.
11. Ibid. 189.
12. Ibid.
13. Harrington 1985, 111.
14. Ibid. 124.
15. Ibid. 113.
16. Ibid. 111.
17. Ibid. 113.

18. Quoted in Isserman 2000, 259.
19. Harrington 1985, 133-134.
20. Harrington 1970, 5.
21. Harrington 1968, 268-269.
22. The essay is reprinted in Nina Howe, ed., *A Voice Still Heard: Selected Essays of Irving Howe* (New Haven: Yale University Press, 2014), 46-73. See also Joseph Dorman, *Arguing the World: The New York Intellectuals in Their Own Words* (New York: Free Press, 2000), 138-43 and 149-150; Irving Howe, "The Fleeting New Left," *The New Republic*, November 9, 1974, 25-8; Neil Jumonville, ed., *The New York Intellectuals Reader* (New York: Routledge, 2007), 317-325.
23. Sale 1973, 212.
24. Ibid. 238.
25. Harrington 1985, 137.
26. Harrington 1973, 140.
27. Ibid. 144.
28. Ibid. 146.
29. Quoted in Isserman 2000, 284.
30. Harrington 1973, 216.
31. Ibid. 217.
32. Harrington 1985, 149.
33. Ibid. 149.
34. Ibid. 150.
35. Ross 2015, 501.
36. Harrington 1985, 150.

Chapter 8

1. Drucker 1994, 270.
2. Ibid. 288.
3. Max Shachtman, "Max Shachtman on Cuba," *Marxists Internet Archive*. https://www.marxists.org/archive/shachtma/1961/05/bayofpigsdebate.html

4. Drucker 1994, 277.
5. Isserman 2000, 194-195.
6. Harrington 1973, 201.
7. Ibid. 202.
8. Isserman 2000, 271-272.
9. Drucker 1994, 308.
10. Harrington 1985, 69.
11. Ibid. 75.
12. Mike Stivers, "Ocean Hill-Brownsville, Fifty Years Later," *Jacobin Magazine*, September 12, 2018. https://jacobinmag.com/2018/09/ocean-hill-brownsville-strikes-1968-united-federation-teachers
13. Harrington 1988, 76.
14. Ibid. 78.
15. Harrington 1973, 222-223.
16. Ibid., 214. See also Ross 2015, 511-512.
17. Quoted in Isserman 2000, 287.
18. Harrington 1973, 212.
19. Drucker 1994, 306-307 and Ross 2015, 508.
20. Quoted in Isserman 2000, 291.
21. Ibid. 292.
22. Harrington 1988, 16. See also Harrington 1980, 309.
23. Quoted in Drucker 1994, 308.
24. Ibid.
25. "Harrington Quits as Socialist Head," *New York Times*, October 23, 1972. https://www.nytimes.com/1972/10/23/archives/harrington-quits-as-socialist-head-assails-partys-attitude-on.html
26. Ross 2015, 516.
27. Drucker 1994, 308.
28. Quoted in Ross 2015, 516.
29. Quoted in Isserman 2000, 299.
30. "Harrington Quits as Socialist Head" and Michael Har-

rington, "Forsaking Debs for Nixon: A Call to American Socialists," *The Nation*, November 13, 1972, 454-455.

31. See Harrington's own postmortem on the election in "The Myth that was Real," *The Nation*, November 27, 1972, 518-521.
32. Quoted in William O'Rourke, *Signs of the Literary Times: Essays, Reviews, Profiles 1970-1992* (Albany: State University of New York Press, 1993), 196.
33. Quoted in Ross 2015, 544.
34. Harrington 1973, 225.

Chapter 9

1. Harrington 1973, 245.
2. Ibid. 245-246.
3. Paul L. Montgomery, "New Socialist Group Plans to Work Within Democratic Party," *New York Times*, October 14, 1973. https://www.nytimes.com/1973/10/14/archives/new-socialist-group-plans-to-work-within-democratic-party.html
4. Harrington 1988, 18.
5. Isserman 2000, 319.
6. "Left Talk in Hard Times: 'Socialist' Labor Fakers Back Democrats," *Workers Vanguard* No. 67 (April 25, 1975): 6. https://www.marxists.org/history/etol/newspape/workersvanguard/1975/0067_25_04_1975.pdf; See also Ross 2015, 545-546.
7. Harrington 1988, 21.
8. Ibid. 36-52.
9. Isserman 2000, 320.
10. Harrington 1988, 25.
11. Ibid. 27.
12. Isserman 2000, 319.
13. Harrington 1988, 22-23.
14. Ibid. 118-119.

15. Ibid. 121.
16. Ibid. 132.
17. Ibid. 91.
18. Ibid. 93-94.
19. Quoted in "Left Talk in Hard Times: 'Socialist' Labor Fakers Back Democrats," 6.
20. Harrington 1988, 92.
21. Ibid. 95-96.
22. Ibid. 97-98.
23. Ibid. 100-103.
24. Ibid. 102-103.
25. Quoted in Isserman 2000, 330.
26. Harrington 1988, 104. See also Michael Harrington, "Carter and the platform: room for the Left," *Democratic Left* Vol. IV, No. 6 (June 1976): 1 and 12-14.
27. Michael Harrington and Peter Camejo, "Should Socialists Have Voted for Carter?" *Militant*, November 26, 1976, 16. https://www.themilitant.com/1976/4045/MIL4045.pdf
28. Ibid.
29. Ibid.
30. Ibid.
31. Ibid. 19.
32. Ibid. 17.
33. Michael Harrington and Peter Camejo, "Should Socialists Have Voted for Carter? Part III," *Militant*, December 10, 1976, 25. https://www.themilitant.com/1976/4047/MIL4047.pdf
34. Michael Harrington, "Electoral victory and full employment challenge," *Democratic Left* Vol. IV, No. 10 (December 1976): 1-4.
35. Mike Davis, *Prisoners of the American Dream: Politics and Economy in the History of the US Working Class* (New York: Verso, 1986), 136.
36. Ibid. 134.

37. Kim Moody, *An Injury to All: The Decline of American Unionism* (New York: Verso, 1988), 149.
38. Ibid.
39. Ibid. 149-152; Moody 2017, 113-114; "Social-Democratic Stirrings," *Revolution* Vol. 4, no. 79 (September 1979): 27-29. https://www.marxists.org/history/erol/periodicals/revolution/rev-4-9.pdf
40. Moody 1988, 150; "Social-Democratic Stirrings," 28; "UAW's Fraser: Prophet of Defeat," *Workers Vanguard* No. 258 (June 13, 1980): 5. https://www.marxists.org/history/etol/newspape/workersvanguard/1980/0258_13_06_1980.pdf
41. Moody 1988, 152-156.
42. Ibid. 152.
43. Harrington 1988, 105-106.
44. Isserman 2000, 334-335.
45. Ibid. 335.
46. Michael Harrington, "Beyond November: The Democrats Remain the Real Home of the Left," *The Progressive* 44 (October 1980), 26. See also Michael Harrington, "No Time for Mourning Now," *Democratic Left* Vol. 8, No. 9 (November 1980): 1-3 and 14; Michael Harrington, "Can the Party Fight Reagan?" *Democratic Left* Vol. X, No. 1-2 (January-February 1982): 1-4.
47. Isserman 2000, 347 and 349.
48. Harrington 1988, 59.
49. Quoted in Ross 2015, 551; See also Max Elbaum, *Revolution in the Air: Sixties Radicals turn to Lenin, Mao and Che* (New York: Verso, 2002), 118-120 and Victor Cohen, ed., "The New American Movement: An Oral History," *Works and Days* 55/56 Vol. 28, Nos. 1 & 2 (Spring/Fall 2010). http://www.worksanddays.net/W&D%202010.html
50. Ross 2015, 552.
51. Harrington 1988, 60.

52. Isserman 2000, 348.
53. Ross 2015, 555; Irving Howe, *Socialism and America* (New York: Harcourt Brace Jovanovich, 1985), 87-88.
54. Michael Harrington, "Democratic Socialism, Israel and the Jews: An Interview with Michael Harrington (1975), with new preface by Mitchell Cohen (2020)," *Fathom Journal*. https://fathomjournal.org/democratic-socialism-israel-and-the-jews-an-interview-with-michael-harrington-1975-with-new-preface-by-mitchell-cohen-2020/
55. Harrington and Camejo, "Should Socialists Have Voted for Carter? Part III," 25; Michael Harrington, "The Middle East: Is Peace Possible?" *Democratic Left* Vol. I, No. 7 (November 1973): 1-2.
56. Harrington 1988, 65. See also Harry Fleischman, "Along the Road to Unity," *Democratic Left* Vol. IX, No. 6 (June 1981): 6-7.
57. Ibid. 66.
58. Ross 2015, 561. For more on the foundation of DSA, see Sandra Chelnov, "Merging at the Base," *Democratic Left* Vol. X, No. 3 (March 1982): 5-7; DSA, "Change the USA, Join the DSA," *Democratic Left* Vol. X, No. 3 (March 1982): center fold; DSA, "All the Way with DSA," *Democratic Left* Vol. X, No. 4 (April 1982): 6-7.
59. Isserman 2000, 349 and Davis 1986, 259.
60. Harrington 1988, 66.

Chapter 10

1. Harrington 1984, 254.
2. Moody 1988, 303-304.
3. Quoted in Sharon Smith, *Subterranean Fire: A History of Working-Class Radicalism in the United States* (Chicago: Haymarket Books, 2006), 246.
4. Quoted in ibid. 246-247.
5. Quoted in ibid. 247.

6. Robert Brenner, "The Paradox of Social Democracy: The American Case (Part Two)," *Verso*. https://www.versobooks.com/blogs/2517-the-paradox-of-social-democracy-the-american-case-part-two
7. Michael Harrington, "Nuclear Threat," *Society* Vol. 18, No. 1 (November 1980): 20.
8. Ibid. 17. See also Michael Harrington, "Finding a Defense Balance," *Democratic Left* Vol. IX, No. 9 (November 1981): 5-6.
9. Michael Harrington and Irving Howe, "Voices from the Left," *New York Times*, June 17, 1984. https://www.nytimes.com/1984/06/17/magazine/voices-from-the-left.html
10. Ibid.
11. Davis 1986, 273.
12. See Jack Fletcher and Ethan Young, "Left Social Democracy Searches for a Program," *Marxists Internet Archive*. https://www.marxists.org/history/erol/ncm-7/lom-dsa.pdf; See also Michael Harrington, "Going on the Offensive," *Democratic Left* Vol. XII, No. 3 (May-June 1984): 3-5; Michael Harrington, "For a Pragmatic Push Left," *Democratic Left* Vol. XII, No. 4 (July-August 1984): 6-7.
13. Manning Marable, "Why Stay with Jesse?" *Democratic Left* Vol. XII, No. 1 (January-February 1984): 8-9.
14. Davis 1986, 283.
15. Alexander Cockburn, *Corruptions of Empire* (New York: Verso, 1989), 370 and 373.
16. Thomas Ferguson and Joel Rogers, "Big Business Backs the Freeze," *The Nation*, July 19/26, 1986. 44. https://www.cows.org/_data/files/1986_Big_Business_Backs_the_Freeze.pdf
17. Selfa 2008, 69.
18. Quoted in Davis 1986, 290.
19. Selfa 2008, 214-215.
20. DSA was split three ways over who to support in 1988, see Eric Thomas Chester, *Socialists and the Ballot Box: A Histori-*

cal Analysis (New York: Praeger Publishers, 1985), 143. Michael Harrington, "Jesse Jackson Breaking Back of a Prejudice," *Los Angeles Times*, March 27, 1988. http://articles.latimes.com/1988-03-27/opinion/op-281_1_jesse-jackson; Michael Harrington, "A Case for Jackson," *Dissent* 35 (Summer 1988): 262-263; Max Elbaum, "Democratic Socialists Debate Jackson Candidacy," *Marxists Internet Archive.* https://www.marxists.org/history/erol/ncm-7/dsa-jackson.pdf

21. Michael Oreskes, "Jackson to Shun Socialist Backing," *New York Times*, December 4, 1987. https://www.nytimes.com/1987/12/04/us/jackson-to-shun-socialist-backing.html
22. Quoted in Herbert Mitgang, "Saluting Veteran of War on Poverty," *New York Times*, July 2, 1988. https://www.nytimes.com/1988/07/02/nyregion/saluting-veteran-of-war-on-poverty.html; See also Michael Harrington, "Democratic Candidates Need A Progressive Program," *Democratic Left* Vol. XVI, No. 1 (January-February 1988): 3; Michael Harrington, "How the Democrats Can Win the Presidency and Govern the Country," *Democratic Left* Vol. XVI, No. 4 (July-August, 1988): 3-4; Michael Harrington, "Victory for Dukakis Is a Victory for the Left," *Democratic Left*, Vol. XVI, No. 5 (September-October 1988): 3 and 12; Michael Harrington, "We Need More than Politics as Usual," *Democratic Left* Vol. XVII, No. 1 (January-February 1989): 2 and 7.
23. Quoted in Selfa 2008, 217.
24. Robert Brenner, "Paradox of Social Democracy (Party Three)," *Verso.* https://www.versobooks.com/blogs/2522-the-paradox-of-social-democracy-the-american-case-part-three
25. Selfa 2008, 227.

Chapter 11

1. Harrington 1988, 137.

2. Ibid. 234.
3. Ibid. 240.
4. Quoted in Isserman 2000, 358.
5. Quoted in ibid 359. See also Paula Span, "The Harrington Perspective," *The Washington Post*, July 1, 1988. https://www.washingtonpost.com/archive/lifestyle/1988/07/01/the-harrington-perspective/80d9d664-2e9f-44e3-8847-3239e192d460/?utm_term=.07004f44d2eb
6. Quoted in Democratic Socialists of America, "DSA-YS Organizing Manual," *Young Democratic Socialists of America.* http://www.campusactivism.org/uploads/YSOutreach.html
7. For tributes to Michael Harrington see *Democratic Left* Vol. XVII, No. 4 (September-October 1989); 3-5 and *Democratic Left* Vol. XVII, No. 5 (November-December 1989) 5-6 and 8.

Conclusion

1. Quoted in Selfa 2008, 229.
2. Quoted in Tatah Mentan, *Socialism: The Only Practical Alternative to Contemporary Capitalism* (Mankon, Bamenda: Langaa Research & Publishing CIG, 2012), 195.
3. Democratic Socialists of America – Political Action Committee, "DSA-PAC Statement on Kerry Campaign," *Democratic Left* Vol. 32, No. 4 (fall 2004): 8.
4. Democratic Socialists of America – Political Action Committee, "DSA-PAC Statement on 2008 Elections," *Talking Union.* https://talkingunion.wordpress.com/2008/08/18/dsa-pac-statement-on-2008-elections/
5. Bhaskar Sunkara, "Project Jacobin," *New Left Review*. https://newleftreview.org/II/90/bhaskar-sunkara-project-jacobin
6. Ibid.; Sunkara has defended Harrington's legacy with former ISO member Joe Allen. See Bhaskar Sunkara, "Lean Socialist," *In These Times*, April 29, 2013.

http://inthesetimes.com/article/14873/lean_socialist/; Joe Allen, "What Harrington Shows Us," *Socialist Worker*, May 2, 2013. https://socialistworker.org/2013/05/02/what-harrington-shows-us; Bhaskar Sunkara, "What We Can Learn from Harrington," *Socialist Worker*, May 6, 2013. http://socialistworker.org/2013/05/06/what-to-learn-from-harrington; Joe Allen, "Taking Sides on Harrington," *Socialist Worker*, May 8, 2013, https://socialistworker.org/2013/05/08/taking-sides-on-harrington

7. Joseph M. Schwartz, "A History of Democratic Socialists of America 1971-2017," *Democratic Socialists of America.* https://www.dsausa.org/about-us/history/
8. Ibid.
9. Ibid.
10. Anna Heyward, "Since Trump's Victory, Democratic Socialists of America Has Become a Budding Political Force: Why an army of young people is joining DSA," *The Nation*, December 21, 2017. https://www.thenation.com/article/in-the-year-since-trumps-victory-democratic-socialists-of-america-has-become-a-budding-political-force/
11. Steve Peoples, "Democratic socialism surging in the age of Trump, and a Maine candidate takes the leap. Maine Democrat Zak Ringelstein is the only major-party Senate candidate to be a dues-paying democratic socialist," *Press Herald*, July 21, 2018.
https://www.pressherald.com/2018/07/21/democratic-socialism-surging-in-the-age-of-trump/
12. DSA, Twitter Post. March 21, 2019. 10:30 PM.
https://twitter.com/DemSocialists/status/1108918838781829120/photo/1; DSA National Political Committee, "Ocasio-Cortez and Omar endorse Bernie and the political revolution," *Democratic Socialists of America*, October 16, 2019. https://www.dsausa.org/statements/ocasio-cortez-tlaib-and-omar-endorse-bernie-and-the-political-

revolution/

13. Andrew Sernatinger, "Bern After Reading: Sanders and Socialist Strategy," *New Politics*, January 28, 2020, https://newpol.org/bern-after-reading-sanders-and-socialist-strategy/
14. Elaine Godfrey, "Thousands of Americans Have Become Socialists Since March," *The Atlantic*, May 14, 2020. https://www.theatlantic.com/politics/archive/2020/05/dsa-growing-during-coronavirus/611599/
15. Former leaders of the Students for a Democratic Society, "An Open Letter to the New Left From the Old New Left," *The Nation*, April 16, 2020. https://www.thenation.com/article/activism/letter-new-left-biden/; Dustin Guastella, "Like It or Not, If We Run Third Party, We Will Lose," *Jacobin Magazine*. April 17, 2020. https://jacobinmag.com/2020/04/third-party-bernie-sanders-democratic-socialism-elections; Jo-Ann Mort, "Unlike Mike," *Democracy: A Journal of Ideas*, May 14, 2020.
https://democracyjournal.org/arguments/unlike-mike/
16. Bhaskar Sunkara, "What Should Socialists Do in November?" *The Nation*, May 4, 2020, https://www.thenation.com/article/politics/socialists-biden-vote-november/; Peter Dreier, "WTF Is Jacobin's Editor Thinking in Voting Green?" *The Nation*, April 28, 2020.
https://www.thenation.com/article/politics/sunkara-jacobin-green-party/; Louis Proyect, "Peter Dreier, Bhaskar Sunkara, and the Green Party," *The Unrepentant Marxist*, May 11, 2020.
https://louisproyect.org/2020/05/11/peter-dreier-bhaskar-sunkara-and-the-green-party/
17. Juan Cruz Ferre, "DSA Votes for BDS, Reparations, and Out of the Socialist International," *Left Voice*. http://www.leftvoice.org/DSA-Votes-for-BDS-Reparations-and-Out-of-the-Socialist-International

18. Maurice Isserman, "Who Are You Calling a 'Harringtonite'?" *New York Times*, September 13, 2018. https://www.nytimes.com/2018/09/13/opinion/who-are-you-calling-a-harringtonite.html
19. Ibid.
20. DSA North Star: The Caucus for Socialism and Democracy, "Statement of Principles," *DSA North Star*. https://www.dsanorthstar.org/statement-of-principles.html; Dan La Botz, "DSA Two Years Later: Where Are We At? Where Are We Headed?" *New Politics*, January 3, 2019. http://newpol.org/content/dsa-two-years-later-where-are-we-where-are-we-headed
21. Ibid.
22. George Fish, "Michael Harrington and Harringtonism: A Critical Assessment," *DSA North Star*. https://www.dsanorthstar.org/blog/michael-harrington-and-harringtonism-a-critical-appreciation
23. Ibid.
24. Seth Ackerman, "A Blueprint for a New Party," *Jacobin Magazine*, November 8, 2016. https://www.jacobinmag.com/2016/11/bernie-sanders-democratic-labor-party-ackerman
25. Ibid. DSA Bread and Roses Caucus member Eric Blanc argues for a nearly identical strategy to Ackerman. Using the apparent successful example of socialists and creation of the Minnesota's Farmer-Labor Party who originally used the Democratic Party to build up their forces, Blanc advocates a "dirty break" strategy of utilizing the ballot line of a capitalist party to construct forces before eventually creating an independent working-class party. See Eric Blanc, "The Ballot and the Break," *Jacobin Magazine*, December 4, 2017. https://www.jacobinmag.com/2017/12/democratic-party-minnesota-farmer-labor-floyd-olson; As Kim Moody notes, the approach of Blanc (and by ex-

tension of Ackerman) was that the Farmer-Labor Party's strategy did not work and was abandoned by socialists in favor of a clean break with the Democrats. See Kim Moody, ""Dirty Break" for Independent Political Action or a Way to Stay Stuck in the Mud?" *New Politics*, June 9, 2020. https://newpol.org/dirty-break-for-independent-political-action-or-a-way-to-stay-stuck-in-the-mud/

26. Joseph M. Schwartz and Bhaskar Sunkara, "Social Democracy Is Good. But Not Good Enough," *Jacobin Magazine*, August 29, 2017. https://www.jacobinmag.com/2017/08/democratic-socialism-judis-new-republic-social-democracy-capitalism
27. Ibid.
28. Joseph M. Schwartz and Bhaskar Sunkara, "What Should Socialists Do?" *Jacobin Magazine*, August 1, 2017. https://jacobinmag.com/2017/08/socialist-left-democratic-socialists-america-dsa
29. Vivek Chibber, "Our Road to Power," *Jacobin Magazine*, December 5, 2017.
https://jacobinmag.com/2017/12/our-road-to-power
30. Ibid.

Appendix

1. Harrington 1976, 2. See also Michael Harrington, "Standing up for Marx," *Democratic Left* Vol. XI, No. 3 (March 1983): 3-4.
2. Michael Harrington, *The Politics at God's Funeral: The Spiritual Crisis of Western Civilization* (New York: Holt, Rinehart and Winston, 1983), 108.
3. Harrington 1965, 93.
4. Harrington 1983, 18.
5. Ibid. 196.
6. Harrington 1976, 17.
7. Ibid.

8. Ibid. 35.
9. Ibid. 36.
10. Ibid. 42.
11. Harrington 1983, 51-54.
12. Harrington 1976, 37.
13. Ibid. 39.
14. Ibid.
15. Ibid. 60.
16. Ibid. 60-61.
17. Ibid. 164.
18. Ibid. 172.
19. Ibid.
20. Ibid. 192.
21. *Marx and Engels Collected Works*, vol. 11, "The Eighteenth Brumaire of Louis Napoleon," (London: Lawrence and Wishart, 1975), 103. (henceforth *MECW*)
22. Harrington 1976, 200.
23. Harrington 1976, 343. See Georg Lukács, *History and Class Consciousness: Studies in Marxist Dialectics* (Cambridge: MIT Press, 1971), 1.
24. Harrington 1976, 26; Michael Harrington, "I Am Not a Marxist, I Am Marx," *The Nation*, December 27, 1971, 694 and Michael Harrington, "Lukács: The Dialectical Career of a Dialectician," *Anvil* Vol. 8, No. 1 (Fall 1957): 18-21. See also my "Karl Korsch's Philosophical Bolshevism," *LINKS International Journal of Socialist Renewal.* http://links.org.au/karl-korsch-philosophical-bolshevism
25. Trotsky 1973, 45.
26. Harrington 1976, 168.
27. George Novack, "Politics and Philosophy in Harrington's 'The Twilight of Capitalism'," 16.
28. *MECW*, vol. 4, "The Holy Family or Critique of Critical Criticism Against Bruno Bauer and Company," 130-131.
29. *MECW*, vol. 49, "Engels to Joseph Bloch in Königsberg –

London, September 21, 1890," 34-35.

30. Harrington 1976, 64.
31. Harrington 1970, 42-54. See also Eduard Bernstein, *Preconditions of Socialism* (Cambridge: Cambridge University Press, 1993), 29-46.
32. Harrington 1970, 50.
33. Ibid. 51.
34. Ibid. 54.
35. Ibid. 53.
36. Harrington 1985, 223-232 and Harrington 1970, 61-62. In both instances, Harrington cites Marx's 1881 letter to Domela Nieuwenhuis where Marx argued that the Commune was not the dictatorship of the proletariat, but "was merely the rising of a town under exceptional conditions, the majority of the Commune was in no sense socialist, nor could it be." *MECW*, vol. 46, "Marx to Nieuwenhuis. 22 February 1881," 66. However, Harrington did not quote the sentence preceding this: "One thing you can at any rate be sure of: a socialist government does not come into power in a country unless conditions are so developed that it can above all take the necessary measures for intimidating the mass of the bourgeoisie sufficiently to gain time – the first desideratum [requisite] – for lasting action." Ibid. This shows Marx was not advocating gradualism, but dealing with the objective conditions for a successful revolution. There was no contradiction in Marx describing the Paris Commune as a "working class government" but not "socialist." The Communard government was composed of working-class representatives, but in the few weeks of its existence, it did not have time to truly implement a socialist program. See Hal Draper, *Karl Marx's Theory of Revolution Volume 3: The "Dictatorship of the Proletariat"* (New York: Monthly Review Press: 1986), 270-271.
37. Harrington 1985, 224.

38. Harrington 1970, 273.
39. Harrington 1989, 25.
40. *MECW*, vol. 23, "On the Hague Congress," 255.
41. *MECW*, vol. 22, "Record of Marx's Interview with The World Correspondent," 606.
42. *MECW*, vol. 22, "Record of Marx's Speech on the Political Action of the Working Class," 618.
43. *MECW*, vol. 23, "On the Hague Congress," 255. See also Soma Marik, *Revolutionary Democracy: Emancipation in Classical Marxism* (Chicago: Haymarket Books, 2018), 150-153.
44. *MECW*, vol. 24, "Critique of the Gotha Programme," 95.
45. *MECW*, vol. 22, "Record of Marx's Speech on the Seventh Anniversary of the International [From the Newspaper Report on the Anniversary Meeting in London on September 24, 1871]," 634. These remarks of Marx were spoken at a banquet in September 1871, and were meant as an anniversary celebration for the International. However, what appears in the *Collected Works* are not Marx's words per se, but actually a report from the banquet that was published in the *New York World*. While both Hunt and Draper are rightly skeptical of the reliability of the bourgeois press in this regard, both believe this report accurately conveys Marx's views on the dictatorship of the proletariat. See Draper 1986, 292-295 and Richard Hunt, *The Political Ideas of Marx and Engels I: Marxism and Totalitarian Democracy, 1818–1850* (Pittsburgh: University of Pittsburgh Press), 308-309.
46. *MECW*, vol. 44, "Marx to Ludwig Kugelmann, April 12, 1871," 132.
47. Quoted in Sidney Hook, *Towards the Understanding of Karl Marx: A Revolutionary Interpretation* (Amherst: Prometheus Books, 2002), 43 [117]. Brackets indicate the page numbers in the updated edition.
48. Michael Harrington, "Wrestling with the Famous Specter,"

The Nation, February 28, 1972, 277.

49. Harrington 1986, 187.
50. Harrington 1989, 297.
51. Ibid. 304 and 308. See also Harrington 1983, 212-216.
52. Harrington 1983, 203.
53. Ibid. 191.
54. Harrington 1976, 311-312.
55. Ibid. 311.
56. Ibid. 313.
57. Harrington 1968, 146 and 150.
58. Harrington 1970, 307.
59. Ibid. 296-297.
60. Harrington and Camejo, "Should Socialists Have Voted for Carter? Part III," 24.
61. Stanley Aronowitz, *The Death and Rebirth American Radicalism* (New York: Routledge, 1996), 96 and Stanley Aronowitz, "The New American Movement and Why It Failed," *Works and Days* 55/56 Vol. 28, Nos. 1 & 2 (Spring/Fall 2010): 23. http://www.worksanddays.net/2010/File03.Aronowitz.pdf
62. I am drawing on the work of Charlie Post here. See Charlie Post, "The Popular Front: Rethinking CPUSA History," *Against the Current*. https://solidarity-us.org/atc/63/p2363/ and Charlie Post, "The New Deal and the Popular Front: Models for contemporary socialists?" *International Socialist Review*. https://isreview.org/issue/108/new-deal-and-popular-front; Charlie Post, "The Popular Front Didn't Work," *Jacobin Magazine*, October 17, 2017. https://jacobinmag.com/2017/10/popular-front-communist-party-democrats
63. Nicos Poulantzas, *Political Power and Social Classes* (London: Verso,1973), 273 and 288. See also Ellen Meiksins Wood, *The Retreat from Class: A New "True" Socialism* (New York: Verso, 1998), 27-31.
64. See my "Nicos Poulantzas: State, class and the transition to

socialism," *LINKS International Journal of Socialist Renewal.* http://links.org.au/node/4543
65. Nicos Poulantzas, *State, Power and Socialism* (New York: Verso, 1978), 128-129.
66. See Charlie Post, "What Strategy for the US Left?" *Jacobin Magazine,* February 23, 2018. https://jacobinmag.com/2018/02/socialist-organization-strategy-electoral-politics
67. Michael Harrington, "Prospects for a Peace Movement," *The Nation,* June 11, 1973, 742.
68. Harrington 1970, 317 and Michael Harrington, "Prospects for a Peace Movement," 742-743. He believed that democratic socialists such as Allende were not doomed to failure, provided there was a democratic left government in Washington to help them. Harrington forgets that it was the liberal governments of JFK and LBJ that worked to overthrow leftist governments in Cuba and the Dominican Republic. See Michael Harrington, "US Capitalism: Partner in Chile's Junta," *Democratic Left* Vol. 1, No. 6 (October 1973): 6.
69. Harrington 1976, 393.
70. Harrington 1968, 211-212.
71. Michael Harrington, *The Vast Majority: A Journey to the World's Poor* (New York: Touchstone, 1977), 124.
72. Ibid. 236.
73. Ibid. 207.
74. Ibid. 250.
75. Ibid. 252 and 201.
76. Harrington 1970, 219.
77. On Tanzania, see Harrington 1977, 189-196.
78. Harrington 1988, 163. For more of Harrington on Grenada and Nicaragua see Michael Harrington, "Against Intervention," *Democratic Left* Vol. XI No 9-10 (November-December 1983): 3-4; Michael Harrington, "Killing Democracy,"

Democratic Left Vol. XIII, No. 2 (March-April 1985): 3-4.

79. Harrington 1988, 217.
80. Ibid. 222.
81. Leon Trotsky, *Writings of Leon Trotsky 1939-1940* (New York: Pathfinder Press, 1973), 206.
82. Leon Trotsky, *The Permanent Revolution & Results and Prospects* (New York: Pathfinder Press, 1970), 101.
83. Ibid. 278-279.
84. Michael Löwy, *The Politics of Combined and Uneven Development: The Theory of Permanent Revolution* (London: Verso, 1981), 89.
85. Harrington 1970, 169.
86. Max Shachtman, "Is Russia a Workers' State?" *Marxists Internet Archive.* https://www.marxists.org/archive/shachtma/1940/12/russia.htm
87. Max Shachtman, "The Crisis in the American Party," *Marxists Internet Archive.* https://www.marxists.org/archive/shachtma/1940/03/crisis.htm
88. Max Shachtman, "On the Russian Question," *Marxists Internet Archive.* https://www.marxists.org/archive/shachtma/1939/10/russiaquestion.html; Marcel van der Linden, *Western Marxism and the Soviet Union: A Survey of Critical Theories and Debates Since 1917* (Boston: Brill, 2007), 84-86.
89. Harrington 1973, 75 and Harrington, "Marxism and Democracy."
90. Harrington 1989, 70.
91. Harrington 1970, 163.
92. Harrington 1965, 128.
93. For a different take, see my "The Chimes at Midnight: Trotskyism in the USSR 1926-1938," *LINKS International Journal of Socialist Renewal.* http://links.org.au/chimes-at-

midnight-trotskyism-ussr-1926-1938
94. Ernest Mandel, "Why the Soviet Bureaucracy is not a New Ruling Class," *Marxists Internet Archive.* https://www.marxists.org/archive/mandel/1979/xx/sovbur.htm; Leon Trotsky, "The Class Nature of the Soviet State," *Marxists Internet Archive.* https://www.marxists.org/archive/trotsky/1933/10/sovstate.htm
95. Leon Trotsky, *The Revolution Betrayed: What is the Soviet Union and Where is it Going?* (New York: Pathfinder Press, 1972), 248-252; Trotsky 1973, 122-123; Tim Wohlforth, *'Communists' Against Revolution: The Theory of Structural Assimilation* (London: Folrose Books, 1978), 84-86.
96. Harrington 1973, 211.
97. Quoted in Isserman 2000, 352.
98. Harrington 1970, 215. See also Michael Harrington, "New vitality in move left, Third World focus," *Democratic Left* Vol. V, No. 1, (January 1977): 1, 5-7; Michael Harrington, "Sharing Socialist Views in Vienna," *Democratic Left* Vol. VIII, No. 4 (April 1980): 3-5; Michael Harrington, "Madrid Conference Gives Strength to Socialists," *Democratic Left* Vol. IX, No. 1 (January 1981): 7-9; Michael Harrington, "Meeting on Socialist Turf," *Democratic Left* Vol. IX, No. 8 (October 1981): 5-6.
99. Quoted in Isserman 2000, 351.
100. Harrington 1988, 201. See also Michael Harrington, "Socialism Reborn in Europe," *The New Republic,* March 11, 1978, 19-22; Michael Harrington, "A specter is helping Europe: Eurosocialism Takes Off," *The New Republic,* May 30, 1981, 17; Michael Harrington, "The British Left: Their Problems – and Ours," *Democratic Left* Vol. 1, No. 3 (May 1973): 4; Michael Harrington, "Willy Brandt May Even Yet Manage Resurrection No. 5," *Los Angeles Times,* March 31, 1987. http://articles.latimes.com/1987-03-31/local/me-1327_1_willy-brandt

101. Harrington 1988, 183.
102. Simon Strong, *Shining Path: Terror and Revolution in Peru* (New York: Times Books, 1992) and Gustavo Gorriti, *The Shining Path: A History of the Millenarian War in Peru* (Chapel Hill: University of North Carolina Press, 1999).
103. Strong 1992, 146-150.
104. Harrington 1988, 218. See also Michael Harrington, "A Better World In Birth," *Democratic Left* Vol. XV, No. 2 (March-April 1987): 10-11.
105. Harrington supported Mário Soares' CIA sponsored Socialist Party during the Portuguese Revolution of 1974-5. See Michael Harrington, "Socialists, soldiers mobilize for Portugal's election," *Democratic Left* Vol. III, No. 3 (March 1975): 1-3.
106. See Ian Birchall, *Bailing Out the System, Reformist Socialism in Western Europe: 1944-1985* (London: Bookmarks, 1986).

Bibliography

Works by Harrington

Harrington, Michael. *The Other America: Poverty in the United States.* Baltimore: Penguin Books, 1962.

----. "Should the Left Support Johnson?" *New Politics* (Summer 1964): 6-10.

http://www.unz.com/print/NewPolitics-1964q3-00006/

----. *The Accidental Century.* New York: Penguin Books, 1965).

----. *Toward a Democratic Left.* New York: The Macmillan Company, 1968.

----. *Socialism.* New York: Sunday Review Press, 1970.

----. "I Am Not a Marxist, I Am Marx." *The Nation,* December 27, 1971: 694-696.

----. "Wrestling with the Famous Specter." *The Nation,* February 28, 1972: 277-278.

----. "The Last Bourgeois." *The Nation,* April 17, 1972: 506-507.

----. "Forsaking Debs for Nixon: A Call to American Socialists." *The Nation,* November 13, 1972: 454-455.

----. "The Myth that was Real." *The Nation,* November 27, 1972: 518-521.

----. "The Left Wing of Realism." *Democratic Left* Vol. 1, No. 1 (March 1973): 5 and 7.

----. "Out Beyond Liberalism," *New York Times,* March 3, 1973.

https://www.nytimes.com/1973/03/03/archives/out-beyond-liberalism.html

----. *Fragments of the Century: A Social Autobiography.* New York: Saturday Review Press,

1973.

----. "The British Left: Their Problems – and Ours." *Democratic Left* Vol. I, No. 3 (May 1973): 4.

----. "Prospects for a Peace Movement." *The Nation,* June 11, 1973: 742-745.

----. "US Capitalism: Partner in Chile's Junta." *Democratic Left* Vol. 1, No. 6 (October 1973): 3-6.

---- "The Middle East: Is Peace Possible?" *Democratic Left* Vol. I, No. 7 (November 1973): 1-2.

----. "Welfare Capitalism in Crisis." *The Nation*, December 28, 1974: 686-693.

----. "Democratic Socialism, Israel and the Jews: An Interview with Michael Harrington (1975), with new preface by Mitchell Cohen (2020)." *Fathom Journal.* https://fathomjournal.org/democratic-socialism-israel-and-the-jews-an-interview-with-michael-harrington-1975-with-new-preface-by-mitchell-cohen-2020/

----. "Socialists, soldiers mobilize for Portugal's election," *Democratic Left* Vol. III, No. 3 (March 1975): 1-3.

----. "Big Lie about the Sixties." *The New Republic,* November 29, 1975: 15-19.

----. "Carter and the platform: room for the Left," *Democratic Left* Vol. IV, No. 6 (June 1976): 1 and 12-14.

----. *The Twilight of Capitalism.* New York: Simon and Schuster, 1976.

----. "Electoral victory and full employment challenge," *Democratic Left* Vol. IV, No. 10 (December 1976): 1-5.

----. *The Vast Majority: A Journey to the World's Poor.* New York: Touchstone, 1977.

----. "New vitality in move left, Third World focus," *Democratic Left* Vol. V, No. 1 (January 1977): 1, 5-7.

----. "Hiding the Other America." *The New Republic*, February 26, 1977: 15-17.

----. "Socialists examine the two souls of liberalism," *Democratic Left* Vol. V, No. 3 (March 1977): 1, 5-7.

----. "Socialism Reborn in Europe." *The New Republic*, March 11, 1978: 19-22.

----. "Marxism and Democracy." *Palinurus*. http://anselmocarranco.tripod.com/id25.html

----. "The New Class and the Left." In *The New Class?* B. Bruce-Biggs, ed., 24-30. New Brunswick: Transaction Books, 1979.

----. "Getting Restless Again." *The New Republic*, September 1, 1979: 12-15.

----. "Sharing Socialist Views in Vienna," *Democratic Left* Vol. VIII, No. 4 (April 1980): 3-5.

----. "Nuclear Threat." *Society* Vol. 18, No. 1 (November 1980): 16-21.

----. *Decade of Decision: The Crisis of the American System.* New York: Simon and Schuster, 1980.

----. "Beyond November: The Democrats Remain the Real Home of the Left." *The Progressive* 44 (October 1980): 26.

----. "No Time for Mourning Now," *Democratic Left* Vol. 8, No. 9 (November 1980): 1-3 and 14.

----. "Madrid Conference Gives Strength to Socialists," *Democratic Left* Vol. IX, No. 1 (January 1981): 7-9.

----. "A specter is helping Europe: Eurosocialism Takes Off." *The New Republic*, May 30, 1981: 15-18.

----. "Meeting on Socialist Turf," *Democratic Left* Vol. IX No. 8 (October 1981): 5-6.

----. "Finding a Defense Balance," *Democratic Left* Vol. IX, No. 9 (November 1981): 5-6.

----. "Can the Party Fight Reagan?" *Democratic Left* Vol. X, No. 1-2 (January-February 1982): 1-4.

----. "Existential Saint." *New York Times*, June 13, 1982. https://www.nytimes.com/1982/06/13/books/existential-saint.html

----. *The Politics at God's Funeral: The Spiritual Crisis of Western Civilization.* New York: Holt, Rinehart and Winston, 1983.

----. "Standing up for Marx," *Democratic Left* Vol. XI, No. 3 (March 1983): 3-4.

----. "Against Intervention," *Democratic Left* Vol. XI No 9-10 (November-December 1983): 3-4.

----. *The New American Poverty.* New York: Holt, Rinehart and Winston, 1984.

----. "Going on the Offensive," *Democratic Left* Vol. XII, No. 3 (May-June 1984): 3-5.

----. "For a Pragmatic Push Left," *Democratic Left* Vol. XII, No. 4 (July-August 1984): 6-7.

----. *Taking Sides: The Education of a Militant Mind.* New York: Holt, Rinehart and Winston, 1985.

----. "Killing Democracy," *Democratic Left* Vol. XIII, No. 2 (March-April 1985): 3-4.

----. *The Next Left: The History of the Future.* New York: Henry Holt and Company, 1986.

----. "A Better World In Birth," *Democratic Left* Vol. XV, No. 2 (March-April 1987): 10-11.

----. "Willy Brandt May Even Yet Manage Resurrection No. 5." *Los Angeles Times,* March 31, 1987. http://articles.latimes.com/1987-03-31/local/me-1327_1_willy-brandt

----. "Democratic Candidates Need A Progressive Program," *Democratic Left* Vol. XVI, No. 1 (January-February 1988): 3.

----. "Jesse Jackson Breaking Back of a Prejudice." *Los Angeles Times,* March 27. 1988. http://articles.latimes.com/1988-03-27/opinion/op-281_1_jesse-jackson

----. "How the Democrats Can Win the Presidency and Govern the Country," *Democratic Left* Vol. XVI, No. 4 (July-August, 1988): 3-4.

----. "A Case for Jackson." *Dissent* 35 (Summer 1988): 262-263.

----. "Victory for Dukakis Is a Victory for the Left," *Democratic Left* Vol. XVI, No. 5 (September-October 1988): 3 and 12.

----. *The Long-Distance Runner: An Autobiography.* New York: Henry Holt and Company, 1988.

----. "We Need More than Politics as Usual," *Democratic Left* Vol. XVII, No. 1 (January-February 1989): 2 and 7.

----. *Socialism: Past and Future.* New York: Arcade Publishing, 1989.

----. "Michael Harrington on the Uniquely Orthodox Radicalism of Dorothy Day." *In These Times,* September 25, 2015. inthesetimes.com/article/18451/pope-francis-dorothy-day-michael-harrington

Harrington, Michael and Irving Howe. "Voices from the Left." *New York Times*, June 17, 1984. https://www.nytimes.com/1984/06/17/magazine/voices-from-the-left.html

Harrington, Michael and Jack Kemp. "Tax Policy and the Economy: a debate between Michael Harrington and Representative Jack Kemp, April 25, 1979." *Archive.org*. https://archive.org/details/TaxPolicyAndTheEconomyADebateBetween-MichaelHarringtonAnd/mode/2up

Harrington, Michael and Peter Camejo. "Should Socialists Have Voted for Carter?" *Militant*, November 26, 1976, 16-19. https://www.themilitant.com/1976/4045/MIL4045.pdf

----. "Should Socialists Have Voted for Carter? Part II." *Militant*, November 26, 1976, 27-29. https://www.themilitant.com/1976/4046/MIL4046.pdf

----. "Should Socialists Have Voted for Carter? Part III," *Militant*, December 10, 1976, 24-25. https://www.themilitant.com/1976/4047/MIL4047.pdf

Anvil. https://www.marxists.org/history/etol/newspape/anvil/index.htm

Democratic Left. https://democraticleft.dsausa.org/

Labor Action Archive. https://www.marxists.org/history/etol/newspape/laboraction-ny/

New International Archive. https://www.marxists.org/history/etol/newspape/ni/issue3.htm

Secondary Sources

Ackerman, Seth. "A Blueprint for a New Party." *Jacobin Magazine*, November 8, 2016. https://www.jacobinmag.com/2016/11/bernie-sanders-democratic-labor-party-ackerman

----. "A New Party of a New Type." *Jacobin Magazine*, July 26, 2018. https://www.jacobinmag.com/2018/07/electoral-rules-third-party-ballot-line-ocasio-cortez-dsa

Allen, Joe. "What Harrington Shows Us." *Socialist Worker,* May 2, 2013. https://socialistworker.org/2013/05/02/what-harrington-shows-us

----. "Taking Sides on Harrington." *Socialist Worker,* May 8, 2013. https://socialistworker.org/2013/05/08/taking-sides-on-harrington

Anderson, Terry H. *The Movement and the Sixties: Protest in America from Greensboro to Wounded Knee.* Oxford: Oxford University Press, 1995.

Aronowitz, Stanley. *The Death and Rebirth American Radicalism.* New York: Routledge, 1996.

----. "The New American Movement and Why It Failed." *Works and Days* 55/56 Vol. 28, Nos. 1 & 2 (Spring/Fall 2010): 21-34. http://www.worksanddays.net/2010/File03.Aronowitz.pdf

Belrose, Nora. "The Left Can Capture the Democratic Party – And Nothing Else Will Work." *NoraBelrose.* https://norabelrose.com/2018/07/20/the-left-can-capture-the-democratic-party-and-nothing-else-will-work/

Bernstein, Eduard. *Preconditions of Socialism.* Cambridge: Cambridge University Press, 1993.

Birchall, Ian. *Bailing Out the System, Reformist Socialism in Western Europe: 1944-1985.* London: Bookmarks, 1986.

Blanc, Eric. "The Ballot and the Break." *Jacobin Magazine,* December 4, 2017. https://www.jacobinmag.com/2017/12/democratic-party-minnesota-farmer-labor-floyd-olson

----. "Democratic Socialists of America Seize the Day." *The Nation,* August 7, 2019. https://www.thenation.com/article/dsa-convention-sanders-atlanta-socialism/

Bloom, Alexander. *Prodigal Sons: The New York Intellectuals and Their World.* Oxford: Oxford University Press, 1986.

Bloom, Alexander and Wini Breines, ed. *"Takin' It to the Streets": A Sixties Reader.* Oxford: Oxford University Press, 2003.

Boggs, Carl. "Gramsci and the New American Movement." *Works and Days* 55/56 Vol. 28, Nos. 1 & 2 (Spring/Fall 2010):

147-15. http://www.worksanddays.net/2010/File12.Boggs.pdf

Brenner, Robert. "The Paradox of Social Democracy: The American Case (Part One)." *Verso.* https://www.versobooks.com/blogs/2508-the-paradox-of-social-democracy-the-american-case-part-one

----. "The Paradox of Social Democracy: The American Case (Part Two)." *Verso.* https://www.versobooks.com/blogs/2517-the-paradox-of-social-democracy-the-american-case-part-two

----. "Paradox of Social Democracy (Party Three)." *Verso.* https://www.versobooks.com/blogs/2522-the-paradox-of-social-democracy-the-american-case-part-three

Brinkley, Alan. *The End of Reform: New Deal Liberalism in Recession and War.* New York: Vintage Books, 1995.

Brody, David. *Workers in Industrial America.* New York: Oxford University Press, 1980.

Buhle, Paul. *Marxism in the United States: Remapping the History of the American Left.* New York: Verso, 1987.

----. *Taking Care of Business: Samuel Gompers, George Meany, Lane Kirkland, and the Tragedy of American Labor.* New York: Monthly Review Press, 1999.

Burnham, James and Max Shachtman, "Intellectuals in Retreat." *Marxists Internet Archive.* https://www.marxists.org/history/etol/writers/burnham/1939/intellectuals/index.htm

Callinicos, Alex. *Trotskyism.* Buckingham: Open University Press, 1990.

Cannon, James P. *The History of American Trotskyism.* New York: Pathfinder Press, 1972.

----. *The Struggle for a Proletarian Party.* New York: Pathfinder Press, 1970.

The Catholic Worker Movement. "The Aims and Means of the Catholic Worker." *The Catholic Worker.* http://www.catholicworker.org/cw-aims-and-means.html

Chelnov, Sandra. "Merging at the Base," *Democratic Left* Vol. X, No. 3 (March 1982): 5-7.

Chester, Eric Thomas. *Socialists and the Ballot Box: A Historical Analysis.* New York: Praeger Publishers, 1985.

Chibber, Vivek. "Our Road to Power." *Jacobin Magazine,* December 5, 2017. https://jacobinmag.com/2017/12/our-road-to-power

----. "Nothing Ventured, Nothing Gained." *Jacobin Magazine,* February 23, 2018. https://jacobinmag.com/2018/02/vivek-chibber-reform-revolution-socialist-strategy/

Cockburn, Alexander. *Corruptions of Empire.* New York: Verso, 1989.

Cozzarelli, Tatiana. "DSA Convention 2019: Sanderism and the Tyranny of the Procedural." *Left Voice.* https://www.leftvoice.org/dsa-convention-2019-sanderism-and-the-tyranny-of-the-procedural;

----. "DSA Convention 2019: This is Not What Democracy Looks Like." *Left Voice.* https://www.leftvoice.org/dsa-convention-2019-this-is-not-what-democracy-looks-like

Cohen, Victor, ed. "The New American Movement: An Oral History." *Works and Days* 55/56 Vol. 28, Nos. 1 & 2 (Spring/Fall 2010). http://www.worksanddays.net/W&D%202010.html

Creegan, Jim. "Left wing of the permissible." *Weekly Worker.* https://weeklyworker.co.uk/worker/1169/left-wing-of-the-permissible/

Davis, Mike. *Prisoners of the American Dream: Politics and Economy in the History of the US Working Class.* New York: Verso, 1986.

Day, Dorothy. *The Long Loneliness: The Autobiography of Dorothy Day.* San Francisco: Harper & Row, 1981.

Democratic Socialists of America – Political Action Committee. "DSA PAC Statement on Kerry Campaign." *Democratic Left* Vol. 32, No. 4 (fall 2004): 8.

----. "DSA-PAC Statement on 2008 Elections." *Talking Union.* https://talkingunion.wordpress.com/2008/08/18/dsa-pac-statement-on-2008-elections/

DSA National Political Committee. "Ocasio-Cortez and Omar

endorse Bernie and the political revolution." *Democratic Socialists of America*, October 16, 2019. https://www.dsausa.org/statements/ocasio-cortez-tlaib-and-omar-endorse-bernie-and-the-political-revolution/

Desan Mathieu and Michael A. McCarthy. "A Time to be Bold." *Jacobin Magazine*, July 31, 2018. https://jacobinmag.com/2018/07/socialism-democrats-alexandria-ocasio-cortez

Deutscher, Isaac. *The Prophet Outcast: Trotsky 1929-1940*. New York: Verso, 2003.

Devinatz, Victor G. "A Cold War at International Harvester: The Shachtmanites and the Farm Equipment Workers Union's Demise, 1946-1955." *Science and Society* 72, no. 2 (April 2008): 182-207.

Dittmer, John. *Local People: The Struggle for Civil Rights in Mississippi*. Champaign: University of Illinois Press, 1995.

Dorman, Joseph. *Arguing the World: The New York Intellectuals in Their Own Words*. New York: Free Press, 2000.

Dorrien, Gary. *The Neoconservative Mind: Politics, Culture, and the War of Ideology*. Temple University Press, 1993.

Draper, Hal. *Karl Marx's Theory of Revolution Volume 3: The "Dictatorship of the Proletariat."* New York: Monthly Review Press: 1986.

Dreier, Peter. "WTF Is Jacobin's Editor Thinking in Voting Green?" *The Nation*, April 28, 2020. https://www.thenation.com/article/politics/sunkara-jacobin-green-party/

Drucker, Peter. *Max Shachtman and his Left: A Socialist's Odyssey through the "American Century."* Atlantic Highlands: Humanities Press International, Inc., 1994.

DSA. "Change the USA, Join the DSA," *Democratic Left* Vol. X, No. 3 (March 1982): center fold.

DSA. "All the Way with DSA," *Democratic Left* Vol. X, No. 4 (April 1982): 6-7.

DSA. Twitter Post. March 21, 2019. 10:30 PM. https://twitter.com/DemSocialists/status/1108918838781829120/photo/1

DSA North Star: The Caucus for Socialism and Democracy, "Statement of Principles," *DSA North Star.* https://www.dsa-northstar.org/statement-of-principles.html

Editorial. "Colonial World in Ferment." *The New International* Vol. XI, No. 8 (November 1945): 229. https://www.marxists.org/history/etol/newspape/ni/vol11/no08/edcomm.html

Elbaum, Max. "Democratic Socialists Debate Jackson Candidacy." *Marxists Internet Archive.* https://www.marxists.org/history/erol/ncm-7/dsa-jackson.pdf

----. *Revolution in the Air: Sixties Radicals turn to Lenin, Mao and Che.* New York: Verso, 2002.

Ferguson, Thomas and Joel Rogers. "Big Business Backs the Freeze." *The Nation,* July 19/26, 1986, 43-47. https://www.cows.org/_data/files/1986_Big_Business_Backs_the_Freeze.pdf

Ferre, Juan Cruz, "DSA Votes for BDS, Reparations, and Out of the Socialist International." *Left Voice.* http://www.leftvoice.org/DSA-Votes-for-BDS-Reparations-and-Out-of-the-Socialist-International

Fish, George. "Michael Harrington and Harringtonism: A Critical Assessment." *DSA North Star.* https://www.dsanorthstar.org/blog/michael-harrington-and-harringtonisma-critical-appreciation

Fisk, Milton. "Socialism from Below in the United States: The Origins of the International Socialist Organization." *Marxists Internet Archive.* http://www.marxists.de/trotism/fisk/index.htm

Fleischman, Harry. "Along the Road to Unity," *Democratic Left* Vol. IX, No. 6 (June 1981): 6-7.

Fletcher, Jack and Ethan Young. "Left Social Democracy Searches for a Program." *Marxists Internet Archive.* https://www.marxists.org/history/erol/ncm-7/lom-dsa.pdf

"For Socialist Democracy! Independent Socialist League Launched on May Day." *Labor Action,* April 25, 1949. https://www.marxists.org/history/etol/newspape/laboraction-ny/1949/v13n17-apr-25-1949-LA.pdf

Forman, James. *The Making of Black Revolutionaries.* Seattle: University of Washington Press, 1997.

Former leaders of the Students for a Democratic Society. "An Open Letter to the New Left from the Old New Left." *The Nation,* April 16, 2020. https://www.thenation.com/article/activism/letter-new-left-biden/

Fryer, Peter. *The Hungarian Tragedy.* London: Index Books, 1997.

Gambino, Lauren. "'We're here to win': US democratic socialists move to center stage." *The Guardian,* August 6, 2019. https://www.theguardian.com/politics/2019/aug/06/democratic-socialists-us-alexandria-ocasio-cortez-bernie-sanders

Glaberman, Martin. *Wartime Strikes: The Struggle Against the No Strike Pledge in the UAW During World War II.* Detroit: Bewick, 1980.

Godfrey, Elaine. "Thousands of Americans Have Become Socialists Since March." *The Atlantic,* May 14, 2020. https://www.theatlantic.com/politics/archive/2020/05/dsa-growing-during-coronavirus/611599/

Gorman, Robert. *Michael Harrington: Speaking American.* New York: Routledge, 1995.

----. "Michael Harrington's Proposals for Democratic Socialism in the United States." *Soundings: An Interdisciplinary Journal* Vol. 87, No. 3/4 (Fall/Winter 2004): 455-479.

Gorriti, Gustavo. *The Shining Path: A History of the Millenarian War in Peru.* Chapel Hill: University of North Carolina Press, 1999.

Greene, Doug Enaa. "Gramsci for Communists." *LINKS International Journal of Socialist Renewal.* http://links.org.au/node/4474

----. "Nicos Poulantzas: State, class and the transition to socialism." *LINKS International Journal of Socialist Renewal.* http://links.org.au/node/4543

----. "The Chimes at Midnight: Trotskyism in the USSR 1926-

1938." *LINKS International Journal of Socialist Renewal.* http://links.org.au/chimes-at-midnight-trotskyism-ussr-1926-1938

----. "Karl Korsch's Philosophical Bolshevism." *LINKS International Journal of Socialist Renewal.* http://links.org.au/karl-korsch-philosophical-bolshevism

Guastella, Dustin. "Like It or Not, If We Run Third Party, We Will Lose." *Jacobin Magazine.* April 17, 2020. https://jacobinmag.com/2020/04/third-party-bernie-sanders-democratic-socialism-elections;

Guastella, Dustin and Connor Kilpatrick. "After the Nevada Blowout, It's Bernie's Party Now." *Jacobin Magazine,* February 22, 2020. https://jacobinmag.com/2020/02/bernie-sanders-nevada-caucus-democratic-primary-win

Hayden, Tom. "Revolution in Mississippi." *A Students for a Democratic Society Publication.* https://www.crmvet.org/info/62_hayden_mccomb.pdf

Heideman, Paul. "It's Their Party." *Jacobin Magazine,* February 4, 2016. https://www.jacobinmag.com/2016/02/democratic-party-realignment-civil-rights-mcgovern-meany-rustin-sanders

----. "Half the Way with Mao Zedong." *Jacobin Magazine,* May 23, 2018. https://jacobinmag.com/2018/05/half-the-way-with-mao-zedong/

Heideman, Paul and Jonah Birch. "The Poverty of Culture." *Jacobin Magazine,* September 16, 2014. https://www.jacobinmag.com/2014/09/the-poverty-of-culture/

Hess, Aaron and Elizabeth Wrigley-Field. "Civil Rights Betrayed: How the Democratic Party Shut Out the Mississippi Freedom Democratic Party." *International Socialist Review.* http://www.isreview.org/issues/38/MFDP.shtml

Heyward, Anna. "Since Trump's Victory, Democratic Socialists of America Has Become a Budding Political Force: Why an army of young people is joining DSA." *The Nation,* December 21, 2017, https://www.thenation.com/article/in-the-year-since-trumps-victory-democratic-socialists-of-america-has-become-a-budding-political-force/

Hirsch, Michael, Ken Schaeffer, Tim Sears, Bogdan Denitch. "Michael Harrington Forum." *The Yankee Radical*, January 2008.

Hook, Sidney. *Towards the Understanding of Karl Marx: A Revolutionary Interpretation.* Amherst: Prometheus Books, 2002.

Howe, Irving ed. *The Radical Papers.* Garden City, NY: Doubleday and Co., 1966.

----. "The Fleeting New Left." *The New Republic*, November 9, 1974: 25-28.

----. "Life in a Sect." *Grand Street* vol. 2, no. 1 (Autumn, 1982): 73-93.

----. *Socialism and America.* New York: Harcourt Brace Jovanovich, 1985.

Howe, Nina, ed. *A Voice Still Heard Selected Essays of Irving Howe.* New Haven: Yale University Press, 2014.

Hunt, Richard. *The Political Ideas of Marx and Engels I: Marxism and Totalitarian Democracy, 1818–1850.* Pittsburgh: University of Pittsburgh Press.

ISL. "Why the Workers Party Formed the ISL." *Labor Action*, May 9, 1949. https://www.marxists.org/history/etol/newspape/laboraction-ny/1949/v13n19-may-09-1949-LA.pdf

ISL Political Committee. "Independent Socialist League's Statement of Dissolution." *New International* Vol. XXIV, No. 2·3 (Spring-Summer 1958): 72-75. https://www.marxists.org/history/etol/newspape/ni/vol24/no02/v24n2-w179-spr-sum-1958-new-int.pdf

Isserman, Maurice. *If I Had a Hammer...The Death of the Old Left and the Birth of the New Left.* New York: Basic Books, 1987.

----. *The Other American: The Life of Michael Harrington.* New York: Public Affairs, 2000.

----. "Who Are You Calling a 'Harringtonite'?" *New York Times*, September 13, 2018. https://www.nytimes.com/2018/09/13/opinion/who-are-you-calling-a-harringtonite.html

Johnson, Alan. "'Neither Washington Nor Moscow': The Third

Camp as History and a Living Legacy." *Nova.* http://nova.wpunj.edu/newpolitics/issue27/johnso27.htm

Jumonville, Neil, ed. *The New York Intellectuals Reader.* New York: Routledge, 2007.

Johnson, Lyndon Baines. "1964 State of the Union Address." *American Rhetoric.* https://www.americanrhetoric.com/speeches/lbj1964stateoftheunion.htm

Kelley, Daniel. *James Burnham and the Struggle for the World: A Life.* Wilmington, ISI Books, 2002.

Klein, Rudolf. "Crumbling the Barricades." *Commentary* (August 1972): 64-69.

La Botz, Dan. "DSA Two Years Later: Where Are We At? Where Are We Headed?" *New Politics,* January 3, 2019. http://newpol.org/content/dsa-two-years-later-where-are-we-where-are-we-headed

----. "DSA Convention 2019 – Overcoming Divisions – Votes to Maintain Strong National Organization." *Medium,* August 6, 2019. https://medium.com/@danlabotz/dsa-convention-2019-overcoming-divisions-votes-to-maintain-strong-national-organization-takes-c3243517e792

Lasch, Christopher. *The Agony of the American Left.* New York: Alfred A. Knopf, Inc., 1969.

"Left Talk in Hard Times: 'Socialist' Labor Fakers Back Democrats." *Workers Vanguard* No. 67 (April 25, 1975): 6. https://www.marxists.org/history/etol/newspape/workersvanguard/1975/0067_25_04_1975.pdf

Le Blanc, Paul and Michael D. Yates. *A Freedom Budget for All Americans: Recapturing the Promise of the Civil Rights Movement in the Struggle for Economic Justice Today*. New York: Monthly Review Press, 2013.

Lenin, V. I. "One Step Forward, Two Steps Back." *Marxists Internet Archive.* https://www.marxists.org/archive/lenin/works/1904/onestep/r.htm

Levy, Peter B. *The New Left and Labor in the 1960s.* Urbana: University of Illinois Press, 1994.

Löwy, Michael. *The Politics of Combined and Uneven Development: The Theory of Permanent Revolution.* London: Verso, 1981.

Lukács, Georg. "What is Orthodox Marxism?" *New International* 23, No. 3 (summer 1957): 179-197. https://www.marxists.org/history/etol/newspape/ni/vol23/no04/v23n4-w177-fall-1957-new-int.pdf

----. *History and Class Consciousness: Studies in Marxist Dialectics.* Cambridge: MIT Press, 1971.

Macdonald, Dwight. "Our Invisible Poor." *The New Yorker,* January 19, 1963. https://www.newyorker.com/magazine/1963/01/19/our-invisible-poor

Mandel, Ernest. "Why the Soviet Bureaucracy is not a New Ruling Class." *Marxists Internet Archive.* https://www.marxists.org/archive/mandel/1979/xx/sovbur.htm

Marable, Manning. "Why Stay with Jesse?" *Democratic Left* Vol. XII, No. 1 (January-February 1984): 8-9.

Marik, Soma. *Revolutionary Democracy: Emancipation in Classical Marxism.* Chicago: Haymarket Books, 2018.

Marx, Karl, and Frederick Engels. *The Collected Works of Karl Marx and Frederick Engels: 50 Volumes.* London: Lawrence & Wishart, 1975.

Matgamna, Sean, ed., *The Fate of the Russian Revolution: Lost Texts of Critical Marxism, Volume 1.* Phoenix Press, London, 1998.

McCarthy, Michael A. "Democratic Socialism Isn't Social Democracy." *Jacobin Magazine,* August 7, 2018. https://jacobinmag.com/2018/08/democratic-socialism-social-democracy-nordic-countries

Meet the Press. "Meet the Press – July 1, 2018." *NBC News.* https://www.nbcnews.com/meet-the-press/meet-press-july-1-2018-n888096

Meyerson, Harold. "What the Socialists Just Did – and Why." *American Prospect,* August 9, 2019. https://prospect.org/article/what-socialists-just-did-and-why

Mentan, Tatah. *Socialism: The Only Practical Alternative to Contemporary Capitalism.* Mankon, Bamenda: Langaa Research & Publishing CIG, 2012.

Miller, James. *Democracy is in the Streets: From Port Huron to the Siege of Chicago.* Cambridge: Harvard University Press, 2004.

Mills, Kay. *This Little Light of Mine: The Life of Fannie Lou Hamer.* New York: Plume, 1994.

Mitgang, Herbert. "Saluting Veteran of War on Poverty." *New York Times,* July 2, 1988. https://www.nytimes.com/1988/07/02/nyregion/saluting-veteran-of-war-on-poverty.html

Montgomery, Paul L. "New Socialist Group Plans to Work Within Democratic Party." *New York Times,* October 14, 1973, https://www.nytimes.com/1973/10/14/archives/new-socialist-group-plans-to-work-within-democratic-party.html

Moody, Kim. *An Injury to All: The Decline of American Unionism.* New York: Verso, 1988.

----. *On New Terrain: How Capital is Reshaping the Battleground of Class War.* Chicago: Haymarket Books, 2017.

----. "The Two Souls of Democratic Socialism." *New Politics* Vol. XVI, No. 4 (Winter 2018). http://newpol.org/content/two-souls-democratic-socialism

----. "'Dirty Break' for Independent Political Action or a Way to Stay Stuck in the Mud?" *New Politics,* June 9, 2020. https://newpol.org/dirty-break-for-independent-political-action-or-a-way-to-stay-stuck-in-the-mud/

Mort, Jo-Ann "Unlike Mike." *Democracy: A Journal of Ideas,* May 14, 2020. https://democracyjournal.org/arguments/unlike-mike/

The New International. "Notes of the Month: A National Service Act." *The New International* Vol. XI, No. 1 (January 1945): 3–7, https://www.marxists.org/history/etol/newspape/ni/vol11/no01/notm.htm

----. "Power of the Third Camp." *The New International* Vol. XX, No.4 (July-August 1954): 196.

https://www.marxists.org/history/etol/newspape/ni/vol20/no04/v20n4-w166-jul-aug-1954-new-int.pdf

New York Times. "Harrington Quits as Socialist Head." *New York Times*, October 23, 1972. https://www.nytimes.com/1972/10/23/archives/harrington-quits-as-socialist-head-assails-partys-attitude-on.html

Novack, George. "The Politics of Michael Harrington." *International Socialist Review* Vol. 34, No. 1 (January 1973): 18-25. http://www.themilitant.com/NI/ISR73/ISR73_01.PDF

----. "Politics and Philosophy in Harrington's 'The Twilight of Capitalism.'" *The Militant* Vol. 41, No. 33 (September 9, 1977): 15-19. https://www.themilitant.com/1977/4133/MIL4133.pdf

O'Rourke, William. *Signs of the Literary Times: Essays, Reviews, Profiles 1970-1992.* Albany: State University of New York Press, 1993.

Oliver, Myrna. "Michael Harrington, Socialist Activist and Author, Dies at 61." *Los Angeles Times*, August 2, 1989. http://articles.latimes.com/1989-08-02/news/mn-565_1_michael-harrington/2

Oreskes, Michael. "Jackson to Shun Socialist Backing," *New York Times*, December 4, 1987. https://www.nytimes.com/1987/12/04/us/jackson-to-shun-socialist-backing.html

Otono, Marcus. "The Political Contradictions of DSA," *Workers Power*. http://www.workerspower.net/us-politics/the-political-contradictions-of-usa

Peoples, Steve. "Democratic socialism surging in the age of Trump, and a Maine candidate takes the leap Maine Democrat Zak Ringelstein is the only major-party Senate candidate to be a dues-paying democratic socialist." *Press Herald*, July 21, 2018. https://www.pressherald.com/2018/07/21/democratic-socialism-surging-in-the-age-of-trump/

Post, Charlie. "The Popular Front: Rethinking CPUSA History." *Against the Current*. https://solidarity-us.org/atc/63/p2363/

----. "The New Deal and the Popular Front: Models for contemporary socialists?" *International Socialist Review.* https://isreview.org/issue/108/new-deal-and-popular-front

----. "The Popular Front Didn't Work." *Jacobin Magazine,* October 17, 2017. https://jacobinmag.com/2017/10/popular-front-communist-party-democrats

----. "What Strategy for the US Left?" *Jacobin Magazine,* February 23, 2018. https://jacobinmag.com/2018/02/socialist-organization-strategy-electoral-politics

Poulantzas, Nicos. *Political Power and Social Classes.* London: Verso, 1973.

----. *State, Power and Socialism.* New York: Verso, 1980.

Proyect, Louis. "Peter Dreier, Bhaskar Sunkara, and the Green Party." *The Unrepentant Marxist,* May 11, 2020. https://louisproyect.org/2020/05/11/peter-dreier-bhaskar-sunkara-and-the-green-party/

RCP. "Social-Democratic Stirrings/" *Revolution* Vol. 4, no. 79 (September 1979): 27-29. https://www.marxists.org/history/erol/periodicals/revolution/rev-4-9.pdf

Robinson, Nathan J. "A Gathering of Comrades." *Current Affairs,* August 7, 2019. https://www.currentaffairs.org/2019/08/a-gathering-of-comrades

Rodden, John, ed. *Irving Howe and the Critics: Celebrations and Attacks.* Lincoln: University of Nebraska Press, 2005.

Ross, Jack. *The Socialist Party of America: A Complete History.* Potomac Books, 2015.

Rustin, Bayard. "From Protest to Politics: The Future of the Civil Rights Movement." *Commentary* (February 1965). https://www.commentarymagazine.com/articles/from-protest-to-politics-the-future-of-the-civil-rights-movement/

----. "The Failure of Black Separatism." *Harpers* (January 1970): 25-34.

Sale, Kirkpatrick. *SDS.* New York: Random House, 1973.

Saunders, Frances Stonor. *The Cultural Cold War: The CIA and the World of Arts and Letters.* New York: New Press, 1999.

Schwartz, Joseph M. "A History of Democratic Socialists of America 1971-2017." *Democratic Socialists of America.* https://www.dsausa.org/about-us/history/

Schwartz, Joseph M. and Bhaskar Sunkara, "What Should Socialists Do?" *Jacobin Magazine*, August 1, 2017. https://jacobinmag.com/2017/08/socialist-left-democratic-socialists-america-dsa

----. "Social Democracy Is Good. But Not Good Enough." *Jacobin Magazine,* August 29, 2017. https://www.jacobinmag.com/2017/08/democratic-socialism-judis-new-republic-social-democracy-capitalism

Scott, Helen, ed. *The Essential Rosa Luxemburg.* Chicago: Haymarket Books, 2008.

Selfa, Lance. *The Democrats: A Critical History.* Chicago: Haymarket Books, 2008.

Sernatinger, Andrew. "DSA 2019 Convention Breakdown." *New Politics*, July 6, 2019. https://newpol.org/dsa-2019-convention-breakdown/

----. "DSA Is Leading the Charge." *Jacobin Magazine,* August 11, 2019. https://jacobinmag.com/2019/08/democratic-socialists-for-america-dsa-convention-2019-atlanta

----. "Moving Targets: DSA's 2019 Convention." *New Politics,* August 21, 2019. https://newpol.org/moving-targets-dsas-2019-convention/

----. "Bern After Reading: Sanders and Socialist Strategy." *New Politics*, January 28, 2020. https://newpol.org/bern-after-reading-sanders-and-socialist-strategy/

Seymour, Richard. *The Liberal Defense of Murder.* New York: Verso, 2008.

Shachtman, Max. "On the Russian Question." *Marxists Internet Archive.* https://www.marxists.org/archive/shachtma/1939/10/russiaquestion.html

----. "The Crisis in the American Party." *Marxists Internet Archive.* https://www.marxists.org/archive/shachtma/1940/03/crisis.htm

----. "Against Both War Camps – For the Camp of World Labor!" *Marxists Internet Archive.* https://www.marxists.org/archive/shachtma/1940/05/mayday.htm

----. "Is Russia a Workers' State?" *Marxists Internet Archive.* https://www.marxists.org/archive/shachtma/1940/12/russia.htm

----. ""Defend the Soviet Union"?" *Marxists Internet Archive.* https://www.marxists.org/archive/shachtma/1941/08/letter.html

----. "On the Twenty-Fourth Anniversary of the Great Russian Revolution." *Marxists Internet Archive.* https://www.marxists.org/archive/shachtma/1941/11/russrev24.html

----. "The Victories of the 'Red' Army and the Struggle for Socialism." *Marxists Internet Archive.* https://www.marxists.org/archive/shachtma/1943/03/stalinism.htm

----. "Left Wing of the Labor Movement?" *Marxists Internet Archive.* https://www.marxists.org/archive/shachtma/1949/09/stalinism.html

----. "Socialist Policy and the War: A Discussion of Position on the Third World War – Part II." *The New International* Vol. XVII, No. 4 (July–August 1951): 204-205. https://www.marxists.org/history/etol/newspape/ni/vol17/no04/v17n04-w149-jul-aug-1951-new-int.pdf

----. "Why Labor Supports Democrats." *The New International* Vol. XVIII, No. 4 (July-August 1952): 186. https://www.marxists.org/history/etol/newspape/ni/vol18/no04/v18n04-w155-jul-aug-1952-new-int.pdf

----. "American Communism: A Re-Examination of the Past." *New International* Vol. XXIII, No. 4 (Fall 1957): 207-244. https://www.marxists.org/history/etol/newspape/ni/vol23/no04/v23n4-w177-fall-1957-new-int.pdf

----. "Max Shachtman on Cuba." *Marxists Internet Archive.* https://www.marxists.org/archive/shachtma/1961/05/bayofpigsdebate.html

Simons, Terry. "Socialism for Our Time: Meeting Michael Harrington." *Counterpunch*, January 29, 2016. https://www.counterpunch.org/2016/01/29/meeting-michael-harrington/

Smith, Sharon. *Subterranean Fire: A History of Working-Class Radicalism in the United States.* Chicago: Haymarket Books, 2006.

Socialist Party-Social Democratic Federation. "A way forward; political realignment in America. Political declaration of the 1960 national convention." *Archive.org.* https://archive.org/details/AWayForwardPoliticalRealignmentInAmerica

Socialist Party-Social Democratic Federation, "To Build a Democratic Left, 1968 Platform: Socialist Party, USA." *Archive.org.* https://archive.org/details/ToBuildADemocraticLeft1968PlatformSocialistPartyU.s.a/page/n0

"Socialist Regroupment: A Discussion." *Labor Action,* May 27, 1957. https://www.marxists.org/history/etol/newspape/laboraction-ny/1957/v21n21-may-27-1957-LA.pdf

Sorin, Gerald. *Irving Howe: A Life of Passionate Dissent.* New York: New York University Press, 2002.

Span, Paula." The Harrington Perspective." *The Washington Post,* July 1, 1988. https://www.washingtonpost.com/archive/lifestyle/1988/07/01/the-harrington-perspective/80d9d664-2e9f-44e3-8847-3239e192d460/?utm_term=.07004f44d2eb

Stand, Kurt. "Looking Backward to Look Forward: DSA's Past, Present, Future." *Medium,* July 30, 2019. https://medium.com/@kurtstand/looking-backward-to-look-forward-dsas-past-present-future-47350c014840

Stein, Arthur. "Indo-Chinese Leader Seeks Deal with French Cabinet." *Labor Action,* March 10, 1947: 7. https://www.marxists.org/history/etol/newspape/laboraction-ny/1947/v11n10-mar-10-1947-LA.pdf

Stivers, Mike. "Ocean Hill-Brownsville, Fifty Years Later." *Jacobin Magazine,* September 12, 2018. https://jacobinmag.com/2018/09/ocean-hill-brownsville-strikes-1968-united-federation-teachers

Strong, Simon. *Shining Path: Terror and Revolution in Peru.* New York: Times Books, 1992.

Students for a Democratic Society. *Port Huron Statement.* Chicago: Charles H. Kerr Publishing Company, 1999.

Sunkara, Bhaskar. "Project Jacobin." *New Left Review.* https://newleftreview.org/II/90/bhaskar-sunkara-project-jacobin

----. "Lean Socialist." *In These Times*, April 29, 2013. http://inthesetimes.com/article/14873/lean_socialist/

----. "What We Can Learn from Harrington." *Socialist Worker*, May 6, 2013. http://socialistworker.org/2013/05/06/what-to-learn-from-harrington;

----. "What Should Socialists Do in November?" *The Nation*, May 4, 2020. https://www.thenation.com/article/politics/socialists-biden-vote-november/

Sutherland, Elizabeth. *Letters from Mississippi.* New York: McGraw Hill, 1965.

Titta, R. "Imperialist Social Democracy vs. Black Liberation." *The Internationalist*, December 2017. http://www.internationalist.org/imperialistsocialdemocracyvsblackliberation1217.html

Trotsky, Leon. *The Permanent Revolution & Results and Prospects.* New York: Pathfinder Press, 1970.

----. "The Class Nature of the Soviet State," *Marxists Internet Archive.* https://www.marxists.org/archive/trotsky/1933/10/sovstate.htm

----. *The Crisis of the French Section [1936-36].* New York: Pathfinder Press, 1977.

----. *The Revolution Betrayed: What is the Soviet Union and Where is it Going?* New York: Pathfinder Press, 1972.

----. *In Defense of Marxism.* New York: Pathfinder Press, 1973.

----. *Writings of Leon Trotsky 1939-40.* New York: Pathfinder Press, 1973.

----. *Writings of Leon Trotsky: Supplement (1934-1940).* New York: Pathfinder Press, 1979.

van Elteren, Mel. *Labor and the American Left: An Analytical History.* Jefferson, North Carolina: McFarland & Company, Inc., Publishers, 2011.

van der Linden, Marcel. *Western Marxism and the Soviet Union: A Survey of Critical Theories and Debates Since 1917*. Boston: Brill, 2007.

Wald, Alan. *The New York Intellectuals: The Rise and Decline of the Anti-Stalinist Left from the 1930s to the 1980s*. Chapel Hill: University of North Carolina Press, 1987.

Workers Vanguard. "UAW's Fraser: Prophet of Defeat." *Workers Vanguard* No. 258 (June 13, 1980): 5. https://www.marxists.org/history/etol/newspape/workersvanguard/1980/0258_13_06_1980.pdf

van der Linden, Marcel. *Western Marxism and the Soviet Union: A Survey of Critical Theories and Debates Since 1917*. Boston: Brill, 2007.

Williams, Juan. *Eyes on the Prize: America's Civil Rights Years, 1954-1965*. New York: Viking Penguin Inc., 1987.

Wohlforth, Tim. *"Communists" Against Revolution: The Theory of Structural Assimilation*. London: Folrose Books, 1978.

----. *The Prophet's Children: Travels on the American Left*. Atlantic Highlands: Humanities Press, 1994.

Wood, Ellen Meiksins. *The Retreat from Class: A New "True" Socialism*. New York: Verso, 1998.

Wright, Terrence C. *Dorothy Day: An Introduction to Her Life and Thought*. San Francisco: Ignatius Press, 2018.

Young Democratic Socialists of America, "DSA-YS Organizing Manual." *Young Democratic Socialists of America*. http://www.campusactivism.org/uploads/YSOutreach.html

About the Author

Doug Enaa Greene is an independent historian living in the greater Boston area. He has been published in *Socialism and Democracy, Links International Journal of Socialist Renewal, MRZine, Counterpunch, Socialist Viewpoint, Green Left Weekly, Left Voice, Jacobin, Cultural Logic, Cosmonaut Magazine* and *Red Wedge Magazine*. He currently blogs at http://blanquist.blogspot.com/

Bestsellers from Zer0 Books include:

Give Them An Argument

Logic for the Left

Ben Burgis

Many serious leftists have learned to distrust talk of logic. This is a serious mistake.

Paperback: 978-1-78904-210-8 ebook: 978-1-78904-211-5

Poor but Sexy

Culture Clashes in Europe East and West

Agata Pyzik

How the East stayed East and the West stayed West.

Paperback: 978-1-78099-394-2 ebook: 978-1-78099-395-9

An Anthropology of Nothing in Particular

Martin Demant Frederiksen

A journey into the social lives of meaninglessness.

Paperback: 978-1-78535-699-5 ebook: 978-1-78535-700-8

In the Dust of This Planet

Horror of Philosophy vol. 1 Eugene Thacker

In the first of a series of three books on the Horror of Philosophy, *In the Dust of This Planet* offers the genre of horror as a way of thinking about the unthinkable.

Paperback: 978-1-84694-676-9 ebook: 978-1-78099-010-1

The End of Oulipo?

An Attempt to Exhaust a Movement

Lauren Elkin, Veronica Esposito

Paperback: 978-1-78099-655-4 ebook: 978-1-78099-656-1

Capitalist Realism
Is There No Alternative?
Mark Fisher
An analysis of the ways in which capitalism has presented itself as the only realistic political-economic system.
Paperback: 978-1-84694-317-1 ebook: 978-1-78099-734-6

Rebel Rebel
Chris O'Leary
David Bowie: every single song. Everything you want to know, everything you didn't know.
Paperback: 978-1-78099-244-0 ebook: 978-1-78099-713-1

Kill All Normies
Angela Nagle
Online culture wars from 4chan and Tumblr to Trump.
Paperback: 978-1-78535-543-1 ebook: 978-1-78535-544-8

Cartographies of the Absolute
Alberto Toscano, Jeff Kinkle
An aesthetics of the economy for the twenty-first century.
Paperback: 978-1-78099-275-4 ebook: 978-1-78279-973-3

Malign Velocities
Accelerationism and Capitalism
Benjamin Noys
Long listed for the Bread and Roses Prize 2015, *Malign Velocities* argues against the need for speed, tracking acceleration as the symptom of the ongoing crises of capitalism.
Paperback: 978-1-78279-300-7 ebook: 978-1-78279-299-4

Meat Market

Female Flesh under Capitalism

Laurie Penny

A feminist dissection of women's bodies as the fleshy fulcrum of capitalist cannibalism, whereby women are both consumers and consumed.

Paperback: 978-1-84694-521-2 ebook: 978-1-84694-782-7

Babbling Corpse

Vaporwave and the Commodification of Ghosts

Grafton Tanner

Paperback: 978-1-78279-759-3 ebook: 978-1-78279-760-9

New Work New Culture

Work we want and a culture that strengthens us

Frithjof Bergmann

A serious alternative for mankind and the planet.

Paperback: 978-1-78904-064-7 ebook: 978-1-78904-065-4

Romeo and Juliet in Palestine

Teaching Under Occupation

Tom Sperlinger

Life in the West Bank, the nature of pedagogy and the role of a university under occupation.

Paperback: 978-1-78279-637-4 ebook: 978-1-78279-636-7

Color, Facture, Art and Design

Iona Singh

This materialist definition of fine-art develops guidelines for architecture, design, cultural-studies and ultimately social change.

Paperback: 978-1-78099-629-5 ebook: 978-1-78099-630-1

Sweetening the Pill

or How We Got Hooked on Hormonal Birth Control Holly Grigg-Spall

Has contraception liberated or oppressed women? *Sweetening the Pill* breaks the silence on the dark side of hormonal contraception.

Paperback: 978-1-78099-607-3 ebook: 978-1-78099-608-0

Why Are We The Good Guys?

Reclaiming Your Mind from the Delusions of Propaganda

David Cromwell

A provocative challenge to the standard ideology that Western power is a benevolent force in the world.

Paperback: 978-1-78099-365-2 ebook: 978-1-78099-366-9

The Writing on the Wall

On the Decomposition of Capitalism and its Critics Anselm Jappe, Alastair Hemmens

A new approach to the meaning of social emancipation.

Paperback: 978-1-78535-581-3 ebook: 978-1-78535-582-0

Enjoying It

Candy Crush and Capitalism

Alfie Bown

A study of enjoyment and of the enjoyment of studying. Bown asks what enjoyment says about us and what we say about enjoyment, and why.

Paperback: 978-1-78535-155-6 ebook: 978-1-78535-156-3

Ghosts of My Life

Writings on Depression, Hauntology and Lost Futures

Mark Fisher

Paperback: 978-1-78099-226-6 ebook: 978-1-78279-624-4

Neglected or Misunderstood
The Radical Feminism of Shulamith Firestone
Victoria Margree
An interrogation of issues surrounding gender, biology, sexuality, work and technology, and the ways in which our imaginations continue to be in thrall to ideologies of maternity and the nuclear family.
Paperback: 978-1-78535-539-4 ebook: 978-1-78535-540-0

How to Dismantle the NHS in 10 Easy Steps (Second Edition)
Youssef El-Gingihy
The story of how your NHS was sold off and why you will have to buy private health insurance soon. A new expanded second edition with chapters on junior doctors' strikes and government blueprints for US-style healthcare.
Paperback: 978-1-78904-178-1 ebook: 978-1-78904-179-8

Digesting Recipes
The Art of Culinary Notation
Susannah Worth
A recipe is an instruction, the imperative tone of the expert, but this constraint can offer its own kind of potential. A recipe need not be a domestic trap but might instead offer escape – something to fantasise about or aspire to.
Paperback: 978-1-78279-860-6 ebook: 978-1-78279-859-0

Most titles are published in paperback and as an ebook. Paperbacks are available in traditional bookshops. Both print and ebook formats are available online.
Follow us at:
https://www.facebook.com/ZeroBooks
https://twitter.com/Zer0Books
https://www.instagram.com/zero.Books